DEVOTIONS®

JANUARY

May m... ...give me understa... *119:169*

Gary Allen, Editor | **Margaret Williams,** Project Editor | Photo © Karen Gruver | Dreamstime.com

DEVOTIONS® is published quarterly by Standard Publishing, Cincinnati, Ohio, www.standardpub.com. © 2012 by Standard Publishing. All rights reserved. Topics based on the Home Daily Bible Readings, International Sunday School Lessons. © 2009 by the Committee on the Uniform Series. Printed in the U.S.A. All Scripture quotations, unless otherwise indicated, are taken from the *HOLY BIBLE, NEW INTERNATIONAL VERSION®. NIV®.* Copyright © 2011 by Biblica, Inc.™ Used by permission of Zondervan. All rights reserved.

Night-lights for Jesus

Let your light shine before others, that they may see your good deeds and glorify your Father in heaven (Matthew 5:16).

Scripture: Matthew 5:13-16
Song: "This Little Light of Mine"

Night-lights just aren't optional for me. I pack one in my suitcase to use in a motel room or when I spend the night at my daughter's. In a pitch-dark room I feel disoriented, especially if I need to get up during the night . . . *Where am I, and where's the door?*

When I'm in the shadows, I feel insecure and uncertain. I can only imagine how it feels to someone who is in the dark about whether or not to believe in God and His Son, Jesus.

Sadly, sometimes whole families live in spiritual darkness. Children grow up getting an education, but have no knowledge of the Son of God. They may be fashion conscious but don't understand being clothed with the Spirit.

It makes me wonder: Could I flip on the night-light for someone by being a little more transparent about my faith?

I used to be a silent witness, but eventually I realized there are many ways to let my light shine for those who need Christ, such as living with integrity, honesty, and heartfelt compassion. These are the lights we can shine every day, all day long.

Light of the world, You said that I am to be a light to this darkened world. May Your brilliance be evident to others through my words, attitudes, and actions. In the name of Christ my Lord I pray. Amen.

January 1–6. **Phyllis Qualls Freeman** lives in Hixson, Tennessee. She loves reading, teaching, and writing for numerous publications. Phyllis and her husband have five grandchildren.

A Mystery Solved

The mystery that has been kept hidden for ages and generations, but is now disclosed to the Lord's people (Colossians 1:26).

Scripture: Colossians 1:21-29
Song: "Show Me Your Glory"

A couple of years ago I discovered what I call "cozy mystery books," such as Cecil Murphey's *Everybody Loved Roger Harden.* Reading a good story or a simple mystery is relaxing when I wrap up in a soft blanket on my glider. My mind searches for hints as I read. I wonder if this could be an important piece of information to keep in mind, or if it is only a detail to make the story more interesting. Sometimes, when the mystery is solved, I clap my hands and say, "I knew it. I knew that had something to do with it."

I have reflected on the clues laid out in the Old Testament regarding the coming Messiah. Then I wonder, *Why didn't someone add up the evidence and figure out that Jesus was the answer to their prayers?* When we look back at the evidence and confirmations, we can clearly see that the Messiah's full identity and mission were hidden until the time God chose to reveal the truth.

Not only is Jesus the Messiah prophesied in the Old Testament, but the New Testament unfolds the mission of this Christ and plants hope in His followers. We can know Christ for ourselves, and we anticipate the time when we'll see His full glory here on earth.

O Lord God, thank You for the solution to the mystery of the ages, revealed in Your Christ. Help me to continue to search for nuggets of truth as I seek to live for Him each day. Reveal more to me through Your Word, I pray. In Jesus' holy name. Amen.

A Treasure to Share

We speak as those approved by God to be entrusted with the gospel (1 Thessalonians 2:4).

Scripture: 1 Thessalonians 2:1-11
Song: "Tell Me the Old, Old Story"

As Office Coordinator of Environmental Services in a small-town hospital, I was expected to type a message to a housekeeper on her pager whenever a patient was discharged so the room could be cleaned. It was important for me to follow through so incoming patients would have sanitary rooms.

All of us accept certain responsibilities for particular tasks. And usually others are depending on us to do our part for the good of all.

The disciples were entrusted with a message to pass on. They were to communicate the gospel of Jesus Christ to the world of their day. And Christ's commission still stands: It was given to all disciples for all generations. Thus, we are commissioned to tell our own world about the Savior.

Sometimes I think of my responsibility this way: If I discovered a cure for a terrible disease, wouldn't I tell everyone about it? This message with which we've been entrusted is beyond even that kind of value.

We can share in different ways about God's love and what it means to us, according to our own personality and the one to whom we speak. But no matter how we do it—it's a great responsibility . . . and a wonderful privilege.

Father, You don't choose angels today to tell about Your Son. Thank You for allowing imperfect human beings this privilege. Help me to be faithful. Through Christ, amen.

Loving with Jesus' Love

It is right for me to feel this way about all of you, since I have you in my heart (Philippians 1:7).

Scripture: Philippians 1:1-7
Song: "Love Lifted Me"

What does it mean to have someone in your heart? Are they in your thoughts? Is it purely an emotional feeling? Is it a matter of loving someone and remembering them?

As children, we sometimes sent valentines to a little boy or girl whom we liked or who liked us. The valentine might have said, "Be Mine," or "I'm thinking of you." The message conveyed the thought that we cared for that person. It was a temporary feeling; the next year we had another special friend and sent another valentine.

Paul told the Christians at Philippi they were in his heart. Later he mentioned that his love for them abounded with the affection of Jesus Christ.

Can we, too, love others with Jesus' love? When His love is in us, it will automatically overflow to others. I like how writer Frederick Buechner spoke of this love: "Turn around and believe that the good news that we are loved is better than we ever dared hope, and that to believe in that good news, to live out of it and toward it, to be in love with that good news, is of all glad things in this world the gladdest thing of all. Amen, and come Lord Jesus."

Loving God, give me a receptive heart for all the grace You send my way. Fill me full to overflowing so Your love will spill out onto those around me. And may I give You all the glory. I pray in the name of Jesus. Amen.

Blazing a Trail

What has happened to me has actually served to advance the gospel (Philippians 1:12).

Scripture: Philippians 1:8-14
Song: "God Will Make a Way"

I can't imagine the courage of the pioneers in the 1800s. With a few covered wagons containing their meager belongings, with limited supplies and big dreams, they endured hardships to reach their goal. Their aim was worth crossing rivers, the possibility of confronting hostile Indians, and facing dangerous wildlife. Courageously, they pursued their destination.

Paul was uncomfortable and inconvenienced by his circumstances. Yet because of his imprisonment he was able to proclaim the gospel among the Roman soldiers. And the brethren became bolder in preaching.

Paul was willing to suffer discomfort, danger, and persecution in order to advance the cause of Christ. When he was a captive, he didn't moan or groan about his plight. Rather, he counted any difficulty an opportunity to gain converts.

Can our present difficulties actually advance the gospel? Here's a way to look at it: Perhaps we are blazing a trail for others to follow, as did the pioneers and Paul. Will others follow God as provider because they see our trust in His provision? Will someone notice our courage and believe that our strength comes from God? May it be so!

Gentle Father, even when my life is full of uncertainty or trouble, give me strength to remain faithful so others can see my faith . . . and Your faithfulness. In Christ's holy name I pray. Amen.

Ready to Stay

I desire to depart and be with Christ, which is better by far (Philippians 1:23).

Scripture: Philippians 1:15-26
Song: "I'll Live for Him"

The author of Philippians desired to be with Christ but was willing to remain and preach the gospel. Paul did experience some rough years. He received stripes on his back, was stoned on three occasions, and suffered shipwreck several times.

Paul knew that, in death, he would enter into the presence of the king of Heaven. He wasn't anxious to die, but he was prepared.

If you were going to meet a king, would you read up on the protocol expected, make sure everything was in order, and prepare yourself thoroughly?

Some day we will meet the King of kings and Lord of lords. Are we ready? Do we know what it takes to enter into His presence? Baptism is the first step—then a lifetime of discipleship.

Paul desired to go to Heaven, but he knew it was best for his followers if he stayed. They depended on him as a leader. He was ready, but he wanted others to be ready too.

Perhaps today you and I can use our influence to make a difference as Paul did. He spoke of God's goodness and taught balanced doctrine until his time came to enter Heaven. I would like to live like that for as long as God allows.

Lord, at times my difficulties can seem overwhelming. Help me, as you did the great apostle, to bloom where I'm planted and be Your witness. Help me depend on the strength and courage You give. In Jesus' name, amen.

The Master Storyteller

Then he told them many things in parables, saying: "A farmer went out to sow his seed" (Matthew 13:3).

Scripture: Matthew 13:1-9
Song: "Tell the Blessed Story of the Cross"

I once told stories professionally and enjoyed searching for the right stories to share with particular audiences. It's fun to watch people's faces as I speak, because everyone loves a good story. I learned that Judges 9:7-15 is perhaps the oldest recorded story in the world, a fable used by Gideon's son Jotham to show the men of Shechem how foolishly they were acting.

Fables and parables are short, simple stories that illustrate a moral lesson. Fables, however, can feature animals, plants, or inanimate objects that are given human qualities, like the trees in Jotham's story. Parables are stories about ordinary people using ordinary things; in them, animals don't talk, wear clothes, or anything like that. Both types of story present an abstract truth in a way that makes it more understandable.

Jesus used parables to teach in a way that made His point plain for anyone who *wanted* to learn from Him. God's kingdom, and the truth about finding it, were clear to those who searched for it.

Yet those who weren't interested wouldn't understand the point of His stories. So, "he who has ears, let him hear" (see Matthew 11:15).

Lord, please open my mind and my heart, that I may hear as You speak to me. Your message is clear; let my ears hear clearly. Through Christ I pray. Amen.

January 7–13. **Maureen McClain** is a freelance writer living in El Paso, Texas, with her husband, Fred. She works with the teens at her church, taking them to Bible quiz competitions.

A Model Garden

The seed falling on good soil refers to someone who hears the word and understands it. This is the one who produces a crop, yielding a hundred, sixty or thirty times what was sown (Matthew 13:23).

Scripture: Matthew 13:18-23
Song: "Little Is Much When God Is in It"

It's been fun looking at seed catalogs and deciding what to plant in our garden this year. Mmmm, let's plant tomatoes. Roma tomatoes, to make salsa! Along with home-grown cilantro and peppers, it should be delicious.

We always buy good, fresh seed from reputable dealers. My husband is good about weeding and regular watering, and he handles all the care of the garden. So we should have a good crop, right? I haven't forgotten anything, have I?

Wait! Is the ground ready? Has it been tilled well? Have we used the right fertilizers?

Jesus told His disciples that even the good seed of God's Word doesn't grow by accident. We need to be ready; you have to want to enter His kingdom.

My garden isn't going to grow if I just toss seed out in the backyard. And we aren't going to enter God's kingdom unless we're ready to hear Him and respond to His call. Even after we've begun to grow in this new life, we'll need to keep nurturing the soil from which spiritual fruit will blossom (see Galatians 5:22).

Father, I want to bear good fruit in Your kingdom. Teach me to prepare my heart so Your Word will grow strong, and my life will show Your character. In Christ, amen.

Wisdom Versus Knowledge

Who is wise and understanding among you? Let them show it by their good life, by deeds done in the humility that comes from wisdom (James 3:13).

Scripture: James 3:13-18
Song: "Fight the Good Fight with All Thy Might"

A good example of human knowledge leading to pride is the *RMS Titanic*. Although the ship was described in trade journals as "unsinkable," it still sank. Why? For one thing, it was traveling too fast for conditions, and the steel and rivets used in the hull were of lesser quality than needed. Furthermore, the wireless radio operators were paid by the Marconi Company to relay messages for the passengers, so they paid no attention to "non-essential" messages . . . warning of icebergs.

Many lives were lost because there were only enough lifeboats for less than half the passengers. People made their decisions based on the knowledge they possessed; they were sure they were right and acted accordingly.

But having knowledge isn't the same as being wise. As the ancient playwright Aristophanes said, "Wise people, even though all laws were abolished, would still lead the same life."

According to the Bible, true wisdom comes from knowing the Lord. And it brings humility, not pride (see Proverbs 9:10; 15:33). That humility will naturally show in our actions—good works, for the good of others and of God's kingdom.

O Lord, open my mind and heart to Your wisdom. Cleanse me of all selfish ambition and envy, that I may live a life that witnesses to Your grace and peace. In the name of Your Son, my Savior, I pray. Amen.

Move Forward in Peace

Bless those who persecute you; bless and do not curse (Romans 12:14).

Scripture: Romans 12:14-21
Song: "Jesus Paid It All"

Corrie ten Boom's story of how she survived the Ravensbruck concentration camp is amazing. But just as amazing is what happened later. After speaking in Germany in 1947, she was approached by a man holding out his hand and smiling. Horrified, she recognized one of the cruelest of the guards who had tormented her and her sister, Betsie.

He was now a Christian, and she knew she must forgive him, since to turn away from him would nullify everything she stood for as a Christian. She had to pray for her arm to move, but at last she was able to reach out and take the former guard's hand. She wrote, "I had never known God's love so intensely as I did then."

In speaking with other victims of Nazi brutality, Corrie reported that those who were able to forgive were the ones who moved beyond the horror of the past most successfully. Taking the hand of a former enemy does more to show God's love than taking revenge.

Jesus died to forgive us for our sins, and we are to forgive others (see Matthew 6:14, 15). May He give us the courage to forgive even our enemies that we might move forward in peace with our own lives.

God, give me the strength to overcome evil with good. Please help me leave any bitterness for past hurts behind me. In the name of Jesus I pray. Amen.

How to Be Great

You know that those who are regarded as rulers of the Gentiles lord it over them. . . . Not so with you. Instead, whoever wants to become great among you must be your servant (Mark 10:43).

Scripture: Mark 10:35-45
Song: "Saved to Serve"

At a dinner in Washington DC, White House adviser Valerie Jarrett caught a glimpse of what she thought was a uniformed waiter behind her and requested a glass of wine. But a closer look revealed the "waiter" to be the nation's second highest-ranking Army officer, General Peter Chiarelli.

Ms. Jarrett was deeply embarrassed, but the general was amused. He didn't humiliate her for her mistake. He didn't get angry. He didn't freeze her out. He brought her a glass of wine, and then he invited her to dinner at his home.

What makes a good leader? Countless books and articles address this question, but they often leave out the most important quality. It surprises many to learn that the best way to become a good leader is to truly care about the welfare of others.

Jesus said that whoever wants to be great must be willing to *serve* others. Does that sound wimpy? It isn't. Jesus was the greatest leader the world has ever known, but how did He describe himself? As gentle and humble in heart (see Matthew 11:29). He washed the feet of His disciples, serving them and setting an example for them—and us—to follow (John 13:15).

Lord, remind me today that I am not important in myself, that I must put others ahead of myself if I am to serve You. In Christ's holy name I pray. Amen.

Serving Others

In humility value others above yourselves, not looking to your own interests but each of you to the interests of the others (Philippians 2:3, 4).

Scripture: Philippians 2:1-4
Song: "Take My Life and Let It Be"

Back in the 50s, my mother would allow my brother and me to ride the bus downtown to see a movie on Saturdays. Because he was older (and a boy!), Kelly always insisted on being "responsible" for the money. Mom always gave us enough for our bus fare as well as popcorn and a drink.

One Saturday, Kelly bought us extra treats without thinking, then discovered after the movie that we didn't have enough bus fare to get home! I was scared and crying, not knowing what we could do. But at the downtown plaza, where all the bus routes converged, Kelly found our bus and simply explained the situation to the driver, promising to bring him the fare when we got home. The driver remembered us and agreed to take us home. But he cautioned us to keep our promise.

When we got home, Mom gave us the bus fare to pay the driver back. It may have been a small thing to him, but I still remember it over 50 years later. That driver looked out for our interests, showing compassion in an unpleasant situation.

Almighty and most merciful God, may I always encourage others, whether in big things or small. Help me to do it humbly and with joy, seeking the good of others over my own good. Thank You for the opportunities You will send my way, and may I always recognize those. In the name of the Father, the Son, and the Holy Spirit, I pray. Amen.

As Great as Shorty?

He made himself nothing by taking the very nature of a servant, being made in human likeness (Philippians 2:7).

Scripture: Philippians 2:5-13
Song: "The Fight Is On"

When I was in high school, I think the most popular person in the school was Shorty. He was an unassuming person, seldom talking about himself, but always looking for ways to help someone. Everyone called him Shorty, since we didn't know his real name or even much else about him. Kids and teachers both went to him with their problems, big or small, and he was always willing to stop whatever he was doing to help.

But who was he? Shorty was the janitor. Although he never acted as though he were more important than anyone else, he never acted as though he were inferior either. He wasn't ashamed of being a janitor, and he was the best one he could be.

He served people with all his heart, whether it was the principal, a teacher, or a new freshman student. When Shorty helped someone, he acted as though that person were the most important person in the school. And maybe, at that moment, they were . . . at least for him.

Jesus described himself as "humble in heart" (Matthew 11:29) and told His followers that "whoever wants to become great among you must be your servant" (Matthew 20:26). So, bottom line: I hope that I'm as great as Shorty was.

Father, I pray for a humble heart, seeking always to serve others rather than myself. Let me follow Your example, since You came to serve, that I will not be ashamed to be a servant. In Christ's holy name I pray. Amen.

See to It

See that you do not despise one of these little ones. For I tell you that their angels in heaven always see the face of my Father in heaven (Matthew 18:10).

Scripture: Matthew 18:10-14
Song: "The Children's Savior"

As a social work major doing my field work, I was shocked at the number of forgotten children I saw. Some of them were permanently disabled due to fetal alcohol syndrome. Others had families who lived in the poorest conditions, and still others had no family at all.

Jesus had a lot to say about children. With each mention, He speaks of them with tenderness, making it clear that children are important to Him. For example, He tells His disciples to make sure they do not despise the children. And He gives them the responsibility to care for the most helpless of society.

When my first child was born, he was placed in an incubator, a controlled environment ideal for promoting healthy growth and development. This transparent box provided the world my son needed in order to thrive in his first days.

Are there children in your life for whom you could be an incubator of sorts? True, we can't change the whole world, but we can change *someone's* world. How can you and I see to it that we care for the little ones in our world?

Lord, help me take up the opportunities to serve and protect the little ones. I pray in the name of Jesus, Lord of all. Amen.

January 14–20. **Margie Sims** is a freelance writer and mother of nine, living in Norwich, New York, who studied social work in college.

Powerful, Compassionate God

Don't be afraid; you are worth more than many sparrows (Luke 12:7).

Scripture: Luke 12:4-7
Song: "Father, Whose Everlasting Love"

"Did you remember to get the lightbulbs?" my husband asked me just this week.

I had to admit, I forgot.

Memory is defined in psychology as an organism's ability to store, retain, and recall information and experiences. I have lost track of the number of times I have forgotten appointments, birthdays, and items at the grocery store. (I just can't remember all my forgettings.) Though I repeatedly forget things, it's so comforting to know that God doesn't forget even the smallest creatures—even a fallen sparrow.

Jesus covers the full spectrum of His Father's character in this passage. He begins by telling the crowd to fear God, who has power over both the body and the soul. Then the 180-degree turn He takes is impossible to miss. Don't be afraid: God does not forget even the tiniest bird, and you are worth more than many of them.

Are you feeling forgotten? If our powerful, compassionate God does not forget the sparrows and keeps up with the number of hairs of our head, He will not forget the details of our daily lives.

O God, Creator of Heaven and earth, help me to remember that Your watchful eye will not forget me. You see me now, and You see my open heart. Meet my fears with Your peace, I pray. Through Christ, amen.

Don't Be a Hypocrite

You have in the law the embodiment of knowledge and truth—you, then, who teach others, do you not teach yourself? (Romans 2:20, 21).

Scripture: Romans 2:17-29
Song: "Only a Sinner"

I couldn't find the tickets I needed to get into the play. I searched my wallet, my purse, even my piles of paper. Finally, I gave up, convinced I didn't get the ticket in the first place. Yet, the more I thought about it, the angrier I became.

I called the box office to inquire about the tickets, thinking perhaps I left them at the window. I was patient at first, but by the time I hung up I had all but accused the poor lady of keeping my tickets herself!

Later that day, I was looking for something in my purse . . . and what did I find? The tickets. The whole time I was accusing the agent of having them, I was actually the guilty one.

I frequently recall that lesson I learned so many years ago: How often we accuse others of the things of which we ourselves are guilty. The apostle Paul says here to check ourselves. If we teach others not to steal, do we steal? If we pride ourselves in keeping the law, do we break the law?

Whether in public or private, we would do well to remember: Don't be a hypocrite.

O Lord my God, You alone are perfect, and I seek to follow in Your ways only by Your strength alone. Please keep me alert to my own faults and shortcomings, as I'm tempted to criticize others. In the name of the Father, the Son, and the Holy Spirit, I pray. Amen.

Hidden Treasure

The kingdom of heaven is like treasure hidden in a field. When a man found it, he hid it again, and then in his joy went and sold all he had and bought that field (Matthew 13:44).

Scripture: Matthew 13:44-53
Song: "Jesus, Priceless Treasure"

Have you ever sat at the beach and watched people with metal detectors searching for hidden treasure? The treasure seekers all seem to have two things in common: they are diligent, and they rejoice when they find something valuable.

Jesus says here that the kingdom of Heaven is like hidden treasure. What makes a hidden treasure valuable? Not only its worth but also that its whereabouts are unknown. The seekers in the parables gave up everything they had for the greatest treasure of all: the kingdom of Heaven. Once that treasure is found, it's certainly worth more than anything else.

Everyone is searching for the hidden treasure of the kingdom of God. All of us long for love, unconditional love. We all seek purpose and meaning, wanting something greater than ourselves to inspire us. And we all look for a "philosophy of life" that explains the world and holds us together in the deepest distress. Isn't all of that—and much more—exactly what the Lord of all offers all of us?

Some diligently seek Him with everything they have, much like the treasure seekers on the beach. Others don't even realize, in all their longing, that they are searching for Him at all.

Lord God Almighty, just as a treasure map guides seekers to a treasure, help me to live my life in such a way that I guide others to You. In Jesus' name, amen.

The Upside-Down Life

Whoever wants to save their life will lose it, but whoever loses their life for me will save it (Luke 9:24).

Scripture: Luke 9:23-27
Song: "If You Would Come After Me"

My family and I were traveling to see our son where he was stationed in Norfolk, Virginia. When we got to the airport, the rental car wasn't ready. We waited for what turned out to be over an hour, which was exhausting for us as we supervised seven tired and hungry children. In spite of the wait, I noticed my husband was very intentional about being kind to the rental agent.

We returned home via the same route, same airport, same rental car company, even the same agent. "Oh, hi!" the young man said to my husband from behind the counter. "I was just talking about you last night with my mother."

"You were?" My husband was puzzled.

"Yes, I told her one of my customers changed my life." He went on to say that my husband's patience and kindness during the wait was impossible not to notice, adding that he would be attending church the upcoming Sunday as a result.

Kindness doesn't come naturally when we're tired or in a hurry. It is upside down, backwards, completely opposite of our natural tendencies.

It is a part of "losing our lives," however. When we deny ourselves to put others first, others take notice.

Lord, You have called me to the upside-down values of Your kingdom. Please change me so that conveying Your character becomes my first response. I pray through Christ my Lord. Amen.

A Safeguard for You

My brothers and sisters, rejoice in the Lord! It is no trouble for me to write the same things to you again, and it is a safeguard for you (Philippians 3:1).

Scripture: Philippians 3:1-6
Song: "Safe in the Arms of Jesus"

"Watch out for the broken glass when you take out the trash today," I tell my teenage son. Because I want to keep my son safe from harm, to warn him like that is no bother to me. I like to give my kids helpful information and guidance.

Paul offers much helpful information to the Philippian church. First, though there are many dangers that threaten their well-being, he tells them to rejoice in the Lord. He then goes on to warn the congregation to watch out for two things—evildoers and . . . confidence in themselves.

Evildoers will bring harm from the outside, he says, followed by a long list of things that could have caused Paul to have confidence in the flesh. Both are equally dangerous. Evildoers can destroy our flesh, and confidence in the flesh will harm our spirits and consequently our walk with Christ.

I wonder: if Paul were writing this letter directly to me, would he warn me about anything particular in my life these days? I am going to examine my life for dangers—both from within and without. Then I'll go to God, asking for help and protection, starting this very day.

O God, help me see when danger is coming and seek protection in Your presence. Guide me in examining my lifestyle. Where confession is necessary, lead me there. Where I see progress, may I rejoice in Your cleansing power. Through Christ, amen.

The Pain and the Power

I want to know Christ—yes, to know the power of his resurrection and participation in his sufferings, becoming like him in his death (Philippians 3:10).

Scripture: Philippians 3:7-11
Song: "Take Up Thy Cross"

Here's one of the great patterns in nature: Seeds lay buried in the dark for a period of time before they sprout through the earth into the light. Darkness comes before dawn; even the change of seasons indicates a time of suffering through the winter before new life comes in the spring.

The same pattern abounds in the Bible. David, Joseph, Noah, Abraham, Paul—all suffered for a season before God fulfilled His promises to them.

And so it is with followers of Christ to this day. We cannot truly know the power of the resurrection without first knowing the fellowship of His sufferings. Having looked to His cross for our salvation, we now take up our own cross of servanthood in His name. We die with him (put to death our "old life") that we may rise to a new life in Him. That is why Paul says here he wants to know both the pain and the power, for both are given by God's grace.

If you are going through a painful difficulty these days, keep your eyes on the power of the resurrection. Your heavenly Father uses both pain and power to complete His work: making you more and more like His Son.

Father, help me to walk steadily with You through both seasons of pain and seasons of power. In the precious name of Jesus my Lord, amen.

Busy as Bees

People were eating and drinking, marrying and giving in marriage, up to the day Noah entered the ark; and they knew nothing about what would happen until the flood came and took them all away (Matthew 24:38, 39).

Scripture: Matthew 24:36-44
Song: "Will Jesus Find Us Watching?"

In my childhood home, honeybees had built their hive in one wall of the upstairs. In fact, it was the wall next to my bed. Though I couldn't see the bees at work, I could hear them at night, even through the plaster and wood. The constant hum told me they were busy doing the things bees do.

They were guarding their queen, birthing more little bees, building up the hive, bit by bit. And, of course, they were manufacturing honey. That is, until the day a man my dad hired came to clean out the hive. The bees, doing what came naturally to bees, had caused damage to our home and had to be eliminated.

Jesus tells of Noah's day, when people too were "doing damage." Like the bees in our house, they went about the business of living without thinking. But their sin led them to wreak havoc on the earth, and God took drastic action. Imagine the people's horror at the flood. Noah had been right.

I thank You, **Gracious Lord,** for my life and for the good news that You'll come again. Impress on me the imminence of Your return while looking forward to that day. In the meantime, help me to live a life that brings You honor and glory. In the name of the Father, the Son, and the Holy Spirit, I pray. Amen.

January 21–27. **Paula Geister** lives in Battle Creek, Michigan. She volunteers in her community and writes for a variety of Christian periodicals.

Wise or Foolish?

The foolish ones took their lamps but did not take any oil with them. The wise, however, took oil in jars along with their lamps (Matthew 25:2-4).

Scripture: Matthew 25:1-13
Song: "Press On, Press On, Ye Workers"

I found a newspaper article in my files listing items to keep in your car in case of emergency. I decided to follow up on the advice and bought a small toolkit for minor repairs. But other suggested items were much simpler, like a roll of paper towels, moist towelettes, and a flashlight—with extra batteries. I thought about some of my past emergencies that were even more stressful because I hadn't been prepared.

How does Jesus distinguish between the wise and foolish virgins? He points to their level of preparedness. How much oil do they bring for the wedding procession? Having a lamp isn't enough if it burns out before the main event.

Christ likens His return to a wedding, so we can take this parable to heart. Are we ready and waiting for Him with anticipation? Are we telling others about Him? Do we fill our "lamp" every day so our relationship with Him glows bright? We don't want our "lamp" to burn out.

The foolish virgins finally arrived, but the bridegroom didn't know them. It was only those who were wise, keeping their fires burning, who enjoyed the wedding feast.

As I watch for Your return, **Precious Lord,** keep me inspired in discipleship, through Scripture reading and prayer. May I keep in mind my first love for You so that my fire won't go out. I pray in Jesus' holy name. Amen.

According to Your Ability

To one he gave five bags of gold, to another two bags, and to another one bag, each according to his ability. Then he went on his journey (Matthew 25:15).

Scripture: Matthew 25:14-21
Song: "Servant of God, Well Done!"

A former classmate of mine works in construction as an independent contractor. Because of the nature of the work, he may be working alongside other subcontractors at a housing site who are also specialists at what they do. But the general contractor is ultimately in charge of hiring the work and making sure it gets done on time.

Sometimes the general contractor must go on the road to visit other construction sites. When he leaves, he puts each subcontractor in charge of his own work. On his return, he expects they'll have been responsible for completing their jobs. He trusts them and their abilities.

It's like that in Jesus' parable. The man expected his servants to work according to their ability when he left them on their own. On a housing project, the electrician cannot do the work of the plumber, or the job suffers. The bricklayer must work steadily to show an increase.

God has given each of us "talents" to use for building His church. He asks us to serve according to our own ability. When we diligently offer what we have, upon His return, we'll hear: "Well done."

Father, thank You for the abilities You've given me—and for the opportunities to serve You and Your people. Help me to use my talents wisely. Through Christ, amen.

Playing Host to Jesus

I was hungry and you gave me something to eat, I was thirsty and you gave me something to drink, I was a stranger and you invited me in (Matthew 25:35).

Scripture: Matthew 25:31-40
Song: "Let My Life Be a Light"

Our congregation was excited. A college choir was coming to visit our church and perform for us. But the event presented a challenge. Where would we house all those students? Members were asked to show up at rehearsal if interested in hosting a student. The people sat in the pews listening to the choir rehearse their last numbers. Then the "assignment" of families began.

As each family and individual met the student they would be hosting, enthusiasm would build. The students were tired from traveling and then rehearsing, but they happily grabbed their bags and left a strange church in a strange town to go home with . . . strangers.

The next day the students seemed refreshed. Their performance was superb.

Hospitality can work wonders amidst any group. And for Christians, it has a wonderful double effect: Jesus says that offering someone a kindness is the same as if it were done to Him, as well. That means every encounter could be an opportunity to serve Jesus himself.

Almighty and gracious Father, I don't want to miss opportunities to serve with a heart of love. Open my eyes to see the needs that matter to You, and give me a heart of hospitality. In the name of Your Son, my Savior, I pray. Amen.

Keep the Goal in Mind

With minds that are alert and fully sober, set your hope on the grace to be brought to you when Jesus Christ is revealed at his coming. As obedient children, do not conform to the evil desires you had when you lived in ignorance (1 Peter 1:13).

Scripture: 1 Peter 1:13-21
Song: "Be Thou My Vision"

Being away at college for the first time is exciting and challenging. A student is, for the first time perhaps, experiencing independence from home. And, of course, college offers opportunities to make the memories of a lifetime.

But there are hazards! Not every classroom will be user-friendly for a Christ follower. Not every club or activity is worthwhile. Without discipline, it's easy to get distracted by the "college scene" and fall away from one's purpose. Students must keep their minds on their work, above all else, because they have a goal in mind.

We never really leave the college scene. We're always learning. In fact, we'll always have to carefully select our friends and activities. We'll need discernment in the "classrooms" in which we find ourselves.

When Peter reminds us to prepare our minds for action and be self-controlled, it's because we too have something to hope for: that day when Christ comes again.

Father, as I go about my day, may I keep the thought of meeting Christ in the fore-front of my mind. When I am prone to distractions, dear Lord, bring me back to You. In Jesus' name, amen.

Citizenship in Heaven

Our citizenship is in heaven. And we eagerly await a Savior from there, the Lord Jesus Christ (Philippians 3:20).

Scripture: Philippians 3:17–4:1
Song: "We Shall Behold Him"

Thanks to a distant cousin who traced our family history, I learned about some ancestors who emigrated from Germany under religious persecution. Their beliefs, while not political, ruffled the feathers of the political system. So it was safer for them to leave and make a new home in the United States.

Once here, the families found work and raised their children. They enjoyed the freedom to worship and express their beliefs as they wished. And, no doubt, some became citizens of their newly adopted country.

It's true that a bold witness can ruffle feathers. However, not all who choose to follow Christ will experience persecution to the extent it's necessary to move from home. And the point isn't the place on earth that we adopt as home. After all, we Christians journey as "aliens and strangers in this world." Furthermore, in the big scheme of things, our time here is short as we anticipate Christ's return.

I believe my ancestors knew the difference between naming their dwelling and claiming citizenship. It didn't really matter if they were earthly citizens of Germany or the United States. Their faith in the Lord made them sure of citizenship in Heaven.

Everlasting Father, sometimes I behave as if earth is my home, as though all I see is what the world offers. I pray for the ability to focus more on You and the heavenly promise of my true home. Through Christ, amen.

On to the Finish

One thing I do: Forgetting what is behind and straining toward what is ahead, I press on toward the goal to win the prize for which God has called me heavenward in Christ Jesus (Philippians 3:13, 14).

Scripture: Philippians 3:12-16
Song: "The Last Mile of the Way"

My friend runs in short races when she gets the chance. One of her most difficult was a race in which the weather was below freezing. She bundled up, as trained as she could be.

But cold is still cold. Her body began to feel the pain all over. Her lungs began to labor in the frigid air. Because the road was snow-covered, footing became the great hazard; she slipped and nearly fell several times. It would have been tempting to quit, but she kept going to the finish line.

The way my friend ran her race is the model for a Christ follower's walk with the Lord. The apostle Paul says we forget what lies behind and strain toward what is ahead. We press on toward our goal.

Following Jesus means that the road is narrow, and few even choose this path. We accept the fact that the path may have slippery spots. The conditions will be stressful sometimes, and we're bound to encounter pain. Yet while a runner in an earthly race may run his race alone, a Christ follower never does. There are others to offer help and support until we finally reach God's heavenly finish line.

Lord, thank You for the strength to keep running the race, even in adversity. Help me forget what was in the past and remember the heavenly call. In Jesus' name, amen.

Knowing Him Better

May [God] give you the Spirit of wisdom and revelation, so that you may know Him better (Ephesians 1:17).

Scripture: Ephesians 1:17-23
Song: "Day by Day"

One way to get to know God better, I have discovered, is to pray for wisdom to understand the Scriptures. For many years I lived my life with one foot in the world and one foot in church. The passage that finally enlightened me was Matthew 11:28-30, "Come to me, all you who are weary and burdened, and I will give you rest. Take my yoke upon you and learn from me, for I am gentle and humble in heart, and you will find rest for your souls. For my yoke is easy and my burden is light."

I learned from these words that I could not continue to live as the world lives and find peace—it was too much of a struggle, and I yearned for God's rest. As I willingly wear His yoke, I find it is indeed easy.

In searching the Bible to know God better, I came across Matthew 5:48, "Be perfect, therefore, as your heavenly Father is perfect." Yikes, that's impossible! How can anyone be as perfect as God? After thinking about this verse, I realized that God meant for me to be a perfect (spiritually mature) Sue Breault, as God is a perfect God. Whew—I don't have to be God—what a relief!

Thank You, **Father**, that You give me wisdom and understanding through Your Word, as I pray and praise You in Jesus' most perfect name. Amen.

January 28, 29, 31. **Sue Breault** writes from Bonita Springs, Florida, where she is active in her church with her husband, Sonny.

What Heavenly Worship!

Blessed is the one who reads aloud the words of this prophecy, and blessed are those who hear it and take to heart what is written in it, because the time is near (Revelation 1:3).

Scripture: Revelation 1:1-6
Song: "Praise Him! Praise Him!"

Some years ago I attended a large praise concert at Brown University in Rhode Island. The auditorium was filled to capacity with worshippers, and the singing grew and grew in volume and intensity.

I felt as if I were in Heaven. I was aware of the magnitude of praise as I looked around at the audience. On my left, up in the balcony, I heard a beautiful harmonious melody. I stood with my mouth open as singing began to flow in waves from the balcony, down to the first floor, back up to the right balcony, around the auditorium and always increasing and decreasing in volume.

"What is this, Lord, what is happening?" As I closed my eyes and joined in the singing, the thought came to me that I should read Revelation 19:6 when I got home. I did, and found out what had happened in the praise concert: "Then I heard what sounded like a great multitude, like the roar of rushing waters and like loud peals of thunder, shouting: 'Hallelujah! For our Lord God Almighty reigns.'"

Thank You, **Father**, for giving me a little taste of heavenly praise. I can't wait to join in with all the communion of saints, angels, and all the heavenly chorus who sing Your praises in worship eternally. Thank You for teaching me to worship You in song, even as I await that greater glory. In Jesus' name, amen.

Who's Praying for You?

My prayer is . . . that all of them may be one, Father, just as you are in me and I am in you (John 17:20).

Scripture: John 17:20-26
Song: "For You I Am Praying"

Our prayer committee was having trouble coming up with any significant plans for the prayer life of our church. One of the main reasons was that each of us felt overwhelmed by personal struggles, such as chronic pain, unbelieving children, loved ones with mental illness, and unemployment. So we decided to just meet and pray for each other.

At the first session, only my dear friend Alma and I could meet. But as I listened to her heartfelt and godly prayer on behalf of my family and myself, tears slid down my cheeks and I felt my burden being lifted. As we all continued to pray for each other, the problems were still there but we were able to broaden our focus to the prayer needs of the church.

Even more than knowing our Christian friends are praying for us, it is such a blessing to know that Jesus "is at the right hand of God and is also interceding for us" (Romans 8:34). In His last recorded prayer on earth, Jesus asked that all His followers would be one. With that kind of prayer support, how can we fail to work together in loving harmony to advance His kingdom.

Thank You, **Father**, for caring friends who lift us up through their prayers and for Your Son, Jesus, who loves us and pleads our case to You. In Jesus' name, amen.

January 30. **Cheryl Frey** is a professional proofreader, an occasional writer, and the teacher of a ladies Sunday school class. She lives in Rochester, NY, close to her two children and three grandchildren.

On Becoming New

If anyone is in Christ, the new creation has come: The old has gone, the new is here! (2 Corinthians 5:17).

Scripture: 2 Corinthians 5:16-21
Song: "Just As I Am"

One evening in May, 1970, I was watching a Billy Graham Crusade telecast while my three children were laughing and playing on the floor. I had just finished thinking about how unhappy I was and wondering what was wrong with me. I had a great husband, three funny, happy children, a nice home. But something was missing. Mr. Graham spoke about a devil who "prowls around like a roaring lion looking for someone to devour" (1 Peter 5:8).

Suddenly I had the answer to an anguished question I had long been asking: "How can God be so cruel to his human race, most of whom are starving, repressed, and miserable?" I came to realize that evil was not of God, but only allowed by Him for His purposes.

Barriers broke down in me and freed me to be open to Mr. Graham's question at the end of his message: "Do you want God?" With tears streaming down my face I answered, "I want God, but I don't know if He wants me." Before that thought completed itself, a drawn-out "yes-s-s" breathed its way through my soul. I knew by that one word that God had been waiting a long time for me to return to Him. The old life was going, and I was entering new life!

Thank You, **God**, for making me a new creation in Christ Jesus. Thank You for loving me just as I am—as You keep forming me into His image. In His name, amen.

DEVOTIONS®

FEBRUARY

"Give thanks to the LORD for his unfailing love . . .
for he satisfies . . ."

Psalm 107:8, 9

Gary Allen, Editor   **Margaret Williams,** Project Editor   Photo © Brand X Pictures | Thinkstock®

DEVOTIONS® is published quarterly by Standard Publishing, Cincinnati, Ohio, www.standardpub.com.
© 2012 by Standard Publishing. All rights reserved. Topics based on the Home Daily Bible Readings,
International Sunday School Lessons. © 2009 by the Committee on the Uniform Series. Printed in
the U.S.A. All Scripture quotations, unless otherwise indicated, are taken from the *HOLY BIBLE,
NEW INTERNATIONAL VERSION®. NIV*®. Copyright © 2011 by Biblica, Inc.™ Used by permission of
Zondervan. All rights reserved. *Holy Bible, New Living Translation (NLT),* © 1996. Tyndale House
Publishers. *King James Version (KJV),* public domain.

Receive His Grace for the Moment

If, by the trespass of the one man, death reigned through that one man, how much more will those who receive God's abundant provision of grace and of the gift of righteousness reign in life through the one man, Jesus Christ! (Romans 5:17).

Scripture: Romans 5:15-21
Song: "Jesus Calls Us"

Ever have one of those days where everything goes wrong? It is so frustrating—makes you feel like spitting nickels (as my mother used to say). I couldn't get on the Internet for days, couldn't make a decision about dental insurance, couldn't find a telephone number, couldn't find my study Bible.

After wasting a whole morning fussing and fuming, I reread Romans 5:17 many times, trying to find something to relate to and write about. It hit me right between the eyes (eventually): "Those who receive God's abundant provision of grace . . ." I wasn't receiving that grace to be calm, to think clearly, to wait for God's answers, and to really listen while waiting.

It amazes me how healing is the reading of Scripture and casting all my cares on Jesus. It amazes me even more how long it takes me to remember: God is in control and gives me the next step in daily living if I just learn to receive the provision of grace He has for me every day.

O Father, teach me to hide Your words in my heart that they would come to me immediately when I'm lost in frustration or worry. In Jesus' precious name I pray. Amen.

February 1–3. **Sue Breault** writes from Bonita Springs, Florida, where she is active in her church with her husband, Sonny.

Following Jesus

"Come, follow me," Jesus said, **"and I will send you out to fish for people"**(Matthew 4:19).

Scripture: Matthew 4:18-25
Song: "I Have Decided to Follow Jesus"

After responding to the invitation to follow Jesus, I became eager to study the Bible. At that time, *The Good News Bible* had just become available, and I so wanted a copy. One Sunday our minister announced that there was a free copy on the back table. I felt someone else probably wanted it, so I didn't take it. I promised myself that if it was still there the next week, I would take it.

The next Sunday I glanced at the table and, sure enough, the Bible was still there. Pointing at the Bible, the minister said to me, "Take it, it's for you." I felt as if God himself had spoken to my heart.

Some friends and I started a neighborhood Bible study, and the first verse we all memorized was "Come follow me and I will make you fishers of men." As we prayed to live out that verse, we felt that through neighborhood studies we could introduce people to Jesus and the Scriptures.

For many years we met and studied with and prayed for stay-at-home folks like ourselves. And through God's grace, we did become "fishers of men."

Almighty and most merciful God, I thank You for Your Word and Your invitation to follow Jesus. I thank You that You placed a desire in my heart to do just that, and then filled me with Your Holy Spirit to enable me to seek and walk out Your plan for my life. In the name of the Father, the Son, and the Holy Spirit, I pray. Amen.

Biblical Hope

He has reconciled you by Christ's physical body through death to present you holy in his sight, without blemish and free from accusation—if you continue in your faith, established and firm, and do not move from the hope held out in the gospel (Colossians 1:22, 23).

Scripture: Colossians 1:12-23
Song: "All My Hope on God Is Founded"

"Exactly what is hope?" I asked God. I know it's more than wishful thinking. As I was listening and waiting for God's still, small voice, the early morning sky began to lighten outside my window. I watched for the sun to begin its rise above the trees beyond the lake. What a beautiful sunrise it was going to be.

Oh, so that's what hope is! It is the expectation of something that hasn't happened yet, knowing in your heart that, without a doubt, it will happen. It seems that God answered with a visual.

So, what is the hope that is held out in the gospel? Verse 22, 23 tell me that it is Jesus' death on the cross that presents me to the Father as holy . . . if I continue in my faith. *If*—a tiny word with a huge impact.

How do I get this hope? Romans 15:13 tells me: "May the God of hope fill you with all joy and peace as you trust in him." Now I understand; God gives me biblical hope as I believe in Him and His work on the cross for me.

Thank You, **God**, for giving me hope and faith. May I remain firm and established in my faith, never moved from the hope held out in the gospel. And may I live for Your glory in the most practical ways today. I pray this prayer in the name of Jesus, my Savior and Lord. Amen.

What I'd Like to Hear

"I am willing," he said. "Be clean!" (Matthew 8:3).

Scripture: Matthew 8:1-4.
Song: "Balm in Secret Prayer"

Wouldn't you love to hear those words from God in reply to an ardent prayer?

"Lord, if you are willing, You can heal my child of the chronic, life-threatening disease that afflicts her."

I am willing. I will do it, immediately.

"Lord, if you are willing, You can find my husband a job so we won't lose our home."

I am willing. He'll get a call today.

This moment in Jesus' life, as He comes down from delivering the Sermon on the Mount with astonishing authority, is preamble to His earthly ministry. The bookend at the other end of His life is another prayer, His own. In the Garden of Gethsemane Jesus prayed, "Father, if it is possible, may this cup be taken from me. Yet not as I will, but as You will" (Matthew 26:39). This prayer, prayed three times, was answered with . . . cosmic silence.

Jesus, my Lord and my Savior, yearned for a different answer than the one He received. But He accepted the silence. And although I want to be the one who's healed immediately, do I have the grace to say, "Not as I will, but as You will?"

Lord, when my prayers are met with silence, I will keep praying, keep listening, keep watching for Your will to be done. Through Christ, amen.

February 4–10. **Liz McFadzean**, married for 37 years, is the mother of two adult children. She serves on the board of a small theater and facilitates a book group in La Cañada, California.

Ears to Hear

The promise is for you and your children and for all who are far off—for all whom the Lord our God will call (Acts 2:39).

Scripture: Acts 2:37-42
Song: "O Be Careful"

As a young, earnest parent, I would cling to Proverbs 22:6 like a life preserver. "Start children off on the way they should go, and even when they are old they will not turn from it." I would do my part—providing moral training—and God would do His part. He would save my children. He promised.

But proverbs aren't promises. They are instructive principles, rules of thumb . . . the way things usually work . . . except when they don't.

When we rely on the idea of certain parental behaviors having sure outcomes with our children, we imply that we somehow control their destinies. But then we realize that the children we so carefully trained aren't perfect, any more than we are. She will sin; he will fall. They will need the Redeemer, just as I did.

So what is the promise in Acts 2:39? Each of us, whom the Lord has called, will be offered that same redemption and infilling Spirit. Our children are mentioned with those who are "far off," despite our best efforts to keep them in the fold. And when any of us are "far off," we are never too far to receive God's grace, if we have ears to hear His voice calling us back.

Father, You hold out to each of us the promise of an eternal relationship with You. Today I pray for all grown-up children—give them ears to hear Your call, especially when they are far off. I'm praying that for myself, as well. In the name of Jesus, amen.

Keep Your Eye on the Ball

Those who live in accordance with the Spirit have their minds set on what the Spirit desires (Romans 8:5).

Scripture: Romans 8:1-5
Song: "Turn Your Eyes upon Jesus"

When my son took up tennis about 14 years ago, it looked like such fun that I started taking lessons too. At my age I may not get faster on the court, but I can get smarter. And in tennis, focus and mind-set are crucial. If you concentrate on form in your execution, have a plan, and keep your eye on the ball, you more often stay in the paint.

Then Court took up hockey, and I became a hockey mom. I learned that if a player takes as many shots as he can, he might score. (If you only play defensively, just to keep the other team away from your goal, you probably won't win.)

Paul talks about mind-set in the Christian life. It's best not to focus on selfish desires and defensiveness. With that kind of mind-set, we turn in on ourselves. But by fixing our eyes on the work of the Spirit in us and through us, worry about our own needs won't overwhelm us. We're free to see God at work and reap the benefits of His grace.

Helen H. Lemmel put it elegantly in her hymn, "Turn your eyes upon Jesus, look full in His wonderful face, and the things of earth will grown strangely dim, in the light of His glory and grace."

Lord, forgive me when I turn my attention to what I'm not getting and away from what You have done for me. Thank You so much for what You are doing through me by Your Spirit's purifying presence. In Jesus' name, amen.

What I Need to Receive

The mind governed by the flesh is hostile to God (Romans 8:7).

Scripture: Romans 8:6-11
Song: "Men Who Walk in Folly's Way"

In 1856 Gustave Flaubert published *Madame Bovary*, a fictional account of a desperate woman haunted by unfulfilled dreams and expectations. He wrote, "Emma was becoming difficult, capricious....Would this misery last forever? Would she never find a way out of it? And yet she was certainly just as good as all those women who lived happy lives. ...She cursed God's injustice; she would lean her head against the walls and cry."

I have never read a more heartbreaking description of today's Scripture passage. Emma is in bondage to her insatiable longing for something—anything—to break through the disappointment of her life. But she is angry at God because He isn't compensating her for her "goodness." She blames God for not rewarding her for being good.

God offers us a mind "governed by the Spirit" and "life and peace" (Romans 8:6). But we cannot earn it by being "as good as all those [others]." It is a gift—the gift of "life to your mortal bodies," as the apostle Paul says (v. 11). This is freedom from the control of envy and disappointment and hopelessness. And I have to ask for it afresh every day.

Thank You, **Lord**, that the Spirit is freely given to those who submit to You. In humility I hold out my hands and my heart to receive life to my mortal body. It is the righteousness of Christ and not my own goodness that has purchased this for me—and how thankful I am! In the name of Jesus, who lives and reigns with You and the Holy Spirit, one God, now and forever, amen.

What I Need to Remember

We know that in all things God works for the good of those who love him, who have been called according to his purpose (Romans 8:28).

Scripture: Romans 8:26-30
Song: "Calm Me, My God"

One of the hardest things for me in any relationship is to have someone misunderstand or misinterpret my actions, or to attribute selfish motives to anything I've done or said. Here's a recent example of the pain this causes me.

My house is on a private street, owned by nine residents. We're all equally responsible for repaving it when necessary, but one neighbor took it upon himself to try to get this work done. When asked about the scope and nature of the work, he hurled accusations at me and the other owners (via the safety of e-mail), saying his efforts were being selfishly sabotaged.

Ouch! That hurt.

But my motives weren't selfish. I was thinking of each of the families on our street. The residents to the south of me, both retirees, are facing drainage problems that come from run-off down the street. The couple to the north bought an older home and upgraded it, planning to "flip it" before the housing market stagnated. I care about these people. They are my neighbors, and I'm called to be a good neighbor, to look not only to my own interests, but also to the interests of others . . . all of the others.

Father in Heaven, sometimes I feel misunderstood, unable to change the negative perception of others. At those times, help me trust that You are at work in ways I cannot see. In the name of Your Son, my Savior, I pray. Amen.

The Whole Truth

Christ Jesus who died—more than that, who was raised to life—is at the right hand of God and is also interceding for us (Romans 8:34).

Scripture: Romans 8:31-39
Song: "Jesus, My Advocate Above"

Jury duty changed my life.

The first time I served on a jury, the judge told us that the miracle of the jury system is that it takes 12 citizens who know nothing about the law, nothing about the case, and nothing about each other. Once they've been given the facts, the jury somehow delivers the right verdict.

In the classic film *Twelve Angry Men*, we meet the panel in the jury room after they've already heard the case. All but one juror is ready to convict. That one hold-out juror asks the others to meticulously go back through all the evidence and testimony—and to confront their own prejudices—to see if their first impressions of guilt are based on the truth. Because one man is willing to intercede for truth, one by one each other person realizes that his initial finding was flawed.

At God's throne each of us will find that there are no flaws in the argument against us. We are all soiled by the guilt of sin and self-centeredness. But we have one righteous man, standing up to intercede for us, in spite of our guilt. And because of Christ Jesus, we can never be separated from the love of God.

Father, I know that at this very moment Christ is at Your right hand interceding for me. I need that reminder, because I can get pretty cavalier about Your love. But it comes at such a price, Christ's death in my stead. Thank You, in Jesus' name. Amen.

Who's Got the Last Word?

Having canceled the charge of our legal indebtedness, which stood against us and condemned us; he has taken it away, nailing it to the cross. And having disarmed the powers and authorities, he made a public spectacle of them, triumphing over them by the cross (Colossians 2:14, 15).

Scripture: Colossians 2:6-15
Song: "Victory in My Soul"

In his 1917 essay on riding a bicycle, Mark Twain wrote, "Try as you may, you don't get down as you would from a horse, you get down as you would from a house afire. You make a spectacle of yourself every time."

The idiom "making a spectacle of yourself" has taken on the connotation of loss of dignity, of looking foolish, of being humiliated. But in ancient cultures, public spectacles were put on for popular amusement or as part of a religious celebration. These could be plays, sporting contests, or even executions.

In our Scripture passage Paul turns the expression on its ear, claiming that in Christ's crucifixion it was not Jesus' death that was the public spectacle, but the total destruction of the powers that thought they could eliminate Him. Not only were they defeated, they were humiliated, made to look powerless and foolish in the light of Christ's victory over sin and death.

In our bodies we experience the sting of death. But how comforting to know that death doesn't have the last word. God does.

Lord, thank You for forgiving all my sins and promising me that, as my guilt is washed away, I experience new life, new power, and new dignity. Fill me with thankfulness, and strengthen my faith. In Jesus' name, amen.

Reaching Out

Immediately Jesus reached out his hand and caught him. "You of little faith," he said, "why did you doubt?" (Matthew 14:31).

Scripture: Matthew 14:22-33
Song: "Take My Hand, Precious Lord"

I know what it is like to be drowning. I know what it's like to cry out to Heaven for help when you have no earthly way for rescue. When I found myself in the ocean and in trouble with no one nearby, I cried out, "God, help me!" That was my prayer, and I didn't even say "Amen."

Like my namesake (Peter) did so many years before me, I was beginning to sink until I had someone rescue me. In fact, two people responded to my pleas. The first one helped me closer to the beach; the second brought me safely to the sand.

I have no idea if those men were angels or not. But my rescuers were likely just two young guys who decided to help a poor drowning older guy (me), who had no business being so far from shore.

In any case, I know this: When we pray, God always responds—Yes, No, or Wait. With Peter, it was an *immediate* Yes, despite the apostle's doubt. Can you find encouragement in that?

Precious Lord, take my hand. Lead me on, let me stand. Help me make those lyrics more than just a song for me today. Through Christ, amen.

February 11–17. **Pete Anderson** lives in Florida with his wife of almost 29 years and their younger son. When not teaching the fourth grade, he enjoys mission trips, leading worship, and preaching.

Of Course Not!

So since God's grace has set us free from the law, does this mean we can go on sinning? Of course not! (Romans 6:15, *New Living Translation*).

Scripture: Romans 6:12-19
Song: "Amazing Grace"

"Dad, am I stupid?" asked the son as he brought his report card to his father.

"Of course not," the dad replied. "But you might need to study harder so you can pass your spelling tests."

Of course not! The phrase tells us the answer is obvious. No, the son is not stupid, he just needs to study more. And when it comes to spiritual life, although we are free from the law, we certainly can't keep on sinning. Of course not!

Jesus gave His all on that Roman cross, holding back nothing. His work of redemption was completed, and love triumphed, bringing God and man together. And now, because our Savior received the judgment for our sin, we can live without the guilt of sin.

Yes, we continue to stumble and fall to temptation. But we do not have license to deliberately choose to keep on sinning. Of course not. We see sin's destructiveness in our lives, the damage it can do. We hope to avoid it by all means. And when we fail, we come before the father and plead forgiveness through the blood of the cross.

But wanting to sin? Of course not.

Father, by Your grace, I can choose to follow Your ways today. Help me in each decision I face to honor You. In Jesus' name, amen.

Love One Another

This is the message that ye heard from the beginning, that we should love one another (1 John 3:11, *King James Version*).

Scripture: 1 John 3:10-17
Song: "Love One Another"

Jesus told His disciples: "A new commandment I give unto you, That ye love one another; as I have loved you, that ye also love one another. By this shall all men know that ye are my disciples, if ye have love one to another" (John 13:34, 35, *KJV*).

Love. On one level, it's quite natural, and hardly a challenge. For example, I find it easy to love my children, my wife, my close friends.

But it's much harder to love an enemy, a lawbreaker, or someone who wants to harm those we love. What about the obnoxious driver in front of me on the highway. What then?

Well . . . we are to love. Love fully, love always, and love wholeheartedly. And this isn't just "pie in the sky," a fuzzy ideal we are to strive for. No, it's a commandment for us to follow, and as someone once put it, "Love is an action word."

We are to love one another in our words and in our actions. That includes everyone from child to child molester, from lover to rapist, and from pious to lawbreaker. We aren't commanded to love their sin, but we are to love the person. After all, what is the one great requirement for anyone to be saved? (Answer: He or she must be a sinner.)

Help me to love others, **Lord**, as You love them—as You love me, a sinner. Open my eyes to those in need around me, those who need Your redeeming love. In Jesus' name I pray. Amen.

How Many Times?

Peter came to Jesus and asked, "Lord, how many times shall I forgive my brother or sister who sins against me? Up to seven times?" (Matthew 18:21).

Scripture: Matthew 18:21-35
Song: "No, Not One!"

"I will never forgive what was done to me—nor will I ever forget." As a minister, I hear something like that quite often. The offended person is often bitter and overwhelmed. Yet, if we are Christians, our response should be to forgive. (And, if we can't just move on, we are to go and seek reconciliation with the one who hurt us.) Hard to do? Sometimes, for sure.

Jesus gave an example of forgiveness in the story that follows today's verse. But, of course, His own life is the best example. I think of Him on the cross, saying: "Father, forgive them, for they do not know what they are doing" (Luke 23:34).

I wonder what we would have done if we were at the foot of the cross. Rescue Jesus from the soldiers? Slay a few bystanders? At least stay with Him through to the end?

No, I suppose we'd probably do what most of the disciples did: leave. But Jesus forgave them too.

So, when we face the next injustice in our lives, let our first step be forgiveness. How many times? Seven times? Seventy times? Always! Will you join me in showing love this Valentine's Day by forgiving someone who has mistreated you?

This is a new day, **Lord**. Help me to forgive others who have wronged me. Help me to pray for those who wrong others. Father, my heart and life are Yours. Let others see Jesus in me as I forgive people who have mistreated me. In Jesus' name, amen.

Remember

The Comforter, which is the Holy Ghost, whom the Father will send in my name, he shall teach you all things, and bring all things to your remembrance, whatsoever I have said unto you (John 14:26, *King James Version*).

Scripture: John 14:25-29
Song: "Teach Me, O Lord, I Pray"

Have you ever been to a high school reunion? If so, you may have heard: "Your face looks familiar, but I can't remember your name." Ah, high school reunions can be such sweet sorrows.

I would actually like to forget a few things of the past, such as things I said or did in anger. Instead, it would be nice to have people remember the "good" things I have done.

Our Savior reminded us that the Holy Spirit would come and "bring all things to your remembrance." He knew we'd likely forget some of His teachings, so the Holy Spirit would remind us. Jesus also knew we would need comforting. So He sent the Comforter to stay with us. Now we are never alone in this world without God's indwelling presence.

Whatever we will face today or tomorrow, isn't it great to know we have someone to help us everyday? He will guide us and direct our paths, if we allow Him to speak to our hearts. We can then respond in loving obedience and faithful witness. Yes, we can have peace if we'll allow the Spirit of God to guide our lives.

Heavenly Father, thank You for the presence of the Holy Spirit. Help me to remember that Your Spirit will be with me, no matter my circumstances today. May I listen closely for His direction. I pray in the precious name of Jesus. Amen.

Give Thanks

Give thanks to the LORD, for he is good! His faithful love endures forever (Psalm 107:1, *New Living Translation*).

Scripture: Psalm 107:1-9
Song: "Give Thanks"

Every Thanksgiving season, we pause and thank God for the many blessings of the year. In the United States, we celebrate that holiday with a big meal and typically watch (or play) sporting events.

Thanksgiving is a wonderful holiday. However, the calendar reminds us that this is February, not November, and Thanksgiving is about nine months away. It happened nearly three months ago, so why are we discussing it today?

Well, actually, the topic is "give thanks"—and we don't have to wait until November to do that. In fact, we can give thanks every day for the many blessings God has poured into our lives. "Everything God created is good, and nothing is to be rejected if it is received with thanksgiving" (1 Timothy 4:4).

Our response to His blessings? Continual gratitude. Thanksgiving day comes once a year, but thankfulness can be our attitude every day. It's a beautiful thing in our lives. As the great preacher Henry Ward Beecher said: "Gratitude is the fairest blossom which springs from the soul."

My great and gracious Lord, thank You for the many blessings You have showered upon me. While I know I have many concerns and problems, today open my eyes to the many blessings I have received. Thank you, especially, for the salvation that comes through Christ. I pray this prayer in His name. Amen.

Walk This Way

Put to death, therefore, whatever belongs to your earthly nature: sexual immorality, impurity, lust, evil desires and greed, which is idolatry. Because of these, the wrath of God is coming. You used to walk in these ways, in the life you once lived (Colossians 3:5-7).

Scripture: Colossians 3:5-17
Song: "Just a Closer Walk with Thee"

Before becoming a Christian, I did all sorts of "things." Oh, I never murdered anyone, but I was no stranger to sin. I walked in the ways of the world (meaning I chose to follow my own path, make my own decisions). That's what we as Christians are supposed to put to death.

Yes, our Scripture passage states we are to "put to death" things such as sexual immorality, impurity, lust, evil desires, and greed. Because of those things, the wrath of God is coming.

"Wrath of God" sounds ominous. But it's no secret that our Holy Lord does not like sin; rather, He calls us to cast off impure things and replace them with pure things, that we might be "re-formed" into the likeness of His Son. And He is going to assist us in doing just that.

The beautiful thing is that we can walk in God's ways each day, allowing Him to be in charge of our lives. That is, we can decide to walk this way today: sexually moral, pure, upright, honest, and led by a godly desire to show the world who the Lord is. Bottom line: It's a question of how we choose to walk.

Father, help me to walk in Your ways today. May I reflect the love of Christ in my life and bring glory and honor to Him. In Jesus' name, amen.

Spiritual Vision

Two blind men were sitting by the roadside, and when they heard that Jesus was going by, they shouted, "Lord, Son of David, have mercy on us!" (Matthew 20:30).

Scripture: Matthew 20:29-34
Song: "Oh Love Divine, That Stooped to Share"

Reading this story in my morning quiet time, I am reminded of another. A poet and an artist were viewing a painting by a French master that depicts this healing of the blind men at Jericho. The artist asked the poet what he saw as the most remarkable thing in the painting. The poet answered by describing the excellent techniques—the grouping of the crowd, the expressions on individual faces, and the depiction of Christ.

"But look," said the artist, pointing to the steps of a home in the background where a discarded cane lay. "One blind man was so sure that he would be healed, that when he heard Jesus passing by, he left his cane and ran to Jesus, fully expecting to see!"

I'm jolted by the image. How did the blind man "see" what the religious leaders of the day, who had witnessed Jesus' miracles, were unable to behold? Could it be that the blind man had an advantage—that he was seeing with his heart and his spirit, not just his eyes?

O Eternal Lord God, I don't want to miss You! Like the blind man, help me in my own blindness to see You with my heart and spirit—that I might follow You more closely. Through Christ my precious Lord I pray. Amen.

February 18–28. **GlenAnn Wood Egan** is an avid hiker, voracious reader, freelance writer, and homemaker. She lives in Centennial, Colorado, with her husband.

Some Things Never Change

He said to them: "It is not for you to know the times or dates the Father has set by his own authority" (Acts 1:7).

Scripture: Acts 1:6-14
Song: "I Sing the Mighty Power of God"

The disciples were so much like us that sometimes they make me smile. Like us, they wondered about the kingdom. What did it look like? When would it come? What would be their role? Like us, they ruminated over their problems, looking to God for immediate answers to questions they naively expected would move the kingdom forward (according to their agendas).

I am like this too. Once, while struggling over some issues in my marriage, I seemed to hear, like a clear bell tone, the Spirit speaking to my heart: "Attend to God, and attend to your husband; don't worry about the rest."

That wasn't what I expected to hear—and not exactly what I *wanted* to hear. But as my heart accepted His authority over the "what" and the "when" of my life, the peace of the Holy Spirit became mine.

What the Lord said to me was certainly not in line with my agenda. But it was part of God's agenda for me—and my path to freedom.

Two thousand years ago, Jesus said much the same thing to the disciples. Today I am grateful to know that some things never change.

O Gracious Father, who is the same yesterday, today and tomorrow, how gratefully I receive Your surprising words of life! Thank You, in the name of the Father, the Son, and the Holy Spirit. Amen.

Knowing Our Stories

We who are strong ought to bear with the failings of the weak and not to please ourselves (Romans 15:1).

Scripture: Romans 15:1-6
Song: "A Charge to Keep I Have"

Head down, as I leave the school this Sunday morning, I feel the same sense of frustration and tension that has for so long characterized my worship experience. Our small church is heading in directions that I see as detrimental to the flock. Speaking with our inexperienced church leadership hasn't helped. So what does it mean "to bear with the failings of the weak" when the ones I see as weak are those leading me?

While praying with my Bible open, I marvel at how Christ was able to always engage with a person in the specific, exact, right way he or she needed.

"Well, He is God," I say to myself. He can see the whole picture of their lives. I on the other hand can never know that I see the whole story about anyone or any situation. Realizing that, I am humbled.

There are things in our leaders' life stories that I can't even guess at. Realizing that, I feel compassion welling up. Whatever I decide to do, I know the Lord would have my actions come from the heart that He has just given me—His heart, which gratefully bears with those who are weak for as long as it is needed.

Almighty God and Father, how easy it is for my heart to harden. Forgive me, Lord, and help me to walk in humility and wisdom toward others for Your sake. I pray through my deliverer, Jesus. Amen.

Warmth of the Son

As for other matters, brothers and sisters, we instructed you how to live in order to please God, as in fact you are living. Now we ask you and urge you in the Lord Jesus to do this more and more (1 Thessalonians 4:1).

Scripture: 1 Thessalonians 4:1-12
Song: "Awake, My Soul, and with the Sun"

In this part of his letter to the Thessalonians, Paul speaks of walking with God in two specific areas of relationship — sexuality and community. Paul's message was as counter-cultural then as it remains today.

But I am captured by the word *live* used here — which literally means, in the Greek text, "walk around" — and the images it invokes in my mind as I walk up a mountain foothills trail close to my home. You see, I have never felt as if I have been to a place unless I have walked around in it. And I wonder if the ancients might have felt the same way, since walking was the most common means of moving about in their world. And in all their walking, I wonder if they felt like they had been to God?

Quite a contrast to my world today, where life is often more of a run than a walk, a race to see how much I can accomplish. I know this is not the walk that God invites us to, and on this morning, I am grateful to be walking with Him as I think He intends. Leisurely, I walk smelling the pine, hearing the call of a meadow lark, feeling both the warmth of the sun and of the Son.

Dear God, how amazing it is that you invite me to walk around with You in all the ways and in all the days of my life. It is such a gift, such a privilege! Help me, Lord, that I may walk well. In Jesus' name, amen.

Listening—or Not?

Guard your steps when you go to the house of God. Go near to listen rather than to offer the sacrifice of fools, who do not know that they do wrong (Ecclesiastes 5:1).

Scripture: Ecclesiastes 5:1-6
Song: "Come, All Christians, Be Committed"

Critics can often rub me the wrong way—as this one seems to be doing to the listeners in this passage of Scripture. I feel exactly the same way about some movie critics, as it is Academy Award season, and I am a film buff.

Sometimes movie critics render me a service in pointing out what I should see and what I should not waste my time on. But at other times I wonder, "What in the world are they thinking?"

Over the years, I have learned to pick and choose among the critics and their opinions. Some share my own taste and values, some don't.

In reading our passage today, I wonder if the people listening to the *Koheleth* (Hebrew for "teacher") are hearing him with similar ears—picking and choosing what they will take to heart from what God is saying. Are they aware of the danger of not listening? Am I?

The risk I take in rejecting advice about a movie is a few dollars and a couple of hours of my time. But the consequences of not listening to God are much greater—my very life and His life in me are at risk.

O Lord, I say that I long to hear You. Yet how often I ignore that still, small voice when it comes. Help me, O God, to not only have ears to hear but a will to *follow* what I hear. In the name of Jesus, my Savior, I pray. Amen.

Second String

See to it that you complete the ministry you have received in the Lord (Colossians 4:17).

Scripture: Colossians 4:7-17
Song: "Have I Done My Best for Jesus?"

Taking a sip of coffee, I am struck by how little I know about the companions of Paul mentioned in this passage. Their names occur but a few times in Scripture, yet I find that they are heroes of the faith! Tychius was the bearer of the letters to the Colossians and Ephesians. Aristachus was with Paul in the riots at Ephesus. Epaphras founded the Colossian church.

I am embarrassed to say that until now, they seemed to me to be sort of a second string in God's story compared to Paul. But each individual was apparently content to play his part, whether large or small. What a contrast to today, with our endless quest to think well of ourselves and be significant.

Decades ago, the writer T. S. Eliot spoke to this impulse, saying, "Half the harm that is done in this world is due to people who want to feel important." I relate to this because one of the driving impulses of my life has been to do something that "really matters." And now I wonder if I have unknowingly done harm in that pursuit. And who am I to decide what really matters? Can I graciously accept, as these relatively obscure men did, whatever role I am given? Can I be the person who is not in the spotlight but the one holding it?

Dear Heavenly Father, forgive me for the ways I try to take control of my life and shut You out. Help me to have more of Your spirit and less of mine. I pray this in the name of Jesus my Lord. Amen.

Hit and Run

Be wise in the way you act toward outsiders; make the most of every opportunity (Colossians 4:5).

Scripture: Colossians 4:2-6
Song: "Open My Eyes, That I May See"

Holding the Bible with one hand, a cup of hot chocolate with the other, I am reflecting on what a funny lot we Christians sometimes are. Especially as new Christians, we can often act enthusiastically but without wisdom. We rush into the work of witnessing, full of good intentions, not realizing that we have no power to do God's work without the Holy Spirit. This truth became quite clear to a friend of mine recently.

On an early summer morning, she was walking a tree-lined bike path, her heart heavy over a hurting relationship. A complete stranger kindly stopped, asking my friend if she was OK. The person quickly began praying for her, and then, just as quickly, continued going on her way. My friend knew the stranger meant well. But rather than feeling cared for, she felt more like the victim of a spiritual hit-and-run attack.

Even though the stranger had Christ to share, the way she went about it did not seem loving. The exchange, my friend said, left her feeling like it was more about the stranger's agenda than her need. But loving others is what we are first, and most, called to do. Be wise, Paul says. I know I cannot be wise without Christ; and I know I cannot be wise without loving.

My gracious God, how patient and kind You are to teach me about Your love. Show me the ways that I miss loving despite my best intentions. Please give me more of Your heart. In the name of Jesus, my Savior, I pray. Amen.

An Excellent Spirit

I have heard that the spirit of the gods is in you and that you have insight, intelligence and outstanding wisdom (Daniel 5:14).

Scripture: Daniel 5:13-21
Song: "Purer in Heart, O God"

It is often written and said that Daniel had an "excellent spirit." The word used here is *ruah*, which means "wind in motion"—a lovely, powerful image of the energy in Daniel's life that made him stand out from others.

George Whitefield, the great evangelist of the 18th century, tirelessly preached across England and America. He established several orphanages and brought thousands to the faith, all the while in a physical condition that today would see him regularly hospitalized.

People like Daniel and Whitefield raise the bar for me. It is hard to think of them as real people. They were not supernatural beings, but they certainly lived like it. How did they do it?

Washing another breakfast plate and reflecting on the ordinariness of my life compared to theirs, I sigh. *Maybe your life is meant to look like yours*, I hear a voice say, *not someone else's*. Hearing those words my heart stirs, a new desire begins rising, and a vision reveals itself. Could I have an excellent spirit too? I start to wonder what if the *ruah* had His full way with me? What would my life look like?

Dear Father, I stand in awe of the ways You show yourself in the lives of Your servants. Help me to live faithfully and fully the life You have given me. In the name of Jesus, my Savior, I pray. Amen.

Dedicated to God

You did not honor the God who holds in his hand your life and all your ways (Daniel 5:23).

Scripture: Daniel 5:22-31
Song: "I Surrender All"

I am struck by the contrast between the two men in our Scripture today, Daniel and Belshazzar. God tells us that it rains on the just and unjust alike. And in the same way, God sometimes also *blesses* the just and unjust alike. Here He has given gifts to both men, but what each has done with his gifts makes all the difference.

For Belshazzar, the party is over. Though he keeps his promise to Daniel, he has not kept faith with God. Instead, exalting himself against the Lord, he even begins using, in sinful ways, the cup dedicated to God. There is no evidence he seeks an opportunity for repentance.

Then there is David, a believer, who is dedicated to God and faithful in all things. Reflecting on his story, I consider the implications for my own life. It is not just praying and going to church. It is everything: Not only my dishware and finances, but all that I have been given and all that I am. It is in these areas where I can be most tempted to compromise. Daniel was faithful to offer everything—and all of himself—back to God. But do I do that?

O God, Creator of Heaven and earth, search my heart for all that is offensive in me, that all of me could be Yours, and that I would know You and love You all the more. I pray this prayer in the name of Jesus, my Savior and Lord. Amen.

Darkness and Light

They could find no corruption in him, because he was trustworthy and neither corrupt nor negligent (Daniel 6:4).

Scripture: Daniel 6:1-10
Song: "Prince of Peace, Control My Will"

It does not seem fair to me that in our time, anymore than in Daniel's time, a person should suffer for doing right. But the ongoing conflict between good and evil put enormous pressures on Daniel, making his life of integrity more inspiring. How did he become such a man? How can I become such a person?

Maybe it begins with everyday events in my life which I might tend to overlook, but where a true battle is raging. One day standing at the checkout counter at a hobby store, I double-checked my receipt and thought the cashier had undercharged me. Bringing it to her attention, I found her surprised but so very grateful.

But I was surprised at the reaction of the women behind me. "You shouldn't have said anything," she said. "They would've never known." Turning to her, I replied, "But I would have known." Then I saw the little girl with her, watching me.

A small moment in my day, yet I couldn't help feeling that a skirmish in the war between darkness and light had been won at that cash register. Daniel's greatest test came at the end of his life. If that proves true for me, I want to be ready.

O Lord, give us eyes to see the real battle being waged in our lives, and in the lives of those we love. Strengthen us to enter the fight with Your wisdom and power. In the name of Jesus, my Savior, I pray. Amen.

Lions and Liberty

The king gave the order, and they brought Daniel and threw him into the lions' den. The king said to Daniel, "May your God, whom you serve continually, rescue you!" (Daniel 6:16).

Scripture: Daniel 6:11-23
Song: "Never Alone"

I have read that in the Old Testament, the image of lions often symbolizes destructive power, disharmony, and the chaos of the universe. That pretty *well* describes my universe right now, I think. My husband and I have just fought, and the experience has left me captive to lions of hurt and discouragement. Sometimes I wonder why God places such a priority on healthy relationships.

But Daniel, right in the middle of the lion's den, was full of peace! He'd already been a conqueror, and in the way that matters most, already rescued.

These thoughts followed me into my workday until, several hours later, a familiar inner voice seemed to say: *You are a rebellious woman, have been for a long time, still are.*

Me, a rebellious woman? Though I would never have used that word for myself, past and present scenes of my rebelliousness began flickering through my mind. Incidents that never made sense to me began connecting. Brokenhearted, yet free, I accepted some hard truths.

Father, how grateful I am for Your life in those who are righteous. But I am even more grateful that there is no place You will not go to rescue those of us who are not. I love You, Lord. In the name of Your Son, my Savior, I pray. Amen.

My Prayer Notes

My Prayer Notes

_____
_____
_____
_____
_____
_____
_____
_____
_____
_____
_____
_____
_____
_____
_____
_____
_____
_____
_____
_____
_____
_____
_____

My Prayer Notes

_____
_____
_____
_____
_____
_____
_____
_____
_____
_____
_____
_____
_____
_____
_____
_____
_____
_____
_____
_____
_____
_____
_____

DEVOTIONS®

MARCH

The prayer of a righteous person is powerful and effective.

— *James 5:16*

Gary Allen, Editor   **Margaret Williams,** Project Editor   Photo © Jostein Hauge | Dreamstime.com

God's Guarantee

I issue a decree that in every part of my kingdom people must fear and reverence the God of Daniel (Daniel 6:26).

Scripture: Daniel 6:24-28.
Song: "With Reverence Let the Saints Appear"

In 30 days a man from our small congregation had to have heart surgery. The doctors gave him a 50/50 chance that he would survive.

He was a leader in the community who owned a construction company. Believing God would see him through the surgery, he asked his fellow believers to pray for him. So our minister announced a 30-day prayer schedule, and people signed up to come and pray 24/7 for this man and the team of doctors. The man survived the surgery and gave the praise and honor to God . . . and thanked the prayer chain!

Thirty days seems to be an important period of time when it comes to scheduling. For example, many products on the market come with a 30-day money-back guarantee.

In our Scripture passage, Daniel received a 30-day challenge: ask things only of the king and do not honor or pray to any other master. He disobeyed the king and was thrown to the lions. But God had a "guaranteed" program in place, didn't He?

O God, the king of glory, I long to glorify You in all I do, and I pray that others will also look to You for salvation. Let them see You in my daily walk, and help me to never forget where the blessings come from. In the name of the Father, the Son, and the Holy Spirit, I pray. Amen.

March 1–3. **Beverly LaHote Schwind** lives in Fairfield Glade, Tennessee, and is active in jail ministry, rehab teaching, and nursing at a homeless shelter.

God of Dreams

In the first year of Belshazzar king of Babylon, Daniel had a dream, and visions passed through his mind as he was lying on his bed. He wrote down the substance of his dream (Daniel 7:1).

Scripture: Daniel 7:1-8
Song: "The Holy City"

My dream seemed so real that I awoke wondering, *Did that really happen?* At times I have written my dreams down, as they were so vivid that I thought they surely must have some meaning. I also write them down so I can remember them and think about them later. And sometimes I've wakened from a good dream and have tried to go back to sleep to finish it! (That usually doesn't work, though.)

In the Bible God frequently spoke to His people in visions and dreams, and lives were thereby changed. For example, Joseph was called "The Dreamer" and was ridiculed as he shared his dreams with his brothers. The wise men were warned in a dream not to tell King Herod they'd found Jesus. And Joseph, the earthly father of Jesus, followed dream-given instructions in his handling of Mary's unusual pregnancy.

In our Scripture today Daniel recorded his dreams as he realized they were special words from God. It speaks of a sincere attentiveness to God's leading. Could we not learn from his example? Let us maintain open, receptive hearts, whether awake or asleep.

Lord God, who never sleeps, I don't want to miss anything You have to say to me today. So speak, Lord, your servant is listening! In the name of Jesus, amen.

God of All

In my vision at night I looked, and there before me was one like a son of man, coming with the clouds of heaven. He approached the Ancient of Days and was led into His presence (Daniel 7:13).

Scripture: Daniel 7:9-14
Song: "Ancient of Days"

When I was a child attending Sunday school, I thought the minister was God. He had white hair and a beard and was such a happy, gentle man. He spoke with a soft German accent.

On Sundays he would come into the classroom and greet us all so cheerfully. I watched in anticipation as he approached our row of chairs to talk with us, bending down to be on our eye level. I didn't know how old he was, but I knew he must be *ancient*. After all, he would speak as if he knew Peter or John and mention questions he wanted to ask Joseph and Abraham some day.

It was easy to honor this man, and I soon realized, as I grew older, how blessed I was to have such a godly role model in this minister. He died years later, but he had been God's obedient messenger through the years. And I saw God through him.

The Ancient of Days sat on the throne in Daniel's dream, with millions of angels ministering to Him. All knees bent before Him, and the son of man was led in. Daniel saw the coronation of the Messiah King whose kingdom shall never be destroyed. We can do no better than to make this king our ultimate pastor, the one who can shepherd us through all of life.

Ancient of Days, You sit enthroned in glory, and to You—when earthly history is ended—all knees will bow. May I honor You in all things this day. Through Christ, amen.

Life on the Line

Daniel resolved not to defile himself with the royal food and wine (Daniel 1:8).

Scripture: Daniel 1:8-15
Song: "When I Survey the Wondrous Cross"

"Recant your Christian faith or die," the judge said. Shoaib Assadullah was arrested in Afghanistan on October 21, 2010, for handing another man a New Testament. He was given one week to decide his fate. A government attorney met with him, offering freedom if only Shoaib would deny his faith. He refused. And he stood alone, as his Muslim family opposed his conversion to Christianity. What would we do in his situation?

In our text Daniel was a captive of the Babylonians. Like Shoaib, he faced a life or death choice: Take a stand for God or possibly perish. He was young and far from home, and compromise would have been easy. Yet Daniel determined to serve God no matter the consequences.

I don't know how things are for Shoaib today. But one news story has said the court relented regarding the death penalty—but that the young Christian remains imprisoned. When interviewed in 2010, Shoaib said: "My life is in the hands of Jesus. Without my faith I would not be able to live." Such boldness shows us the way whenever we face the temptation to deny our Lord in word or in deed.

Father, please help me to be faithful to You no matter my circumstances. I rely on You for that kind of courage today. Thank You, in Jesus' name. Amen.

March 4–10. **Diana Stewart** is a retired insurance agent living in Oklahoma City. She teaches a Bible study at her church and serves as an online missionary for Campus Crusade for Christ.

Time to Recollect?

To these four young men God gave knowledge and understanding of all kinds of literature and learning. And Daniel could understand visions and dreams of all kinds (Daniel 1:17).

Scripture: Daniel 1:16-21
Song: "Some Day He'll Make It Plain"

My 15-year-old grandson is close to obtaining his learner's permit for driving. However, his parents have issued a stern, formal warning: "Obedient behavior and a sure demonstration of responsibility must be evident before any driver's permit can be obtained." Eathan's choice to obey must precede his parents' blessing to drive a car.

In our text Daniel is a prisoner of the Babylonians. He is only a teenager, but his obedience to the Lord becomes more and more obvious. He resisted the temptation to "go along with the crowd" and just fit in. Instead, he chose to obey God, even in his choices of food and drink. In other words, Daniel put God first. And the result? God prospered Daniel in all he did.

Today, I'm evaluating my own priorities. Am I putting the Lord first? And what, exactly, does that mean in practical terms? For one thing, it must surely mean that I will stop to remember during my day, as often as possible—remember that I am God's child, that I belong to Him, and that following His ways will bring my greatest good.

Heavenly Father, forgive me for letting so many other things diminish my sense of Your presence amidst my daily routines. Help me to remember! You alone are worthy of praise and glory—and of all my obedience. In Jesus' name, amen.

Amazing Remodeling

What the king asks is too difficult. No one can reveal it to the king except the gods, and they do not live among humans (Daniel 2:11).

Scripture: Daniel 2:1-11
Song: "Only Trust Him"

"It's impossible!" I moaned. For 25 years I'd shared Jesus with my grandfather, and the results were always the same. He listened patiently, patted me on my pumpkin head, and said he'd think about it. He'd embraced the mistaken idea that people were like dogs. When they died they became nothing— extinguished—with no hope of Heaven.

Persevering, I visited with my grandfather again shortly after his 85th birthday, and he told me he wanted to give his life to Jesus. I was shocked! But should I have been? I'd prayed diligently for him, so why didn't I expect the seemingly impossible . . . to become possible?

The wise men in the king's court were asked to do something they believed impossible: tell what the king had dreamed. But not knowing the almighty God, they underestimated His power. "It can't be done!" they declared.

I wonder, as God's children, do we sometimes make the same mistake? What is it that God can't do? It's as if the Lord is a building contractor: He specializes in the impossible, remodelling it to the possible.

Lord, I'm sorry for my lack of faith. You know the end from the beginning, and there is no power greater than Yours. Your goodness and mercy endure forever. Thank You for hearing my prayers. Please help me to trust You more. In Jesus' name. Amen.

Apply Some Wisdom Today

When Arioch, the commander of the king's guard, had gone out to put to death the wise men of Babylon, Daniel spoke to him with wisdom and tact (Daniel 2:14).

Scripture: Daniel 2:12-16
Song: "Eternal Wisdom, Thee We Praise"

Jim slammed the door as once again his new bride greeted his arrival with a laundry list of complaints. "Why do you have to act that way?" his wife whined. "I just need to talk!"

I was blessed with a godly mother-in-law who helped me navigate this common problem. Her wisdom taught me that instead of greeting my husband at the door with my day's distress, to pour him a glass of tea and allow him to unwind for a minute. After letting him talk first, he would be ready to hear the challenges of my day. This small gift of wisdom brought great rewards.

But ultimately, wisdom comes from God. So, how do we get it? James 1:5 says we can simply ask God for it, and He'll give it to us generously. It begins with learning God's Word. Then, as we apply the Word to our lives, we grow in wisdom.

Daniel received word of his impending execution. What would he do? Panic or trust God? He chose trust and spoke to the commander with respect, using wisdom and tactful speech. This approach brought an audience with the king—and eventually saved lives.

Father, I need wisdom. There are family members watching my life just as I watched my mother-in-law's. May I put You on display by my choices and my words. Teach me Your ways, Lord, and fill me with godly wisdom. Through Christ, amen.

God Knows the Future

The king said to Daniel, "Surely your God is the God of gods and the Lord of kings and a revealer of mysteries, for you were able to reveal this mystery" (Daniel 2:47).

Scripture: Daniel 2:36-49
Song: "Have Thine Own Way, Lord!"

A health crisis changes everything. After surviving a sudden heart attack, my husband, Mark, endured a multitude of tests, including a chemical stress test. He hated this test and vowed never to repeat it. However, just two years later, he needed the dreaded test again.

Mark wasn't happy! He argued, but the doctor wouldn't budge—and Mark failed the stress test. Even though he'd resisted all the way, God knew there was a life-threatening problem that needed fixing. Emergency bypass surgery was scheduled, and his heart was repaired.

Daniel knew God was all-knowing. So he asked Him to intervene by meeting the king's demand for dream interpretation. This intervention would save their lives. Furthermore, remember the result of Daniel's faith: the king canceled the execution order and fell on his face, praising the true God.

Like Daniel, we too can trust God in difficult, pressurized situations. He knows the end from the beginning and wants what is best for us. Our job is to stop being afraid and trust Him. Then we too can fall on our faces, praising God.

Lord, I thank You for walking with us through medical trials. You know all things, Lord, and I am so grateful to rest in Your care. Knowing you're never caught off guard like I am, please help me to trust You more. In Jesus' name, amen.

Gracious Forgiveness Awaits

Now, Lord our God, who brought your people out of Egypt with a mighty hand and who made for yourself a name that endures to this day, we have sinned, we have done wrong (Daniel 9:15).

Scripture: Daniel 9:15-19
Song: "Repent, the Kingdom Draweth Nigh"

A small flash outside the kitchen window caught my friend David's attention. He saw his young son, Chris, playing with matches. A little later, a father-son discussion ensued at the kitchen table. "But I haven't played with matches!" Chris kept saying . . . punishment was coming.

The Hebrews were living in the faraway land of Babylon where they'd been taken captive. Why were they there? Because of sin. God saw their wrongdoing and confronted them, time and again. Sadly, the people denied it, refusing to repent. Yet Daniel, himself a captive, continued to pray for his people, knowing that, before freedom could be realized, they needed to recognize their rebellion and reverse their ways.

Before you and I can be right with God, we too must lay down our stubbornness and face our sin head-on. The Father clearly knows what we've done, just as David knew about Chris's transgression. Shall we deny the obvious, or admit it? God's gracious forgiveness awaits us.

Father, thank You for helping me come clean about my own sin and for sending Jesus to pay its penalty in my place. You've forgiven me and cleansed me from all unrighteousness. For that I am eternally grateful! May my gratitude show forth in how I live throughout this day. In Jesus' name. Amen.

God Is Good; We Aren't

We have sinned, and have committed iniquity, and have done wickedly, and have rebelled, even by departing from thy precepts (Daniel 9:5).

Scripture: Daniel 9:4-14
Song: "Lord, I'm Coming Home"

For my friend Carol, college meant freedom. "Let the good times roll!" replaced church. Though her feelings of guilt were terrible, the appeal of the world was stronger. Several years into her rebellion, the stresses of Carol's lifestyle began to show: she found that running from the Lord was hard work! So she repented and returned to the Lord.

Daniel and his fellow countrymen languished in Babylonian captivity for one reason: the Israelites' willful rebellion. So Daniel offered up an eloquent prayer of repentance for himself and his nation.

The great deception of our modern age is that because God is love, He will not punish anyone. So why repent? In his book *God Has a Wonderful Plan for Your Life: The Myth of the Modern Message*, Ray Comfort gives the illustration of a man convicted of a brutal murder. At his sentencing the man tells the judge, "I believe you are a good man and will overlook my sins."

The judge replies, "Because I am a good man, I am going to see justice done." According to Comfort, "On the Day of Judgment, the goodness of God will be the very thing that will condemn [lost sinners]."

As Daniel knew, even for a "good guy" like himself, repentance is always appropriate.

Lord, thank You that You honor genuine repentance and have provided for our salvation through the death of Jesus, our Lord. In His name, amen.

Heart-warming Thought

As soon as you began to pray, a word went out, which I have come to tell you, for you are highly esteemed (Daniel 9:23).

Scripture: Daniel 9:20-27
Song: "Leaning on the Everlasting Arms"

For years I'd heard of the "empty nest syndrome" and was adamant that I'd never fall to it. However, a few years ago when our nest became officially empty, I unexpectedly plunged into depression. Even though I had made plans to stay extra busy with writing projects, along with involvement in the local jail ministry, my gloom persisted.

I finally realized: I hadn't been petitioning my heavenly Father about my loss. In my efforts to stay busy, I had pushed away the one who could help me. Pouring out my heart to the Lord, I soon felt a weight lift off my shoulders.

Oh, I still feel twinges of melancholy when I reflect on those years of child rearing. Yet I have come to accept this new chapter in my life. Now I spend more time praying for my kids, remembering that the Lord can see them when I cannot. And, no doubt, the Lord of all creation loves them even more than I do. That "my" children are actually His—and knowing He has their best interests at heart—warms my own heart.

Heavenly Father, I thank You for the gift of my children. Help me to accept the changing seasons in my life and in theirs, knowing that You have a wonderful plan for all of us. I pray this prayer in the name of Jesus my Lord. Amen.

March 11–17. **Connie Sturm Cameron** is an author and speaker who enjoys prison ministry and Kenyan missionary work. She lives with her husband of over 30 years in Glenford, Ohio.

Angels Watching over Us

See, I am sending an angel ahead of you to guard you along the way and to bring you to the place I have prepared. Pay attention to him and listen to what he says. Do not rebel against him (Exodus 23:20, 21).

Scripture: Exodus 23:20-25
Song: "Angels Watching over Me"

It was to have been a simple surgery for my mother, but something went terribly wrong. Mom became seriously ill following the procedure and needed another corrective surgery. The night before her second operation, I couldn't sleep. Though I'd visited her earlier that day at the hospital, I hadn't prayed with her . . . she seemed so afraid when I left. Finally, around 2 a.m., I desperately cried out, "Lord, please send someone to my mother to pray with her."

The next day when I visited Mom in the recovery room, even though she was heavily sedated, there was no mistaking the sparkle in her eyes. "A very pregnant nurse visited me late last night," Mom whispered. "I've never seen her before. She asked me if I was afraid. When I said 'yes,' she asked if she could kneel by my bed and pray with me. I was so grateful."

Mom stayed in the hospital a few more days. While there, she inquired of several staff members about that nurse so she could thank her. Amazingly, no one knew of a pregnant nurse.

Almighty and most merciful God, forgive me for holding onto my burdens and for forgetting to turn to You during my time of need. Thank You for sending Your ministering angels to me and to my loved ones. Lest I forget, remind me that no problem is too big for You to handle. In the name of Jesus, amen.

Choose Your Friends Wisely

[God said,] "You shall not make a covenant with the people of this land, but you shall break down their altars.' Yet you have disobeyed me. Why have you done this?" (Judges 2:2).

Scripture: Judges 2:1-5
Song: "Jesus Is My Best of Friends"

"Mom, why can't I spend the night at Trisha's house?" my preteen daughter wailed. "It's not fair; a lot of my friends are allowed to!"

"Your father and I haven't met her yet," I gently explained. "You know the rules. Let's invite her over for dinner soon."

As parents, we try to teach our children to make good choices, especially when it comes to choosing friends. Hopefully, we have made good choices in our friendships and are examples of what healthy friendships look like.

God warned the people of Israel not to associate with certain people groups—for their own good. Yet they chose not to listen and suffered some painful consequences.

We can regularly share such teachable Bible lessons with our children, explaining to them that the people we socialize with can have a positive or negative influence on us. We need to warn our children, while they are young, of the consequences of associating with the wrong crowd. It could prevent having a prodigal teen down the road.

Father, help us to train up our children in the way they should go, speaking to them about You "when [we] lie down and when [we] get up" (Deuteronomy 11:19). Remind us that those seeds we plant today in their moldable, teachable hearts will help protect them as they approach adulthood. I pray in the name of Christ. Amen.

Trust God's Word

You will be silent and not able to speak until the day this happens, because you did not believe my words, which will come true at their appointed time (Luke 1:20).

Scripture: Luke 1:8-20
Song: "Above the Hills of Time"

After praying for Ashley in our women's prayer group and asking God to restore her marriage, we gathered our coats to start for home. That's when I overheard Ashley talking about her plight to Megan. "I don't know what I'm going to do. I'm so afraid of losing my marriage."

Megan wisely reminded her that we had just asked the Lord to help. Ashley could trust that God had heard our prayer and was at work in her life and marriage. Now she could walk forward in faith, seeking by God's strength to be a patient, loving, and forgiving wife to her mate.

When Zechariah and Elizabeth didn't believe the angel's message that they would have a child, God closed Zechariah's mouth from speaking until their baby, John, was delivered. The point was clear: Don't doubt God's Word.

Nothing is impossible for God. He can restore an ailing marriage and bring life to a lifeless womb. Our part is to pray, believing He hears us, walking in faith. He will answer us in His way and in His time.

Heavenly Father, help me to believe that You hear my petitions and pleas and then to be patient enough to wait on Your perfect timing. I know You have my best interests at heart. Use me to remind others of the same, giving them hope in You. In Jesus' precious name I pray. Amen.

Promise Keeper

"I am the Lord's servant," Mary answered. "May your word to me be fulfilled" (Luke 1:38).

Scripture: Luke 1:26-38
Song: "Precious Promise"

Have you ever noticed how children hold onto our every word? They have complete trust in us and usually remember the most trivial of promises.

"Yes, I'll read you two books tonight," the harried mother responds to her demanding toddler. But when bedtime arrives, the exhausted mother can barely keep her eyes open to finish the first book.

"I'll read you two books tomorrow," she says, yawning. "But Mommy, you *promised!*" the bright-eyed toddler responds.

We have all made promises, and at times we were not able to come through. And we have also been on the opposite side: counting on someone's word, only to be disappointed.

In the early 1990s, Bill McCartney recognized the need for men of faith to keep their promises. His passion to help fathers and husbands become men of integrity eventually became the powerful men's group, Promise Keepers.

Our heavenly Father is the original promise keeper. Thankfully, we can turn to Him with the faith of a little child. (His desire, though, is that we keep our word.)

Father in Heaven, I thank You for not going back on Your word to me, but for fulfilling every promise. Forgive me for those times when I have broken my promises to You and to others, and strengthen me to be a person of integrity. I pray this prayer in the name of Jesus, my merciful Savior and Lord. Amen.

Where Is Your Treasure?

Understand that the vision concerns the time of the end (Daniel 8:17).

Scripture: Daniel 8:1, 13-18
Song: "God Will Take Care of You"

Almost immediately following a natural disaster, a path appears through the destroyed area. The debris flanking the pathway represents once-prized possessions: photo albums, stamp collections, books. Now it's all just trash.

Recently I found an article with a similar theme. A trader in the Indian state of Bihar had lost his life savings after termites infested his bank's safe deposit boxes and ate up his paper money and stock certificates. The bank had posted a sign about the problem, but the man hadn't been to the bank for months. Since the safe had not been broken into, the bank wasn't liable. And the man had been keeping the money from his wife and family, due to some family conflicts.

God allows our riches to turn into trash every day. Why? It could be to get our attention and to help us to see that we have our priorities confused. God calls us to wake up to what truly matters: our relationship with Him and our loved ones. While there is nothing wrong with having stuff, the problem comes when the stuff has us. Today may we remember that money is a tool to carry out the will of God.

O Lord, thank You for lifting my vision now and then to see the end of all earthly things. May I keep my possessions loosely in my hand, being ready and willing to give them away at Your command. Remind me that where my treasure is, there my heart is also (see Luke 12:34). Thank You, Father. Amen.

God's Perfect Timing

I am going to tell you what will happen later in the time of wrath, because the vision concerns the appointed time of the end (Daniel 8:19).

Scripture: Daniel 8:19-26
Song: "He's an On-Time God"

Our choir was in place, and the worship music had begun. But there was no sign of the soloist. Finally, at the last possible second, Heather dashed to the front, breathlessly singing out the most appropriate lyrics, "He's an on-time God, yes He is!" We erupted in laughter as God's sense of humor and His perfect timing made such a practical impact on us.

Whenever I reflect on that morning, I can't help but smile. It reminds me that what might appear to be a delay can actually be God's appointed time. And that is what I try to pray for regularly: God's appointed timing.

Instead of asking, "Father, help me to get there on time," I now pray, "Father, help me to get there at Your appointed time." Such a simple change in prayer has made all the difference in how I move through my days. It immediately calms me down and reminds me that God is in control.

While I do my best to be punctual, if something unforeseen happens, I am able to accept it—as "grist" for my own growth process. As difficult as it is to wait, I want God's timing, not mine.

Heavenly Father, thank You for Your reminders that You are in control of my day, not me. Please keep my eyes open to the fact that any interruption could actually be a divine appointment. In Jesus' name, amen.

Remember It All

For seven days eat unleavened bread, the bread of affliction, because you left Egypt in haste—so that all the days of your life you may remember the time of your departure from Egypt (Deuteronomy 16:3).

Scripture: Deuteronomy 16:1-8
Song: "Servant of God, Remember"

I loved attending the shows when my husband was singing with the Highland Harmonizers, a barbershop harmony chorus in Colorado Springs. The songs were beautifully sung and choreographed, the skits hilarious, and the quartets spectacular.

Most of the songs are overwhelmingly nostalgic. They hearken back to the good old days, the times gone by, with rather intense longing. For barbershoppers, *memories* is a key word.

It's human nature to recall the good times of the past. But what about the tough times? In our Scripture God calls the people to observe—with annual memories and a ritual meal—how they were driven out into a desert. Eating the "bread of affliction" would help them remember. Thankfully, the point was to recall the faithfulness of God in finally leading them *out* of affliction. After many trials, they entered a promised land.

Let us refuse to blot from our memories the difficulties we've encountered through the years. Aren't those the very times when we have seen God's hand most powerfully at work?

Lord, thanks for the blessings You've poured into my life in the past. I also acknowledge the ways You've worked in the midst of my struggles. In Jesus' name, amen.

March 18–24. **Carol Wilde** works as a web development manager for ValPak in Naples, Florida. Previously, she spent many years as a marketing director in Christian publishing.

Try a Body Prayer?

Then the people bowed down and worshiped (Exodus 12:27).

Scripture: Exodus 12:21-27
Song: "Before the Lord We Bow"

In our church there is time in each service for us to "bow down" as we worship. We lower our upper bodies when we sing the ancient *sanctus et benedictus,* based on Isaiah 6:1-3 and Psalm 118:26 — "Holy, holy, holy, Lord God of Hosts: Heaven and earth are full of thy glory."

Then it feels as if my whole self is praying, not just my mind, but all of me. And I can "say" to the Lord, with my posture, that I am humbled in His presence, that I adore His holy name.

When God instituted the Passover for His people, he was doing something infinitely gracious. They had no hope of leaving their slavery in Egypt until He took drastic measures. If Pharaoh would not relent, the firstborn of the land would be killed by an angel *passing over* them.

The gracious part is this: Any home that displayed blood sprinkled above and on the sides of the doorposts would be spared.

What was the peoples' response to this gift of their salvation, every time they recalled it? They bowed down and worshipped.

I invite you to find a time this week in which you can offer a posture prayer. What heartfelt thankfulness or adoration would you like to express? Might it involve a bow or a bended knee?

O God, the King of glory, I honor Your name, and I bow to Your greatness. Thank You for being the Holy Lord of all! I pray this prayer in the precious and holy name of Christ my Lord. Amen.

You Can Trust Him

They left and found things just as Jesus had told them. So they prepared the Passover (Luke 22:13).

Scripture: Luke 22:7-13
Song: "The Lamb's High Banquet We Await"

As your driving along, wondering about the route, do you ever stop to ask for directions? It can be scary asking a total stranger which route to take — especially if you're heading up into high mountains or facing the prospect of crossing a hot, dry desert. You may wonder, *Did he tell us the right thing? Was she herself confused?*

Even if the person giving the directions is sincere and wanting to help, who knows whether he or she may be misinformed? or impishly playful? or downright mean?

Not so with Jesus! When it was time for the preparation of the Passover meal, He told two of His disciples exactly where to go, what to do and say, and what would occur. And later, of course, they "found things just as Jesus had told them."

The point is: Jesus is trustworthy, then and now. The next point is: Sometimes I forget this.

Shakespeare once said: "Don't trust the person who has broken faith once." And that seems right to me. But with the Lord, the opposite side of the coin can bring any of us followers great confidence and peace: "Has our Master ever broken trust, even once?"

Almighty and most merciful God, I praise You for Your trustworthiness today. Your promises and decrees are set in stone, and I can "take them to the bank." That is a great comfort to me, and I thank You, in Jesus' name. Amen.

Beware the Linkage!

Is not the cup of thanksgiving for which we give thanks a participation in the blood of Christ? And is not the bread that we break a participation in the body of Christ? (1 Corinthians 10:16).

Scripture: 1 Corinthians 10:14-22
Song: "In the Quiet Consecration"

The apostle Paul wanted his Corinthian readers to be aware of what we might call the "unintended linkages." What do I mean? Well, if they felt perfectly free to eat meat that had been sacrificed to idols, on one level, that would be perfectly OK. All Christians know that any honoring of idols is pure illusion. But there is a linkage: when we *associate* ourselves in any way with something less than pure, we "participate" in it.

So let us beware of divided loyalties. We might feel perfectly free to do something that is in a gray area for Christians, activities about which believers disagree. Perhaps our minds do not condemn us when we do these things. But the linkage, the participation, may come back to haunt us. A friend who sees us doing it may receive a wound to her conscience.

The glory of this passage is that it teaches a profound respect for the Lord's Supper. The word *participate* in the Greek text is *koinonia*, often translated communion, or sharing, or fellowship. In taking the bread and cup, we have communion with Christ, we share in His life, death, resurrection, and ascension, and we enjoy fellowship with our brothers and sisters in Christ.

Thank You, Lord, for the privilege of sharing in Your life. This comes to me by pure grace, so I can only lift my hands and give You praise. In Christ, amen.

Which Meal Is the Focus?

Don't you have homes to eat and drink in? Or do you despise the church of God by humiliating those who have nothing? What shall I say to you? Shall I praise you? Certainly not in this matter! (1 Corinthians 11:22).

Scripture: 1 Corinthians 11:17-22
Song: "In Sweet Communion"

I've noticed something interesting about our coffee hour at church. Over the years it has become much more than some donuts and coffee for folks to enjoy after the church service. There is, on most Sundays, an entire kitchen crew armed with saucepans and skillets, focused on eggs, bacon, toast, hash browns, and any number of variations on traditional and untraditional breakfast themes. What happened?

And there's another aspect to this: I've overheard some conversations that make me think the breakfast might be a seriously important part of any given Sunday for some of the folks—and I include myself!

Has it become too important? Problem is, it can be pretty tempting to sit in a pew and let my mind wander to the approaching eggs and bacon when I should be focusing on hymns and prayers. (Is Helen in the kitchen today? Love her biscuits!)

But I digress . . . where was I? Right, let us stand and sing.

P. S. I wonder what the apostle Paul would say about all this. Wait! I know. It's right here: "Shall I praise you? Certainly not in this matter!"

Let me take to heart, **Lord,** the apostle's warning about confusing the sacred meal and the ordinary dinner. May I honor the Lord in both. In Jesus' name, amen.

Ready for Communion?

Whoever eats the bread or drinks the cup of the Lord in an unworthy manner will be guilty of sinning against the body and blood of the Lord (1 Corinthians 11:27).

Scripture: 1 Corinthians 11:23-32
Song: "Do This: Remember Me"

Susie had spent Saturday night partying with friends. There was quite a bit of drinking, and when she woke up she really couldn't remember what else might have happened at Carrie's house. But it was time to get up— she'd promised Mom she'd be in church today, ready to take communion. *But am I ready?*

Jim erased every trace of the history cache on his computer, knowing he wouldn't want any of his family members to see where he'd been surfing on the web. Of course, what they didn't know couldn't hurt them, so no harm done, right? *I still feel a little guilty, though . . . but time for church!*

Bob and Mary had the most explosive argument about the Sunday paper. Mary had torn out some coupons and advertisements, obliterating an article Bob wanted to read. Too late to put the pieces back together—Bob was helping serve communion today, and it was time to head to church. Both of them still fuming, the couple slammed the car doors. *We'll finish this little fight after church—and I know who's going to win!*

Dear reader, in light of Paul's words about taking the bread and cup "worthily," what are your observations about our friends above? If they were to come to you for counsel, what would you say?

O Lord, give me pause as I look forward to taking the bread and the cup. Do I discern the Lord here? Have I confessed my sins to Him. Am I ready? Through Christ, amen.

Better to Serve

Who is greater, the one who is at the table or the one who serves? Is it not the one who is at the table? But I am among you as one who serves (Luke 22:27).

Scripture: Luke 22:14-30
Song: "Who Is on the Lord's Side?"

It was a big banquet at my college, and it was the first time I'd ever served as a waitress. Yes, I was chosen to help serve the big dinner on a parent-student visitation day. Prospective students from around the country were there to check out our college, so we wanted to make a good impression.

My lack of experience in serving did *not* make the desired impression. I spilled a glass of water on one lady. And then, as I was whisking away an empty plate, I failed to remove the silverware first. A bread knife flew off at a right angle and landed nicely in the coat pocket of the gentlemen seated two chairs away. I politely retrieved it (if one can be considered "polite" while rummaging through another's clothing).

Jesus points to the privilege of serving others. He tells His followers that it is a high calling and that He, himself, is on a mission to do exactly that: *serve*.

We can enjoy being served. But let us remember that an even greater enjoyment can flow from being the one who serves. It comes with its present-day pleasures. But, according to Jesus, we will have a future reward beyond compare: reigning alongside the King of kings.

Make me a servant at heart, **Lord,** for I know that the kingdom values have little to do with the world's perspectives on success. In the name of Christ, amen.

Release Jesus!

I will punish him and then release him (Luke 23:16).

Scripture: Luke 23:13-25
Song: "Hallelujah! What a Savior!"

"I find no basis for your charges against him." But the crowd kept shouting, "Crucify Him! Crucify Him."

"Why?" Pilate asked.

My question today is: Why would Pilate release the man who had been thrown into prison for insurrection and murder, while surrendering the innocent Jesus to their will?

His words to the crowd were, "I have examined him in your presence and have found no basis for your charges against him" (v. 14). So why was he persuaded by the crowd to do what he knew was wrong? He decided to listen to the crowd instead of his conscience.

Why do we let people curse Him, deny Him, turn their faces against Him? Is it the crowd? But the crowd might not let us be in their circle of friends. The crowd might make us feel uneasy if we talked with them. They might not let our children be involved in sports. So many reasons, so many times, so many people determine what we choose to do.

But the crowd! Get away from the crowd and listen to God. Do not be a Pilate.

Help me, **Lord**, to listen to Your voice above the noise of the crowd. I love You, and I want to live for You. I certainly don't want to crucify You again in any way. I ask these things in Your holy name. Amen.

March 25–31. **Francine Duckworth,** of Brush, Colorado, has written for several devotional publications over the years.

King of the Jews

There was a written notice above him, which read: THIS IS THE KING OF THE JEWS (Luke 23:38).

Scripture: Luke 23:32-38
Song: "Lead Me to Calvary"

He is the king of the Jews. He is our king too.

Crucified, dead, and buried. People watched, rulers sneered, soldiers mocked. "If you are the king of the Jews, save yourself" (v. 37). We weren't there, but we can think about what we might have done if we were. *Would I have been part of the crowd who watched and sneered or part of the crowd who cried and prayed?*

Those who cried for Jesus' death—had they read the Scriptures, had they heard the prophecies?

Maybe they had.

Maybe they knew.

Maybe they were just caught up in the crowd.

Maybe they just found it easier to go along with their friends.

It happens today in our town and with our families. We love Jesus. We want to live for Him. We know He is our king. But someone says Jesus Christ this, or God that, and we sit silently.

Are we letting that person crucify Him again? Can you speak up? Can I? Can we tell the world that He is still the great King?

"Yes, He is the King of kings! Yes, He died for me. Yes, He died for you."

O Lord, You are here in my world, risen from the dead. Thank You for being with me this day—for dwelling within me by Your Holy Spirit. I want people to know You are the King of kings. I want them to know You died for me and for them. Help me to demonstrate these things by the way I live my life. In Jesus' name, amen.

Trust Him for the Courage

The centurion, seeing what had happened, praised God and said, "Surely this was a righteous man" (Luke 23:47).

Scripture: Luke 23:44-49
Song: "Praise God, from Whom All Blessings Flow".

"Surely this was a righteous man"(v. 47) said the centurion, the eyewitness who saw what unfolded on the hill of Golgotha. And we too know that Jesus was guiltless.

We know He was morally upright. In fact, those of us who have placed our faith in Him believe He was perfect in every way—tempted, yet He did not sin (see Hebrews 4:15). We have God's Word to show us what He did and why He did it. This soldier had only what he had seen. Then he praised God for all He witnessed in the stellar character of the Christ.

Some people who witnessed this horrible crucifixion, beat their breasts and went away. On the other hand, "All those who knew him, . . . stood at a distance, watching these things" (v. 49).

Two groups: The ones who beat their breasts and those who knew Him. So I wonder: Where do I stand? In which group am I?

I want to be like the centurion who praised God and said, "This was a righteous man" (v. 47).

Let's be the ones who love Jesus enough to stay with Him, faithful to the end. We can do it, if we'll trust God for the courage.

O God, the King of glory, there are so many things I have to praise You for this day. I pray that if suddenly a multitude of difficulties pour into my life today, I will still praise Your holy name. You are worthy of all honor and praise. In the name of Jesus, my Lord and Savior, I pray. Amen.

They Rested

They rested on the Sabbath in obedience to the command-ment (Luke 23:56).

Scripture: Luke 23:50-56
Song: "Under the Atoning Blood"

Joseph, a good and upright man, asked for Jesus' body. He had not consented to the crowd's actions, and this frustrated him. He had come from his hometown waiting for the kingdom of God. He ended up asking for Jesus' body.

How lovingly he must have prepared the body for burial. As he wrapped it in linen cloth and placed it in the tomb, I'm sure he was wondering what would happen.

Some women followed Joseph and watched as he laid Jesus in the tomb. They went home, prepared spices and perfumes, and rested on the Sabbath as the commandment told them to do. Then they were the first ones to see that Jesus had risen.

A good thing to do today: Obey the commandments.

Flying, traveling, telling others about Jesus, that was me during our furlough year. When on the plane I witnessed. When traveling on the bus, I shared about God's love. At churches I enjoyed telling what God had done on our mission field.

But I too needed to obey the Lord's commandment, just as those ladies did on a Sabbath so long ago. I needed to rest. This coming Sunday, let's take a moment to ask ourselves: Where am I going? What am I doing? Why?

Dear God, Your Word says, "Come to me, all you who are weary and burdened, and I will give you rest" (Matthew 11:28). I do need to rest today. I want to see You, spend time with You, hear from You, and be guided by You. In the name of Jesus, amen.

Never Said a Word

He did not open his mouth (Isaiah 53:7).

Scripture: Isaiah 53:3-9
Song: "He Has Surely Borne Our Sorrow"

Lied to and about, I just kept working. Coworkers asked others to write letters about me. Nevertheless, I taught each day and did what I thought was right. Told I wasn't competent for the position, I kept saying to myself, "Jesus never defended himself. I'm not going to say a word." People told me to go to the office and fight. But I kept hearing these words of Scripture: "Let your gentleness be evident to all" (Philippians 4:5).

"Francine, you're going to lose your job." Concerned friends talked to my husband. "I've lived with Francine long enough to know she'll turn to God. Don't worry about her," he said.

But I didn't want to turn to God. I wanted to scream and say, "This isn't right!" But I kept going to God's Word. "If it is possible, as far as it depends on you, live at peace with everyone" (Romans 12:18). I tried. I thought of Jesus.

No one I know has ever gone through what Jesus went through. No one I know has been despised and rejected as He was. "He was oppressed and afflicted, yet he did not open his mouth" (v. 7). What an example for us. What I went through was hard, but nothing like what Jesus went through for us. And He never said a word.

Lord Jesus, I know that some Christians have suffered greatly. But no one has given up the glories of Heaven to take upon the sins of the world for all time. I can't imagine the horrible pain of the burden that You carried. I can only thank You for this sacrifice. In Your precious name I pray. Amen.

They Told All!

They told all these things to the Eleven and to all the others (Luke 24:9).

Scripture: Luke 24:1-12
Song: "Tell the Blessed Story"

He has risen! Exciting news! "Remember how he told you . . . [He] must . . . be crucified and on the third day be raised again." It happened. They saw the empty tomb. The women told all these things to the 11 apostles and all the others.

Rosa told all these things to family and friends. She had been coming to our church for about six months. A new Christian, she attended the ladies Bible study. "We have this gift of eternal life," she said. "I feel like I need to share it with everyone."

And that she did. The first year she was in our church, she invited her family members, and they came. Friends came with her to Wednesday night study hour. Coworkers said, "I want to see what has made such a difference in Rosa's life."

Last Sunday morning Rosa had a 5-year-old relative with her. She had let him spend Saturday night at her house, so he could come to church with the family on Sunday.

I'm 66-years-old, a Christian since I was 9. I know Jesus is alive and working in my life. But do I have this zeal? The Lord has worked miracles in our family and with our friends. Have I told all these things to others?

Rosa did. You can. I will.

Dear Heavenly Father, help me to tell the good news with a winsome but courageous spirit. It is a blessed story, and people of this world need to hear it from someone who is willing to first be their friend. It is Your command. In Christ's name, amen.

Eyes Wide Open

Then their eyes were opened and they recognized him (Luke 24:31).

Scripture: Luke 24:13-21, 28-35
Song: "We Would See Jesus"

Resuscitated, on oxygen, and in an ambulance, Julie opened her eyes. Through the two windows in the back of the ambulance, she saw two white crosses. It was at that moment she decided to give her life to Jesus. From that day on, Julie wanted to make all of her decisions based on Jesus' life and His love.

Abused, a runaway, and needing someone, Julie had looked for love. She had heard about Jesus, read about Him, had even gone to a church when her grandmother was alive. All those things came back to her now. How had she been so blind? Why had she turned away?

"Then their eyes were opened and they recognized him, and he disappeared from their sight" (v. 31).

But that day in the ambulance, Jesus did not disappear. He stayed with Julie, and she had His assurance that He would be with her always.

Have all of Julie's problems vanished? No. But her eyes were opened, and she claimed Him as her Savior. Jesus has begun a marvelous, transforming work in Julie's heart.

Daily He transforms each of us who seek to know Him.

Loving Father, open my eyes. Help me to recognize Your presence when I am teaching. I want to see You as I work at serving others. I'm Yours, and You are mine. Thank You for Your love, in Jesus' name, amen.

DEVOTIONS®

APRIL

Remain in me . . . No branch can bear fruit by itself;
it must remain in the vine. Neither can you bear
fruit unless you remain in me.

—*John 15:4*

Gary Allen, Editor   **Margaret Williams,** Project Editor   Photo: Stockbyte | Thinkstock®

DEVOTIONS® is published quarterly by Standard Publishing, Cincinnati, Ohio, www.standardpub.com. © 2012 by Standard Publishing. All rights reserved. Topics based on the Home Daily Bible Readings, International Sunday School Lessons. © 2009 by the Committee on the Uniform Series. Printed in the U.S.A. All Scripture quotations, unless otherwise indicated, are taken from the *HOLY BIBLE, NEW INTERNATIONAL VERSION®. NIV®.* Copyright © 1973, 1978, 1984, 2011 by Biblica, Inc.™ Used by permission of Zondervan. All rights reserved. Scripture quotations marked (*NASB*) *are* taken from the *New American Standard Bible®.* Copyright © 1960, 1962, 1963, 1968, 1971, 1972, 1973, 1975, 1977, 1995 by The Lockman Foundation. Used by permission. (www.Lockman.org). All rights reserved. Scripture quotations marked (*NKJV*) are taken from the *New King James Version®.* Copyright © 1982 by Thomas Nelson, Inc. Used by permission. All rights reserved.

Taking a Stand

Now I make known to you, brethren, the gospel which I preached to you, which also you received, in which also you stand (1 Corinthians 15:1, *New American Standard Bible*).

Scripture: 1 Corinthians 15:1-8
Song: "Stand Fast for Christ Thy Savior"

When German church reformer Martin Luther was challenged by the established church in 1521, he appeared before the legislative body known as the Diet in the city of Worms. Luther was proclaiming *sola fide*, "faith alone," and church officials demanded he recant his message. "Unless I am convinced by the testimony of the Scriptures or by clear reason," he said, "I cannot and will not recant anything." Then, according to tradition, he continued: "Here I stand, I can do no other. May God help me. Amen."

Luther's firm stand was based on the secure foundation of the eternal validity of the gospel of grace. It was the same gospel, Paul reminded the Corinthian believers, that was the basis of their faith.

The gospel of grace still encounters challenges. In fact, sometimes I'm tempted too: "Surely it's not enough just to believe in Christ. I must add something to get God's approval." But, of course, I can contribute nothing to my salvation. The full work was done at the cross.

Father, I know so well when I stand on the gospel of grace that I stand on an eternal, unshakable reality. In Christ's name, amen.

April 1–7. **Anne Adams,** who resides in Houston, Texas, has been a freelance writer for more than 30 years, publishing in both secular and Christian publications.

Remember to Remember

She turned around and saw Jesus standing there, and did not know that it was Jesus (John 20:14, *New American Standard Bible*).

Scripture: John 20:11-18
Song: "In the Garden"

Some years ago, I sang at a statewide conference with our church choir. Also, I was on the staff of another church in our denomination, so I knew I'd see many of those friends there.

As the program started, because of the large number of attendees, conference-goers were being seated in the choir area. Among these was Randy, a member of the church where I worked. As he took his seat, he saw me and looked confused. I knew he was puzzled because I was in a place he didn't expect to see me. However, then he nodded and smiled, and the program began.

Mary Magdalene must have experienced something similar outside Jesus' tomb. Did she also do a "double take," as Randy did? No doubt Mary failed to know Jesus at first because she could hardly expect to see Him outside the tomb where He'd been laid . . . cold and dead. But when He spoke to her, she recognized Him.

Sometimes, like Mary, I fail to recognize the Lord's presence in my life, usually because I don't expect Him to be there. It's as if I forget that He is *always* with me. And isn't that the challenge for all of us: to keep remembering?

Lord God, help me learn to be constantly aware of Your presence in my life. And grant that I may trust that reality as I serve You. In Jesus' name, amen.

Verifying Scars

Unless I see in His hands the imprint of the nails, and put my finger into the place of the nails, and put my hand into His side, I will not believe (John 20:25, *New American Standard Bible*).

Scripture: John 20:24-29
Song: "I Saw His Scars"

In 1803 in New York City, a carpenter named Thomas Hoag disappeared. Two years later, his sister-in-law encountered a man she claimed was Hoag, and the man was arrested and charged with family desertion. At his trial, he was identified by his wife, his employer, a close friend, and by a scar on his forehead.

Nevertheless, the accused claimed his name was Joseph Parker. Despite the evidence presented, the judge wanted more proof. Then a friend remembered something else. The real Hoag had a long scar on the sole of his foot. When the defendant removed his boots and displayed a scar-free foot, the case was settled. Though Hoag never surfaced, Parker was cleared.

Thomas was ready to believe in Jesus' resurrection, but he wanted proof—and he got it. While the lack of a scar cleared Parker, with Jesus the *presence* of scars clearly identified Him.

I also have soul-tarnishing scars of sin and failure—marks that I know sadden my Lord. Yet, it is Christ's scars, representing His sacrifice for me, that assure me of His acceptance and His call to take up my own cross for Him.

Father, help me remember that the verifying scars prove not only the reality of the resurrection but also of Christ's sacrifice. I'm so thankful that His atoning work frees me of guilt and allows me to serve You. In Christ's name I pray. Amen.

Worketh While You Waiteth

Simon Peter said to them, "I am going fishing." They said to him, "We will also come with you" (John 21:3, *New American Standard Bible*).

Scripture: John 21:1-8
Song: "If Thou but Suffer God to Guide Thee"

Many years ago I purchased a wall plaque that used a "religious" format and Gothic type to express a humorous but true statement: "Everything cometh to him who waiteth, as long as he who waiteth worketh like heck while he waiteth."

I put it up in my office because, as a writer, I'm quite familiar with the concept. It reminds me that when I submit something to a publisher I should remain busy with other projects while waiting for a response.

Did Peter have the same idea when he returned to his fishing business after Jesus' resurrection? While the Lord had constantly been with the disciples before, now He appeared less often. So while waiting, Peter fished. And there on the beach Jesus met him.

Waiting for the Lord is an important part of the Christian life, but it can be frustrating. So what to do? When He wants me to wait for Him then, to paraphrase the plaque, I must keepeth busy in God's service while I waiteth until I meeteth Him.

Almighty and most merciful God, I wait upon You to lead me into service in Your kingdom. What You have planned is far superior to anything I could ever conceive, so help me to patiently follow You, step by step each day. In the name of Jesus, who lives and reigns with You and the Holy Spirit, one God, now and forever, amen.

Food and Fellowship

Jesus came and took the bread and gave it to them, and the fish likewise (John 21:13, *New American Standard Bible*).

Scripture: John 21:9-14
Song: "Break Thou the Bread of Life"

A teacher in a Christian elementary school had a class composed of children from various churches. One day she encouraged her students to bring in, and talk about, something that was distinctive to their particular faith community.

A young boy began: "I'm Catholic, and this is my rosary." Next on the program was a girl. "I'm an Episcopalian," she said, "and this is my *Book of Common Prayer*." Then there was another girl. "I'm a Methodist," she said, "and this is my casserole dish."

One amusing aspect of this story is that there are different versions in which the third child is a Baptist or Presbyterian or Lutheran or . . . you name it. Also, as I know from personal experience, casseroles—and by extension, church dinners—are entirely interdenominational.

Obviously, food and the accompanying fellowship are a uniting factor for all believers. Likewise, when Jesus and the disciples had breakfast on the beach, it served to unite and encourage, as well as instruct.

Whether it's a church dinner or a quick cup of coffee with a Christian friend, indeed food serves to unite us. But it also provides the setting to encourage, to listen, to share, and maybe even to pray.

Father, thank You that the Bread of Life is with me. Please help me always be attuned to the spiritual nourishment I can only get from Him. In Christ's name, amen.

Following Closely

He said to him, "Follow me!" (John 21:19).

Scripture: John 21:15-19
Song: "Where He Leads Me"

"What happened when I came over to your house yesterday?" Mary asked her friend Sue. "Jackie had just run out the door, and you were chasing him. Part of the 'Terrible Twos'?"

"You got it. His latest trick is to run away when I want him to do something," Sue replied. "Last night I'd told him it was bedtime just as you came over. So he laughed and ran out the front door. He was hard to see in the dark, but I just followed the lights on his shoes."

At Mary's puzzled expression, Sue explained. "Remember those little sneakers my in-laws got him? The ones with the flashing lights on the back? He loves them, but he didn't realize they stymied his trick. I easily caught him—just followed the lights."

Jesus completed His word to Peter with a simple statement: "Follow me!" And Peter did—faithfully and devotedly—until his death.

Our Lord gives the same invitation today. So how do we follow Him? Perhaps we do it best when we become so close to Him that we are constantly aware of His presence and guidance. Then we find that following Him is a blessing indeed.

Lord, I know that following You is a lifetime commitment, and that sometimes Your path involves struggle. Help me to see that I can only grow when I move through difficulties with a trusting heart. In Jesus' name, amen.

True Identification

Look at my hands and my feet. It is I myself! (Luke 24:39).

Scripture: Luke 24:36-53
Song: "Were You There?"

In 1920 when an unidentified young woman was hospitalized in Berlin, Germany, some claimed she was actually Anastasia, daughter of the late czar of Russia. They thought she had somehow escaped the murder of the Russian royal family by Communists in 1918. Others said she wasn't Anastasia but a missing, mentally ill Polish woman. Over the next years, as her true identity was widely discussed, she gradually became known as Anna Anderson.

Anna came to the U.S. in 1968, and died in Virginia in 1984. Then the remains of the czar, his wife, and all five children were discovered and identified. So who was Anderson? Final identification came from DNA tests that showed she wasn't related to the Russian royal family but did show a connection to the Polish woman's family. Science provided a true identification.

It was vital that the disciples truly identify the risen Christ. They had to know for sure, since their lives depended on a *living* Lord.

How do we identify Christ in our lives? What is alive will grow. Thus His living presence in us keeps producing the fruits of His beautiful character.

Father, I know that the Christ that challenged the disciples so long ago also challenges me today. Help me use this knowledge to completely and totally serve You. In the name of Jesus I pray. Amen.

Don't Cancel Those Words!

Whoever has my commands and keeps them is the one who loves me (John 14:21).

Scripture: John 14:18-24
Song: "I Love You, Lord"

I suppose that innocent bystanders would be sickened: my wife and I must say "I love you" to each other at least a dozen times a day. Whether upon waking or just before falling asleep—or at some unexpected time during the day—one or the other of us will start that quick exchange. We enjoy and treasure the comfort, the closeness, the intimacy of that simple phrase.

But the only reason it carries any weight is that we see it reinforced in a hundred different ways. It's borne out in how we speak to each other, the consideration we show. It's in food cooked, clothes picked up, a door held open, a new cabinet built, a meal served to friends, dishes washed. It's in the courtesy and respect. It's in everything we do.

Singing "I Love You, Lord," is a fine thing, when it's borne out in our obedience to Him: His commands to return good for evil, to endure ill treatment, to show love to someone who has mistreated us. Confessions and professions mean nothing if our actions cancel them out.

O gracious God, help me to show my love for You in my daily attitudes and actions—by obeying everything You have commanded. May this way of living be a witness to Your marvelous grace working within me. I pray this prayer in the name of Jesus, my merciful Savior and Lord. Amen.

April 8–14. **Doc Arnett** directs institutional research at the oldest college in Kansas, Highland Community College. He and his wife, Randa, live in Blair, Kansas.

Love Through Bearing Fruit

If you do not remain in me, you are like a branch that is thrown away and withers; such branches are picked up, thrown into the fire and burned (John 15:6).

Scripture: John 15:1-7
Song: "More Love, More Power"

Along the fence line, a strand of trees grows between the neighbor's field and ours. You don't have to look too long or too closely to see some reminders of the ice storm that devastated our area three years ago. Branches as large as 6 inches thick still hang in some of the trees, caught by lower branches when the weight of the ice snapped them like twigs.

Around other trees, branches broken by that storm or by the winds since then, lie about the base, scattered in clumps. If plans hold to purpose, I will spend this weekend picking those up and hauling them over to our burn pile.

It's a simple rule of nature: only that which holds to its source can grow and flourish. The branch has to be held to the trunk to receive its water and nutrients from the roots. Without that connection, no amount of sunlight, carbon dioxide, and moisture can produce a single bit of food for the tree.

Even on a social level, we humans like to take our nourishment with a connection to others. As an old proverb quips: "He who eats alone chokes alone." And our connection to Christ is certainly more precious, more imperative. It is our anchoring in Him that gives us life and lets us bear fruit to His glory.

O Lord God, root me deeply and securely in You. Fill me with Your Spirit and Your Word, and let me never be cut off from the true vine. In His name I pray. Amen.

God Within Us

I tell you, it is for your good that I am going away. Unless I go away, the Advocate will not come to you; but if I go, I will send him to you (John 16:7).

Scripture: John 16:1-11
Song: "Be with Me, Lord"

I started using battery-powered carpenters' tools when Randa gave me a small circular saw for Christmas about 10 years ago. With only 12 volts it could still saw through 15 or 20 boards before it had to be recharged.

Since then, I've bought at least three upgrades. Each time, I'm still impressed with how much more power the newer model has and by how much longer each charge lasts. And it's great to forget about the extension cord when working outdoors.

But at times I'll still use my handsaw. It'll cut through timbers that are much too thick for the battery saw. But the power on the handsaw depends solely on me. Frankly, that power depletes pretty quickly and takes a lot longer to recharge!

Jesus tells His disciples that His leaving is a good thing. How can that be? How can it be that they would actually *gain* through His return to Heaven?

It is by the incredible gift of the Holy Spirit. Our power, our strength, our wisdom, our capacity are no longer limited by the confines of human flesh; we are energized by the very power of God himself. Instead of having God with us, we now have God within us.

Father, thank You for the gift of Your Holy Spirit that indwells in those who love You. Let me never resist His work in me but always yield to His leading. Through Christ, amen.

The Privilege of the Spirit

In the last days, God says, I will pour out my Spirit on all people (Acts 2:17).

Scripture: Acts 2:17-21
Song: "Sweet, Sweet Spirit"

Ever since I was a child, I've marveled at the stories of the prophets and how they were filled with the Holy Spirit. I picture Elijah doing battle with the prophets of Baal, taunting them, having them soak his sacrifice with barrels of water, and then calling down the fire of God upon the altar. I think of Elisha and his healings and miracles. I remember the strength of Samson and how he ripped the gate of the city off its hinges and carried it up the side of the mountain. I see Daniel standing before Nebuchadnezzar, interpreting a dream the king couldn't even remember.

As we read through the pages of the Old Testament, we see that millions of God's people never received the Holy Spirit. Rather, there were just a privileged few who ever knew that power and blessing, and that responsibility.

In addition to the salvation God poured out into the world at Pentecost, there is the fulfillment of that wonderful prophecy from Joel. No longer was the Holy Spirit granted only to a select handful of men. He was given to all believers, regardless of gender, ethnicity, history, geographic origin or any other distinction. In this gift, Jesus proves His love for us and His power in us.

Lord, great and holy are You in all Your ways. Open the hearts of believers throughout the world that they may embrace the gift of Your Holy Spirit. Through Christ, amen.

The Joy of the Path

You have made known to me the paths of life; you will fill me with joy in your presence (Acts 2:28).

Scripture: Acts 2:22-28
Song: "Follow On"

For 20 years, Randa had been telling me about the wonderful joys of hunting mushrooms. I'd gone out with her a few times, and she'd only found a couple. Otherwise, the fine delicacy of morels at our house depended upon the generosity of others. I began to suspect that hunting mushrooms was a bit like hunting snipe: it was a trick to play on some poor ignorant wretch.

Then, last April, we finally hit pay dirt over at Bluff Woods, a public conservation area in northwest Missouri. On our first morning, we found three or four little patches that provided us with enough for two or three repasts of buttered delight.

I was hooked. As soon as I got off work each day, I'd rush over and spend a couple of hours hiking a few miles, searching for and finding those delectable fungi.

My enthusiasm kept me out after dark a time or two, and once I ended up missing the trail back to the parking area. After a half hour of increasing anxiety, I stumbled upon the creek and followed it until I got back to the trail. What a relief! No longer afraid of being lost in the woods in the dark, I rejoiced because I knew where the trail led.

When we follow God's Holy Spirit, we know the path of life and rejoice in His presence as we walk along.

Heavenly Father, I pray, lead me always in the path of peace and wisdom, the path of righteousness and obedience. In the name of Jesus, amen.

The Loving Touch

Exalted to the right hand of God, he has received from the Father the promised Holy Spirit and has poured out what you now see and hear (Acts 2:33).

Scripture: Acts 2:29-36
Song: "Revive Us Again"

Even though three of my six children are now in their 30s, I've never gotten over the longing to pick them up and hold them again. The hugs that we share during our sporadic reunions are warm and strong. But not a day goes by that I don't wish I could sit them on my lap, read Shel Silverstein, *The Berenstein Bears*, or *Br'er Rabbit* and rock them to sleep as I did when they were small (before they scattered across the continent).

Facebook and text messages—even phone calls—can't supplant the pleasing expression of physical contact. Talking face to face, the occasional pat on the back, the squeeze of an arm, and the light kiss of affection all fill a void in my heart and soul that nothing else can fill. There is, at a primeval level, something special and sacred in such fellowship between parent and child.

It is that fellowship, in a much purer and more divine form, which Jesus accomplished when He poured out his Holy Spirit upon all flesh. By this, He achieved a literal fellowship of being within each and every believer. How blessed we are to have such intimate association with Him who made us.

Merciful God, thank You for the blessing of earthly relationships—and much more for the incredible privilege of communion with You and all believers through Your Holy Spirit. I pray in the name of the one who, by His death, purchased the privilege of bestowing this fellowship upon those who love Him. Amen.

A Promise Fulfilled

All of them were filled with the Holy Spirit and began to speak in other tongues as the Spirit enabled them (Acts 2:4).

Scripture: Acts 2:1-16
Song: "Standing on the Promises"

I had promised Randa, "It will be worth the effort." Getting up at five in the morning, we hiked the steep trail from the parking lot up to the ridge, dim light filtering through the tall hemlock, poplar, and oak trees. As the first pink began to tinge the eastern sky, we'd hiked the half-mile along the top of Natural Bridge. Then we'd made the challenging climb up the bare face of a huge, blunted spike past Lovers Leap.

We sat quietly, almost reverently, watching the morning mist slide down the slope of a valley several hundred feet below us. The sky colored and brightened, until finally a red-ball sunrise crested the distant hills of the horizon, flooding the eastern Kentucky mountains with its light.

The peace of Randa's expression and the glow in her eyes told me that I'd kept my promise. What joy!

Imagine the joy Jesus must have felt on the Day of Pentecost when He kept His promise to His disciples that He would not leave them alone. He'd also fulfilled the prophecy He'd made through His prophet Joel hundreds of years earlier. It's a promise and prophecy that continues to bless us nearly 2,000 years later.

O God, Creator of Heaven and earth, how incredible are Your power and love, how great is the comfort that You give us each day through Your Holy Spirit. Thank You, in the holy name of Jesus my Lord. Amen.

We've Lost Our Way

Like the blind we grope along the wall, feeling our way like people without eyes (Isaiah 59:10).

Scripture: Isaiah 59:9-15a
Song: "Turn Your Eyes upon Jesus"

The Sexual Revolution was not a good idea. For those without a relationship with God, traditional morality seemed restrictive and stifling. They didn't trust the one who designed sexual intimacy to bond a man and woman as one. But with the casting off of such restraints, the results have been devastating.

A 2010 study by *Time* magazine and the Pew Research Center compared attitudes about marriage in 1960 and 2010. Cohabitation has increased, according to the survey, not just because economic times are hard, but because 40% of Americans in 2010 viewed marriage as obsolete.

The biggest impact of the moral shift falls on the children. Compared to 1960, the survey showed that eight times as many babies were born out of wedlock (41%) and three times as many children lived in single-parent homes (25%).

Christians who care about kids can often lead these children to the Lord by serving as Big Brothers or Sisters. These young parents need mentors because many didn't have stable role models when they were growing up. They're groping their way along the wall of parenting.

You are Father to the fatherless, **Lord,** and Savior to the desperate. Help families to find You, and use me in the process. In Jesus' name, amen.

April 15–21. **Patty Duncan,** living in Eugene, Oregon, teaches fifth grade at Eugene Christian School. She loves teaching art to children after school and during a week-long art camp in the summer.

He Himself Shows Up

He saw that there was no one, he was appalled that there was no one to intervene; so his own arm achieved salvation for him, and his own righteousness sustained him (Isaiah 59:16).

Scripture: Isaiah 59:15b-21
Song: "At the Cross"

Jeff Yellow Owl grew up on a Blackfeet reservation amid poverty and rampant alcoholism. As a disillusioned young man, Jeff drank daily. Seeing the boy's despair, his father helped him get off the reservation and find work in Washington State.

Jeff kept drinking and began taking drugs, but a new friend pestered him to go to church, and eventually Jeff agreed to attend just once. That night he heard the gospel and committed his life to the Lord.

The new convert went to his first 4th of July service at a large church, and the minister extolled the founding fathers and America's Christian heritage. He was shocked. "The white men lied, murdered, deceived, and broke all their promises to us—and *that's* Christianity?" He was angry!

Back at his apartment he fumed, wanting to get back at the minister. But then the Lord seemed to speak to his heart: "I took it on myself—on my back—when they beat me. I took it on my body on the cross. Justice has been served at the cross." Over time Jeff realized the impact of this truth and now shares the message of reconciliation with the church where he ministers.

God, my sins divide me from people. Forgive me. Help me listen and feel for people who have been treated unjustly. In the name of Jesus, amen.

Raised to Walk in New Life

All my longings lie open before you, Lord; my sighing is not hidden from you. My heart pounds, my strength fails me; even the light has gone from my eyes (Psalm 38:9, 10).

Scripture: Psalm 38:9-15
Song: "As the Deer"

Distraught over her fiancé's decision to end their engagement, Mikki Loomis ran a red light, and a truck crashed into her car at full speed. Two months after the accident, she still lay in a coma with severe brain damage. The doctors told her family they didn't expect her ever to wake up. They sent her to a nursing home, and her family's prayers intensified.

Incredibly, within a couple of weeks her eyes began to flutter, and within days Loomis regained consciousness. Her body was partially paralyzed on one side and shook on the other. With the mentality of an infant, she had lost her sense of self and simply wanted to die.

As time passed, though, her brain function improved. When therapists told her to accept her condition, she put Scriptures on the wall because she couldn't memorize them. With the door closed, she taught herself to walk again.

For a long time, Mikki had felt God's presence in the room but refused to speak to Him. She turned her head away, telling God she hated Him. But eventually she gave God a chance, praising Him in three-word sentences for 10 minutes each day. She made a remarkable recovery and lives a full life today.

Father, You are strong—and so willing to heal our injuries and infirmities. Praise You for Mikki's life and for the way You've worked in my life too! In Jesus' name, amen.

What's the Probable Explanation?

He did not waver at the promise of God through unbelief (Romans 4:20, *New King James Version*).

Scripture: Romans 4:16-25
Song: "God of Wonders"

What prompted Abraham's confidence that God was able to give him and Sarah a child in spite of old age and infertility? He knew the God of creation. God designed the human body and knew how to fix it, in all its intricacy.

Many modern churches have lost this vital emphasis on God as Creator. Christian philosopher Nancy Pearcey notes in her book *Total Truth* that the teachings of Darwin have cut deeply into the foundations of Christian faith. Young people presented with evolution-as-fact in school question how the creation story in Genesis can be real if Darwin's theory is true. In secular colleges, anti-Christian professors attack the faith of students as foolish fairy tales.

In response, Pearcey urges Christians to study and confront the theory of a materialistic evolution. For starters, remember that the scientific method can only proceed by observation and the recording of data. Thus it can describe the "what" quite well.

But when it comes to "how," and especially "why," it must enter the realm of philosophical faith, just as religion must. Yes, both must seek self-evident first principles in the realm of philosophy. In that sense, they begin on equal footing, asking: which is the most probable explanation for all we see?

God of wonders, I see Your fingerprints on stars and grains of sand. Everywhere I note the work of my Creator. Praise You, through Christ my Lord. Amen.

The Truth Cannot Lie

God did this so that, by two unchangeable things in which it is impossible for God to lie, we who have fled to take hold of the hope set before to us may be greatly encouraged (Hebrews 6:18).

Scripture: Hebrews 6:13-20
Song: "Only Truth"

"There will come a time," my minister said this morning in his sermon, "when ministers in the pulpits of America will be commanded to not preach on some topics. It will become illegal to preach God's Word on certain politically incorrect subjects."

He went on to declare that he intends to preach God's truth anyway. "When I told my wife that," he continued, "she said 'You could go to jail,' and I replied, 'I know.'"

The young minister of the church I attend takes a bold stand for scriptural truths because he passionately believes God doesn't lie. All that the Lord has conveyed to us through Scripture for our encouragement, instruction, and guidance must be taught, and he will teach it.

As he preaches his way through a book of the Bible, he doesn't skirt difficult issues. When he comes to a passage that deals with sin, he carefully explains, emphasizing God's love for us in calling for repentance from self-destructive deeds. For example, when he came to Matthew 19, he clearly defined marriage as one man and one woman who become one flesh for one lifetime.

Lord, I trust what You say. In a world where morality is seen as relative—and almost any truth can be questioned and adjusted to suit human nature—I find so refreshing the clear teaching of Scripture. Thanks for this blessing! In Jesus' name, amen.

Not Finished Yet

The Root of Jesse will spring up, one who will arise to rule over the nations; in him the Gentiles will hope (Romans 15:12).

Scripture: Romans 15:7-13
Song: "'Tis So Sweet to Trust in Jesus"

My friend Jo Ann told me she was a closet Christian. Growing up in an observant Jewish family in Denver, as a child she longed for the beauty and fun of Christmas. Her strict father would allow nothing that hinted of Christmas in the house, not even a pine cone from a school art project. "But Hanukkah didn't satisfy my craving for festive decorations," she said.

One December, Jo took matters into her own hands. She saved her allowance and bought green felt, then found a toilet plunger in the bathroom and took it to her room. Always an artistic child, she carefully draped the felt over the upright plunger, shaping it to resemble a Christmas tree. Then she crafted little ornaments from odds and ends and delicately hung them on the tree. She hid her creation in her closet.

"So, literally, I was a closet Christian," Jo said, laughing, as she finished her story.

She doesn't need to hide her celebration now because she's an adult and a marketplace Christian. Her life and stories enrich my appreciation for being grafted into the root of God's chosen people, the Jews. God is not finished with them . . . or me.

Almighty Jehovah, I'm so grateful to be included in Your family and attached to the root of Jesse, my Lord Jesus. Thank You for sharing Your favor with me, a Gentile. In Messiah's name I lift up this prayer. Amen.

Hope Beyond Death

Brothers and sisters, we do not want you to be uninformed about those sleep in death, so that you do not grieve like the rest of mankind, who have no hope (1 Thessalonians 4:13).

Scripture: 1 Thessalonians 4:13–5:11
Song: "Christ the Lord Is Risen Today"

During the last month of my mother's life, my brother and sister-in-law and I visited her daily and helped feed her. As we watched her weaken and slip away from us, I commented, "She's folding her tent in peace. She'll pitch it again in Heaven."

I see that same peace in my friend, Susan. Her husband is now on 24-hour-a-day hospice care for her. He lies in a hospital bed in the living room, and she sleeps on the couch at night. I talked with her recently at church, and she looked calm, beautiful, and radiant.

When the husband of another friend died, she sent a long e-mail describing the details of her last moments with her beloved mate. She recounted the grace and tenderness of the Lord in allowing the event to unfold just as it had.

Another friend's mother-in-law voiced her desire to go home to be with the Lord by saying "I just want Jesus to come and pick me up."

As Christians we have every reason to approach our own death—and the passing of those we love—with hope instead of despair. We will see them again.

Father, someday You will take me home to live with You forever and be with loved ones who have gone before me. I thank You that they remain in the blessed fellowship of Your church, awaiting the resurrection along with us. Through Christ, amen.

Into God's Light

We praise you, God, we praise you, for your Name is near (Psalm 75:1).

Scripture: Psalm 75
Song: "Holy God, We Praise Thy Name"

I watched my husband, John, grow weaker and weaker. The doctors couldn't stop the bleeding in his colon, and it seemed as if his life was fading away. After four transfusions, his situation didn't improve, and John slept most of the time. When he did, sometimes I walked outside the hospital and into the sunlight.

Out there, it was as if God shined His light into my darkness, and I felt the warmth of His presence. When John awoke, I opened the shades in his room so he could experience the light from God too. Before leaving each day, I prayed for him and could see hope in the midst of his suffering.

At eleven o'clock one evening, the surgeons came into John's room. "We're going to take out the part that's bleeding," they said. Following John's gurney down to the operating room, I stayed and prayed with him for as long as I was allowed.

After the emergency surgery, John grew stronger and his sense of humor returned. I knew we had come out of a terrible darkness into God's marvelous light. John knew too, and he thanked God for helping us through our time of trouble.

Thank You, **Father,** for shining Your light into our dark moments. And thank You for extending Your healing hand upon those we love. In the name of Jesus, Lord and Savior of all, I pray. Amen.

April 22–28. **Sue Tornai** lives with her husband, John, and dog, Maggie, in Carmichael, California. She has taught Sunday school for more than 20 years and enjoys camping and fishing.

Even When I Can Breath!

But for you who revere my name, the sun of righteousness will rise with healing in its rays (Malachi 4:2).

Scripture: Malachi 4
Song: "His Name Is Wonderful"

Vivid rainbow colors of sea life thrilled me as I swam underwater at Monastery Beach near Monterrey, California. Fascinated by the beauty, I forgot about the high surf I'd descended into. The surge rocked me gently back and forth (giving me a false sense of comfort), and I became tangled in the kelp. My scuba instructor cut the sea vines off me, dropped my weight belt, and sent me around the kelp bed.

After swimming all the way around the vines, I began to feel the sand under my hands. Instead of planting my fingers and holding on through each wave, I panicked and tried to climb up the beach. The surge pushed me onto my back, and my mask and regulator slid off my face. The surf tossed me around like a beach ball, and my life passed before me. *What will happen to my children?* I wondered. Desperate to cry out to God, the only thing I could say was the name of Jesus.

It took seven men to pull me out of the tumultuous waves that day. Laying exhausted on the beach, I prayed, "Thank You, Jesus. Thank You, Jesus." Today when words to prayers don't come easily, I still simply say the name of Jesus, and I know He is near.

Thank You, **my Lord and Savior,** that all I need to do is call Your name to know You are with me. But help me remember to converse with You throughout every day—even when I'm not drowning! I pray through Your precious name. Amen.

Beauty: Wherever He Is

How lovely is your dwelling place, Lord Almighty! (Psalm 84:1).

Scripture: Psalm 84
Song: "Better Is One Day"

Majestic French Gothic architecture makes the Notre Dame Cathedral in Paris, France, the finest structure in Europe. Hymns roared from the huge organ pipes, light shown through the stained glass windows, and the sculptures, candles, and incense created an awesome sense of holiness inside the church. It was a religious holiday when we visited the great Notre Dame.

She is rich in beauty, never to be forgotten. Even in the midst of many tourists, her elegance spoke of God's dwelling place. I lifted up my heart in thanks and praise as I stood beside a large pillar; I wanted to linger a little longer.

As magnificent as the cathedral is, from the inside as well as out, I am thankful God's presence can't be confined to a mere building. By Him all things exist, and in Him all things consist—and He chooses to dwell in the hearts of His people. His courts, His people, and His ways encourage and strengthen me.

Whether traveling through life's valleys or enjoying mountaintop experiences, I know God is with me. It is comforting for me to know that I don't have to get to His house to experience His nearness. All I need to do is whisper His name.

Lord God, I would rather spend time in Your courts—with You and Your people—than anywhere else. Thank You for all the beauty of Your creation and for the creative works of human hands that seek to honor You. Yet You are not bound in beautiful sanctuaries, and for that I am thankful as well. Through Christ, amen.

Communion with God

My help comes from the LORD, the Maker of heaven and earth (Psalm 121:2).

Scripture: Psalm 121
Song: "Blessed Assurance"

Leaving my mom in a Texas hospital room to go back to my home in California was the hardest thing I've ever done. We had spent 10 days reading the Bible, singing hymns, and watching our favorite movies. Since Mama's disease would soon take her life, I knew I would never see her again this side of Heaven.

The last day I was with her, I wrote her favorite verses on a strip of paper. "I lift up my eyes to the mountains—where does my help come from? My help comes from the Lord, the Maker of heaven and earth" (Psalm 121:1, 2). Then I taped them to Mama's bedrails. Tears spilled down my cheeks when she reached up and touched my hand.

"What are you doing?" she asked.

"I have to go back to work, Mama. But when no one is here to give you your Bible or read it to you, these words will remind you that God is near. He will never leave you."

"I love you, Susie."

"I love you too, Mama."

Holding Mama's hand, I prayed with her one last time. It was what she taught me to do. But this time it was more. It was our final communion together with God.

Thank You, **Lord God,** the maker of Heaven and earth, for Your help in my darkest of times. And thank You for the privilege of serving You, both in the church and in my family at home. In the name of Jesus, I pray. Amen.

Constant Cleanup

When the kindness and love of God our Savior appeared, he saved us, not because of righteous things we had done, but because of his mercy. He saved us through the washing of rebirth and renewal by the Holy Spirit (Titus 3:4, 5).

Scripture: Titus 3:1-7
Song: "You Are My King

After spending the day cleaning house, I stopped to eat dinner. My fluffy white puppy ran into the family room and then jumped up on the sofa and chairs. Drenched in mud, she was a mess, and she made a muddy mess of my clean house.

"Maggie, *no!*" I picked her up to wash her in the sink, but her legs kept running as if they were still on the ground. Mud splattered all over my white shirt. Holding her under the clear, warm water, and looking out the window, I could see the hole she'd dug. It was nearly as big as she was.

That day Maggie reminded me of what I must have looked like when God reached down and rescued me. I wasn't lovely to look at, and His picking me up meant that my mess got on Him. I've never understood how He could exchange my ugliness for His righteousness.

I didn't deserve His warmth and love, but He took me as His daughter, with all my sin and failure. I'm thankful He didn't leave me that way. He washed me in baptism and by His mercy, He keeps cleaning me up daily—making me more like Jesus.

Thank You, **Lord,** for Your mercy and grace. Thank You for not waiting until I was good enough or worthy enough to be Your child. Thank You for transforming me, day by day, into the person You want me to be. I pray in Jesus' holy name. Amen.

Affirmations

May your whole spirit, soul and body be kept blameless at the coming of our Lord Jesus Christ (1 Thessalonians 5:23).

Scripture: 1 Thessalonians 5:23-28
Song: "The Lord Bless You and Keep You"

I washed the feet of my seventh-grade Sunday school students. It was the last Sunday I would spend with them, and I wanted our time to be meaningful. We talked about things we'd learned together over the past year, things like the call to tell others about God's amazing love and how we could be ready when Jesus returns. Then I prayed for each student.

As much as I prepare and pray over each lesson, I'm not always certain how the young people will receive the message. This particular Sunday, after I finished washing and drying those precious feet that would go from that day into the big world, my most challenging student stepped forward and offered to wash my feet. Tears welled up in my soul as I took off my shoes to receive her gift and prayer.

Paul taught the people in the church at Thessalonica and wrote tender, loving letters to them when he couldn't be with them. When he prayed for them, he also asked them to pray for him. Knowing that they grew in their faith kept Paul preaching and teaching. For me, seeing my students grow in their faith encourages me to keep teaching Sunday school. May the spirit, soul, and body of us all be kept blameless till Jesus returns!

Thank you, **Lord**, for blessing me as I serve You with all my heart. Thank You, especially, for tender surprises along the way that keep me showing up to teach Sunday school. Through Christ I pray. Amen.

A Blessed Rebuke

Stand firm and hold fast to the teachings we passed on to you, whether by word of mouth or by letter (2 Thessalonians 2:15).

Scripture: 2 Thessalonians 2:1-4, 8-17
Song: "Loyalty to Christ"

Waiting in the salon for my hair appointment, I heard my hairdresser, Sharon, talking about her relationship with God. Then while she cut my hair, I talked about growing up in a Christian home, telling about how my mom read the Bible with me and took me to church and Sunday school. Sharon stopped for a minute and wrinkled her brows at me.

"You have me confused," she said.

My heart fell, knowing she referred to the sinful way I lived. After my divorce, I ended up in one broken relationship after another. Nothing and no one satisfied my longings. Loneliness and despair were my daily companions. Sharon's words penetrated my heart and caused me many sleepless nights until I decided to seek God for a new way to live.

Had Sharon failed to rebuke me, no doubt the God of Heaven would have sent someone else. That's the way He is. His amazing love changed me, and He himself became my deepest longing.

Little by little, His ways became my ways. I know now that although the world's values may seem attractive and tempting, it's better for me to stand firm in the truth—the truth of God's love and the assurance of spending eternity with Him.

Thank you, **Dear Lord,** for never giving up on me. Thank You for faithfully rebuking me when I need it, because You have my best at heart. Through Christ, Amen.

Strength and Hope in Trials

Then I would still have this consolation—my joy in unrelenting pain—that I had not denied the words of the Holy One (Job 6:10).

Scripture: Job 6:8-13
Song: "Rescue"

Job had been through struggles and the testing of his faith like few of us will ever know. He had literally lost everything because of his belief in God.

We all go through times when we feel like the weight of the world is on us, and the world offers little or no help. It wants to heap even more on us, almost like testing to see if we will deny our maker and our faith in Him.

Through all of his trials, however, Job knew that he had to put his trust in God and took comfort in knowing that he remained loyal to His Lord. We need to do the same, knowing that Jesus has been through it on our behalf. He has overcome this world and all the temptations and pressures it places on us. In Him, we are victorious.

Jesus is there for us whenever we need Him. While all the pressures placed on us may not immediately go away, we know that He will walk with us through everything to the end. "For my yoke is easy and my burden is light" (Matthew 11:30).

Lord, I trust You in those times of life when everything seems out of control. I need You to help guide me through the trials and remind me of Your sustaining presence. Through Christ I pray. Amen.

April 29–May 1–3, 5. **John Oxford** has worked as a reporter in Moultrie, Georgia, for seven years. An Atlanta native, he is happily married to his wife, Ashleigh.

Sleepless Nights

When I lie down I think, "How long before I get up?" The night drags on, and I toss and turn until dawn (Job 7:4).

Scripture: Job 7:1-6
Song: "Cry Out to Jesus"

Our struggles can tend to separate us from the things that are so important: family, friends, church, and even times of rest. Job wondered when his trials would end, becoming discouraged enough to ask God to end his life. Yet, in the end, God more than blessed Job for his faithfulness, knowing Job had ultimately stood strong in the face of adversity (see Job 42:12).

I like how the great nineteenth-century preacher Henry Ward Beecher spoke of Job's kind of adversity: "Affliction comes to all not to make us sad, but sober; not to make us sorry, but wise; not to make us despondent, but its darkness to refresh us, as the night refreshes the day; not to impoverish, but to enrich us."

Can you see it this way, no matter what trials you face at the moment? There is a goal to be accomplished amidst our struggles: spiritual growth. That is why, when trouble hits, we need spend little time asking "*Why* did this happen?" The better question to ask is: "What is the way for me to *respond*—the way that will help me become more like Jesus?" Then we can move through the difficulty with the confidence of Job, who finally said: "I know that you can do all things; no purpose of yours can be thwarted" (Job 42:2).

Lord, when I enter a tough time, help me to focus on this: "How will You use this for my good and Your glory?" Thank You, in the name of Jesus. Amen.

My Prayer Notes

DEVOTIONS®

May

Each of you should use whatever gift you have received to serve others, as faithful stewards of God's grace.

—1 Peter 4:10

Gary Allen, Editor   **Margaret Williams,** Project Editor   Photo Steve Mason | Photodisc | Thinkstock®

DEVOTIONS® is published quarterly by Standard Publishing, Cincinnati, Ohio, www.standardpub.com. © 2012 by Standard Publishing. All rights reserved. Topics based on the Home Daily Bible Readings, International Sunday School Lessons. © 2009 by the Committee on the Uniform Series. Printed in the U.S.A. All Scripture quotations, unless otherwise indicated, are taken from the *HOLY BIBLE, NEW INTERNATIONAL VERSION®. NIV®.* Copyright © 1973, 1978, 1984, 2011 by Biblica, Inc.™ Used by permission of Zondervan. All rights reserved. Scripture quotations marked (*NLT*) are taken from the Holy Bible, *New Living Translation.* Copyright © 1996. Used by permission of Tyndale House Publishers, Inc., Wheaton, Illinois 60189. All rights reserved.

He's Got It Covered

My offenses will be sealed up in a bag; you will cover over my sin (Job 14:17).

Scripture: Job 14:7-17
Song: "East to West"

Job was feeling very low when he cried out to God, wailing over the depths of his sin. We go through something similar when we feel the weight of the guilt of our sin bringing us down.

For us, thankfully, Jesus has already paid the price for our sin with His death and resurrection. Because of Jesus, our sin has been cast far away from us, to the depths of the deepest oceans and farthest distances. Our sin does not have to weigh us down.

For all Christians, however, truly experiencing freedom from sin is a lifelong process. Initially, in baptism, we take on the new life Christ has offered us (see 2 Corinthians 5:17), but we're still pulled to certain attitudes and actions from our old life. Those things that seem normal, even comfortable, are what we cling to the most.

In a process of growth, by the power of the Spirit within us, we begin to shed the ways of our old life. Sometimes it's quite uncomfortable, but abandoning the old sinful nature is our goal. Thankfully the Lord Jesus "covers" our sin, even as He washes it away.

Lord, thank You for the freedom from my sin. I pray You continue to reveal yourself to me so I can walk in Your light and not in the darkness of my sinful nature. I want to be Your child in all I do and say, not a child of the world. Through Christ, amen.

May 1–3, 5. **John Oxford** has worked as a reporter in Moultrie, Georgia, for seven years. An Atlanta native, he is happily married to his wife, Ashleigh.

The Greatest Love

Because of all my enemies, I am the utter contempt of my neighbors and an object of dread to my closest friends — those who see me on the street flee from me (Psalm 31:11).

Scripture: Psalm 31:9-16
Song: "My Jesus"

Was David paranoid? Not likely. As the old quip tells us: "It's not paranoia if you really *are* being followed." It was certainly the real-life case with David, who was hunted down by King Saul out of pure jealousy. The king spread lies about the young man, making David feel like an outcast. His words in Psalm 31 tell of his pain.

David was so weighed down by the burden of another's vengeance that it showed through in his visage and manner. In effect, when people saw him walking toward them, they would cross to the other side of the street — or head for an alley!

It's not easy being "an object of dread" to our friends and neighbors. But sometimes, because of the sinful actions of others, it can't be helped.

What to do? Follow the way of David: Cry out to God and admit your pain; keep coming back to the strength and wisdom of the Lord who sustains you. Ultimately, the beautiful words of praise that came from David's heart will be upon your lips too.

And never seek payback. As Francis Bacon once said: "A man that studieth revenge keeps his own wounds green, which otherwise would heal and do well."

Lord, help me to flee to Your protective arms when I'm under attack and falsely accused. Help me to know and feel that You are there, giving me the peace that passes all understanding. Thank You, in the name of Jesus. Amen.

Greatness of God

Praise be to the LORD, for he showed me the wonders of his love when I was in a city under siege. In my alarm I said, "I am cut off from your sight!" Yet you heard my cry for mercy when I called to you for help (Psalm 31:21, 22).

Scripture: Psalm 31:19-24
Song: "You Are My Hope"

Some folks just don't believe in miracles. When someone is healed of a disease that was thought to be life-threatening, those people shrug it off: the doctors must have misdiagnosed it. But I believe that God blesses those who truly trust in Him for everything. And sometimes He really does intervene with miraculous result.

In our psalm today, David speaks of that kind of intervention. He recalls the days of being in a city surrounded by the enemy, with no way out. No doubt the food and water were running low, and discouragement threatened—let alone a slow and painful death. Yet his cry was heard in Heaven; help descended.

Now David can give sage advice to all who may face a daunting challenge of any kind, even in our modern day. His advice is simple: "Be strong and take heart, all you who hope in the Lord" (v. 24). We may not always see the healing or some other thing we ask; God most often works through natural and ordinary means—especially through the compassion and hard work of His kingdom citizens. But we can trust that the Lord works all things "for the good of those who love him" (Romans 8:28).

O God, I thank You that You have given me so much in this world! May I be a good steward of Your blessings, the wonders of Your love. Through Christ I pray. Amen.

What Compassion and What Joy!

Because of the LORD'S great love we are not consumed, for his compassions never fail. They are new every morning; great is your faithfulness (Lamentations 3:22, 23).

Scripture: Lamentations 3:19-24
Song: "Trading My Sorrows"

The prophet Jeremiah, writer of the book of Lamentations, knew the Lord's compassion, even in the most trying times of imprisonment. Like so many of God's prophets, he faced persecution and the threat of death.

I think of Richard Wurmbrand, the Anglican minister imprisoned by Romanian Communists for almost 15 years in the mid-twentieth century. Listen to his words: "The cruelty of atheism is hard to believe when man has no faith in the reward of good or the punishment of evil. There is no reason to be human. There is no restraint from the depths of evil which is in man. My Communist torturers often said, 'There is no God, no hereafter, no punishment for evil. We can do what we wish.'"

Yet Wurmbrand trusted in God's compassion, even after years of beatings that left permanent scars. In fact, he was a joyful believer, able to say: "I have found truly jubilant Christians only in the Bible, in the underground church, and in prison."

Can we praise the Lord amidst all circumstances? Jeremiah did, Wurmbrand did, and so can we.

Lord, keep building up my faith in You. I know I will go through hard times, but I trust You will guide me and show me the path as I walk through. In Jesus' name, amen.

May 4. **Gary Wilde** is the editor of *Devotions®* and also a minister serving in Bonita Springs, Florida, where he lives with his wife, Carol, and Yorkie, Robbie Burns.

His Most Precious

These have come so that the proven genuineness of your faith—of greater worth than gold, which perishes even though refined by fire—may result in praise, glory and honor when Jesus Christ is revealed (1 Peter 1:7).

Scripture: 1 Peter 1:3-16
Song: "Last One Standing"

In Tolkien's famous fantasy novel, *The Lord of the Rings,* there is a rather despicable character named Gollum. He was driven to insanity by his obsession over the One Ring, enslaved to the ring's power, and desperately trying to get it back after losing it. He called the Ring "My Precious."

In a similar way, Jesus Christ—of distinctly opposite character!—pursues after us and seeks our growth in holiness. That is, He wants us back (wants to redeem us) whenever we have lost ourselves in some form of sinning. He may do so by allowing us to go through a fire of refinement, where our faith will finally be revealed as genuine.

But it's a painful process, isn't it? Jesus, however, is obsessed with us, loves us with all His being, even going to the cross on our behalf. And Christ's refinement of our faith reveals His true nature to us and allows us to see Him in all His glory. He burns sin away and calls us "My Precious" as He makes us one with Him!

Lord, I ask You to remove everything from my life that keeps me from true fellowship with You each day. Only through Your refinement, though it can be a painful process, will I grow into a person of genuine and abiding faith. Make me purer than the most precious minerals in Your sight! In the name of Jesus, amen.

What Holy Ambition!

It has always been my ambition to preach the gospel where Christ was not known (Romans 15:20).

Scripture: Romans 15:14-21
Song: "Everybody Praise the Lord"

We haven't heard from Pastor Andrew in New Delhi for months. Years ago, he put a simple but desperate prayer on the Internet. He wanted to share the good news of Christ with all who came into his life. He wasn't asking for money or goods, but for friends to pray for the churches he helped establish. He wanted communication with those who did not fear persecution for practicing their faith in Jesus.

It was risky, but we connected by phone and e-mail for several years. Andrew and his fellow ministers worked low-paying jobs to fund their church's ministries. They did whatever it took to get Bibles for their members. For a short time, we were able to send money to help them.

Then contact with Andrew ended. Months later, we received a single e-mail. Andrew had been imprisoned, his colleagues scattered. His family was safe, but in hiding. The last we heard, they asked for prayer to continue in ministry.

Andrew, his family, and his church members have become dear friends. As the silence continues, we pray with heavy hearts for their safety, for all those who have the most holy ambition—simply to preach the gospel.

O Lord, help me value the freedom to worship You in safety, and show me ways to help and encourage those who are on the front lines. Through Christ, amen.

May 6–12. **SanDee Hardwig,** a retired English teacher, lives and writes in Brown Deer, Wisconsin, while caring for her two perky cats, Odie and Milo.

Fools Despise Wisdom

The fear of the LORD is the beginning of knowledge, but fools despise wisdom and instruction (Proverbs 1:7).

Scripture: Proverbs 1:2-7
Song: "Show Me Your Ways"

Have you ever foolishly ignored good advice? I have and as a result learned some valuable lessons (the hard way). I can relate to the church father Augustine's biographical *Confessions*, even though he lived so long ago: from AD 354–430.

Augustine's mother tried to raise him with Christian ethics and wisdom, but he chose to go another way. He confessed to much lying, to deceiving his tutors and parents, stealing, fighting, and even fathering a child out of wedlock.

But what a contrast between Augustine's youthful foolishness and his life after baptism at age 31! With his foundational theological teachings, the church was able to flourish in northern Africa and beyond. In fact, most scholars consider Augustine the most important figure in the ancient Western church's history.

Like us, Augustine was foolish and sinful when he was without God. And like us, when he asked God for forgiveness, God heard his cries. With the "fear of the Lord," he became a humble man of God whose written words can still speak to our hearts.

Father God, how wonderful to be reminded of Your love and everlasting goodness through the testimony of great Christian leaders! Show me Your way, Lord, that I too may be of value in Your kingdom work. In the name of Jesus, amen.

Got Some Unfinished Business?

That you might put in order what was left unfinished and appoint elders in every town, as I directed you (Titus 1:5).

Scripture: Titus 1:5-9
Song: "Laying It Down"

"What do you want to be when you grow up?" Grandpa asked me on my 10th birthday. "I want to be a teacher and write books," I answered, with no hesitation. That's what I knew I would do: teach school and write books. I taught high school English for 22 years, but I've never published a book.

I wrote a children's book, *Jacoby and the Red Unicorn*, but the manuscript still sits on my shelf. So that doesn't count, does it? Then I started a romance novel for teenagers in 1985. I wrote eight chapters and shared the first three with a well-respected editor. He said, "This promises to be an unusual love story." He liked the characters and my writing style and encouraged me to send it to him when finished. That was in 1990, and I never wrote another word. Why not? Fear of failure? Fear of success?

In Paul's letter to Titus, he lists character traits that are desirable and undesirable in an elder of the church. He must be "one who loves what is good, who is self-controlled, upright, holy and disciplined" (v. 8). Perhaps those are character traits we should all strive for, whether we are in the running for church eldership or not. (In other words: Are you like me with good intentions and unfinished business?)

Heavenly Father, I confess I often procrastinate. Help me utilize Your time and gifts more fully. Make me more aware of Your constant presence and guidance. Fill me with energy and joy as I go about Your business. Thank You, in Jesus' name. Amen.

He Who Stands Firm

Then you will be handed over to be persecuted and put to death, and you will be hated by all nations because of me (Matthew 24:9).

Scripture: Matthew 24:9-14
Song: "The Righteous Cry Out"

The attackers were clad in shawls when they fired their guns on Shahbaz Bhatti, March 2, 2011. His death followed two months after Punjab governor Salman Taseer was killed for supporting Asia Noreen, the first Christian woman sentenced to death in Pakistan on blasphemy charges. Christians there are accused of blasphemy when they profess belief in Christ.

A TV anchorperson stated that Minister Bhatti repeatedly asked the government for safer housing near the capital where most government officials are housed. He was told there were no vacant houses. In a BBC interview Bhatti said, "I am ready to die for a cause[Christianity]. I'm living for my community and suffering people and I will die to defend their rights"

When asked about "the end of the age," Jesus warned, "Because of the increase of wickedness, the love of most will grow cold, but the one who stands firm to the end will be saved" (vv. 12, 13). How can we—who have freedom of religion— stand firm upon our rights and do what we can to help those who are persecuted for the faith?

Lord God, we are many individuals, but Your Word says we form one body in Christ. Help me pray faithfully for those who suffer for Your sake. Sometimes I run out of words, so fill me with Your loving presence and teach me to pray even without words. In the precious name of Jesus, amen.

The Giant Plus Sign

There is one God and one mediator between God and mankind, the man Christ Jesus, who gave himself as a ransom for all people (1 Timothy 2:5, 6).

Scripture: I Timothy 2:1-7
Song: "Jesus, Lover of My Soul"

Have you seen the 2011 television series, *Fairly Legal*? The main character, Kate, is a feisty young attorney who left law practice to become a legal mediator (a dispute-resolution expert). In one episode, Kate helped avoid an international incident when she was summoned by diplomats from a Mideastern embassy. Little Naji's mother died, leaving the girl in the custody of an American stepfather. But the maternal grandmother took the little girl and sought asylum in the embassy of her own country. Needless to say, it was a volatile situation.

Naji was confused, frightened, caught between Daddy and her beloved grandmother. Kate appealed to the common love of the adults. She helped Naji express what she wanted. Thanks to Kate's wisdom, peace and reconciliation won the day.

Yes, it is a fictional story—but it helps me see the nature of a good mediator: he or she represents all parties. Today's Scripture assures us that Jesus mediates for us. God's holiness must be honored and maintained, yet His mercy is infinite. Thus, through the sacrifice of Christ on the cross, the two are brought together. In fact, the cross is like a giant plus sign: holiness and mercy come together there, for our everlasting salvation.

O Lord, thank You for being in my corner and rescuing me from the effects of my sin. Thank You, especially, for the mediating work of atonement! Through Christ, amen.

Blessed Counsel

Do not repay evil for evil or insult with insult. On the contrary, repay evil with blessing, because to this you were called so that you may inherit a blessing (1 Peter 3:9).

Scripture: 1 Peter 3:8-12
Song: "Living for Jesus"

"I want to hurt her! Kianna's mother punched my little girl in the nose! They won't let me see her." Chip's 5-year-old daughter was in the emergency room, doctors were trying to stop the bleeding. Chip, Kianna's father, is battling addictions, falling behind in child support, but has just landed a much needed job. He and Kianna's mother often battle over finances, visitation, and custody.

"Do you want to jeopardize your new job, your progress in recovery, and risk never seeing your little girl?" I asked. Chip sobbed, "No! I just want to see Kianna, hold her and comfort her." Then he asked me to pray with him. As we prayed, Chip recited a Scripture he'd read in recovery group. "His divine power has given us everything we need for a godly life" (2 Peter 1:3). God does give us wisdom for meeting our earthly struggles in His Word.

Yesterday Chip called, praising God. He had spent time with his daughter, avoided an ugly confrontation, and even sympathized with the mother's heartfelt remorse for hitting their child. They plan to go for family counseling for the sake of their children. Have you found blessed counsel in the Bible recently?

O Father God, You will always be there for me. Thank You for loving me just as I am. Help me to love and accept others just as they are—and lend a helping hand whenever I can. I pray in Jesus' holy name. Amen.

Remember Your Cleansing

Whoever does not have them [the qualities of godliness] is nearsighted and blind, forgetting that they have been cleansed from their past sins (2 Peter 1:9).

Scripture: 2 Peter 1:2-15, 20, 21
Song: "Redeemed"

My clock's red digits glowed brightly as they signaled every hourly change while I tossed and turned through the night. Fitful dreams and bad memories reminded me of one foolish childhood sin. "Oh God, forgive me" I cried into my pillow. But could God ever forgive my past, so I could find peace?

The apostle Paul wrote, "Abraham believed God, and it was credited to him as righteousness" (Romans 4:3). "The words 'it was credited to him' were written not for him alone, but also for us, to whom God will credit righteousness" (Romans 4:23, 24). We can forget about this precious credit to our account and the gracious cleansing from our past sin! Sometimes we hang onto old guilt and torture ourselves with it. We keep going over poor decisions we've made, making ourselves miserable. With me, it's the temptation to imagine how life would have gone if I'd made better choices. If only . . . .

That night I sobbed, "Forgive me, Lord. I've messed up so many times." Just before dawn, Jesus answered—the words came almost audibly: "Why do you dwell on past sins? I no longer remember them. You are righteous in me." Then the peace which passes all understanding washed over me.

Lord, You remind me that no one is saved by good works, but by the good work of Christ on the cross. Keep me trusting in His righteousness. In Jesus' name, amen.

Clothed in Love

If that is how God clothes the grass of the field, which is here today, and tomorrow is thrown into the fire, how much more will he clothe you—you of little faith! (Luke 12:28).

Scripture: Luke 12:22-28
Song: "Give of Your Best to the Master"

My friend Delores, 85, has lived a long life and worked hard for most of it. For many years she worked as nurse and later as a fabric store clerk. Currently, Delores's family keeps her busy: five children, dozens of grandchildren, great-grandchildren, and great-great-grandchildren.

Some would say she deserves to take it easy at her age and simply manage her own affairs. She need not concern herself with helping young orphans around the world. But that is not Delores's way.

It only took a few minutes of watching a news broadcast for her to decide to sew clothes for poverty-stricken children in Africa. "The reporter said many children in Africa never live past the age of 5," said Delores. "Pretty little sundresses may give them hope and teach them that they matter." She also sews shirts and shorts for little orphaned boys.

People like Delores help fulfill God's promises of caring for others. Through generous spirits and talented hands, His Word is fulfilled, and lives are changed.

O God, help me to be willing to work with my hands in ways that will help others. I pray in Jesus' holy name. Amen.

May 13–19. **Kayleen Reusser** has written nine children's books and had stories in Chicken Soup books. She cofounded a Christian writing group and speaks to adults and children about writing.

Left Holding the Bag?

Provide purses for yourselves that will not wear out, a treasure in heaven that will never fail, where no thief comes near and no moth destroys (Luke 12:33).

Scripture: Luke 12:29-34
Song: "How Firm a Foundation"

It scared the wits out of me for years. "They knock your feet right out from under you," said one friend. "Don't walk in alone," advised another. "Go with a group of people."

Each fall a certain manufacturer of colorful, stylish cloth handbags, backpacks, luggage, and coin purses conducts an outlet sale at a mega store close to my home. The event attracts thousands of shoppers each year.

I had avoided attending the outlet sale. After all, who looks forward to being stampeded by female shoppers looking for good deals? However, last year I decided to attend and purchase Christmas presents. I left a note at home, so if I were indeed trampled to death, my husband would know where to find me.

Needless to say, I survived. The experience was even somewhat pleasant. Customers shopped companionably beside each other with no serious fighting (not even a bloody nose!).

Later, while walking to my car, I wondered about the fuss. Jesus warned against obsessing over possessions that have no eternal significance. Problem is: they'll all eventually wear out.

Dear Heavenly Father, You know my needs and desires so well. Please help me to use my resources in ways that honor You. All praise to You, in the name of Jesus my Lord. Amen.

The Perfect Butler

It will be good for those servants whose master finds them ready, even if he comes in the middle of the night or toward daybreak (Luke 12:38).

Scripture: Luke 12:35-40
Song: "Arise, My Soul, Arise!"

I love to watch old movies. One of my favorites is the Alfred Hitchcock thriller, *Notorious*. In one scene, a butler shrugs into his topcoat as he hurries toward the main door. It is the middle of the night, and he has been resting, but the master and his wife have come home from their honeymoon and need assistance. The butler doesn't hesitate to put aside his own physical needs in order to serve his master. He takes their wraps and inquires about preparing a meal. The offer is declined as Ingrid Bergman and her husband retire for the evening.

To be ready, 24/7, to fulfill the wishes of one's master is a sign of true dedication. Rarely do we see such commitment today, except in some marriages.

Most people prefer to think of their own needs first. Yet the Lord calls us to just the opposite attitude as we await His sudden, blessed return in glory.

We aren't allowed to wait obediently for Him one day and practice sinful habits the next (see Galatians 5:16-21). Jesus wants us to be true to Him all of the time. Are you practicing patient watchfulness?

Lord God Almighty, it can be easy to slack off in my diligence as I await Your coming. Please give me confidence and patience so my actions continue to honor You, day by day. I pray in Jesus' holy name. Amen.

No Vegging Out Allowed!

From everyone who has been given much, much will be demanded; and from the one who has been entrusted with much, much more will be asked (Luke 12:48).

Scripture: Luke 12:41-48
Song: "Beautiful Garden of Prayer"

Since 2008, each summer my friends Bill and Penny have traveled 290 miles north of Fairbanks, Alaska, to teach the residents of Arctic Village how to garden. This generous couple—he is a carpenter and she is a high school math teacher—believe that eating fresh vegetables will greatly improve the health of the 140 villagers. You see, they usually eat bush meat, which causes digestive problems. They also hope to plant seeds of interest about their Christian faith.

The gardening was a challenge for them. "I had never transplanted a seedling before going to Alaska," said Bill. "Penny and I stumbled our way through that first year."

Other obstacles arose. The couple endured some suspicious attitudes from villagers. And they had to live in a tent for the entire summer. "The first year Penny asked me, 'Why us?'" recalled Bill. "She wondered what we were doing. All I could say was that I had a gut feeling we were called by God to do this."

By the end of summer 2010, the villagers had cultivated a cornucopia of healthy veggies. Bill and Penny knew they could help people with their skills and dedication. I wonder what I can do to advance God's work with the gifts He's given me.

Lord, the needs of people are everywhere around us. Help me to use my hands in work that is pleasing to You. In Jesus' name I pray. Amen.

Thanks for the GAPs

Every good and perfect gift is from above, coming down from the Father of the heavenly lights, who does not change like shifting shadows (James 1:17).

Scripture: James 1:12-18
Song: "God Has Given You His Promise"

While memorizing Bible verses as a 10-year-old child at church camp one summer, I tried to find easy connections to assist me. With James 1:17 I lucked out. The first letters of each word in "good and perfect" formed GAP. This short word stuck with me years later whenever something monumental happened in my life.

Upon getting engaged, I knew God had given me a GAP gift with my fiancé. When my dad died unexpectedly following surgery, I realized through my grief that it, too, was a GAP gift. We'd be reunited in Heaven someday. And when my children were born, my heart filled with thanks for God's GAPs.

But the death of a friend's husband, leaving her a widow with children to care for, was a difficult GAP gift to understand. Yet over the years, my friend found a job and successfully raised her daughters to be responsible, adventurous women. God's GAP gifts to her became evident over time.

Life is full of GAP gifts. Some events may take years before they appear as such. But if we remember God's goodness and that He always has our good in mind, we'll find it and see all of life is filled with promise.

Lord, may I recognize the good and perfect gifts You pour into my days. Deepen my trust in Your constant care, no matter the circumstances. In Jesus' name, amen.

In the Little Things

Whoever can be trusted with very little can also be trusted with much (Luke 16:10).

Scripture: Luke 16:10-13
Song: "The Solid Rock"

A few years ago, I wrote a book on Indonesian crafts and recipes for middle-school children. The editor asked me to photograph the 20 completed projects using children as models. Thankfully, parents of children I knew from my church were happy to sign permission forms for their children's photos to appear in the book. And, as I worked at the public middle school, I arranged with parents to take the children home with me after school to work on the projects.

Each day for several weeks, this was the process. It was tiring—but so much fun! What amazed me most was the parents' trust in me. Some were my good friends; others hardly knew me. All seemed confident about my being alone with their child in my home.

It humbled me. Yet, I knew they had seen my three children grow up to be responsible adults. They had seen me teach Sunday school and Vacation Bible School and knew of my work at the school.

The book, *Recipe and Craft Guide to Indonesia,* turned out well. Each time I look at the photos of the children with their projects, I think of the trust of their parents. And I am thankful.

God, I learn best by starting out with a little to care for, then gradually increasing my responsibility. Help me to keep my eyes on You for wisdom in being accountable for things both large and small. In Jesus' name, amen.

Persevering with Your Gift

Each of you should use whatever gift you have received to serve others, as faithful stewards of God's grace in its various forms (1 Peter 4:10).

Scripture: 1 Peter 4:1-11
Song: "We Give Thee but Thine Own"

I've been a writer for 20 years, beginning before our family owned a computer and before we had an Internet account. Writing without these resources was slow and often painful. And discouragement was a constant companion as rejection letters streamed through my mail box.

When our family purchased a computer and signed up for Internet services, the ability to meet other writers through e-mail, chat rooms, and writing classes was such a blessing. Better yet was meeting my new writing friends in person at conferences and at coffee shops. We'd sit and talk about writing for hours on end.

Today, I'm the cofounder of a Christian writing group. Our goal is to provide companionship and encouragement to fellow writers. We may not all be writing explicitly biblical materials, but we're using our articles, stories for children, and personal essays to bring other people closer to God. We consider the desire to write for God a gift that we can use to serve Him. What is your gift? How can you expand it to serve others?

Almighty and most merciful God, thank You for the gift of writing. It is often a challenge to find time to use it—and sometimes doubt about my talent creeps in. However, please keep my goals focused on pleasing You. In the name of the Father, the Son, and the Holy Spirit, I pray. Amen.

Loveless Lovers

People will be lovers of themselves . . . not lovers of the good (2 Timothy 3:2, 3).

Scripture: 2 Timothy 3:1-9
Song: "More Love to Thee"

Butch and I stood in his office one day talking. "I don't love my wife," he told me. "People love their cars and love their houses and love their dogs. So as far as I can tell, love doesn't mean much. No," he went on, "I don't love my wife. I *respect* my wife."

In our passage today the words *lover* or *love* appear a half-dozen times. But love paints no pretty pictures here. No valentines or hearts—or any semblance of true love or respect—graces the description of the "terrible times in the last days" (v. 1).

As I read these words, I hold up the scriptural mirror. Am I a lover of God? Or am I only a lover of myself, my money, and my pleasure? Do I sully the word or act of love by my unlovely or unloving ways? Do I spend time with others guilty of love-lessness too? If so, God tells me, "Have nothing to do with such people" (v. 5).

God's love for me is pure and holy. So, may my love for Him spring from awe of who He is and thanksgiving for what He's done for me in Jesus Christ.

God of love, transform me by Your love. Help me love the things You love and the people You cherish. Through Christ, who loved me and gave himself for me, amen.

May 20–26. **Kathy Douglas**, of Swanton, Ohio, is an avid in-line skater who enjoys drinking sweetened, iced coffee while writing.

Red Dog

Let my true messengers faithfully proclaim my every word. There is a difference between chaff and wheat! (Jeremiah 23:28, *New Living Translation*).

Scripture: Jeremiah 23:23-32
Song: "Thy Word"

I had always wanted to ride on a combine. Last fall the man who farms the land around our one-acre homestead accommodated me. As the huge combine cut its way through the rows, what was left of the stalks and husks littered the field. Corn filled the hopper behind us. The waste saturated the air around the combine, only to dissipate like morning fog.

"Chaff that the wind blows away," I, the former city slicker, mused aloud.

"Red dog."

"What?"

"I call it 'red dog,'" the farmer said. "That's what the 'chaff' of corn is." As I looked at the corn dust swirling around my neighbor and me that day, I saw its reddish glint.

As Jeremiah preached to the farming community of his day, he spoke of God's true words as grain. But he told his hearers to beware of the "lying prophets, who prophesy the delusions of their own minds" (v. 26). Their words were chaff—maize's red dog.

Can I distinguish between God's truth and man's error? Am I careful to examine all things in the light of Scripture?

Thank You, **Lord,** for the Bible. Thank You that it doesn't just contain truth, but is truth. Thank You, as well, for those who teach your Word truly and truthfully. In Jesus who is the Way, the Truth, and the Life, I pray. Amen.

Money Matters

You have hoarded wealth in the last days. Look! The wages you failed to pay the workers who mowed your fields are crying out against you (James 5:3, 4).

Scripture: James 5:1-6
Song: "What Is the World to Me?"

Our friend Mike is a self-made millionaire. He never went to college, but early on became an expert tool and die maker. He built his company and his reputation as both a savvy businessman and a man of integrity. His company, which now has operations in two states, has flourished.

Mike pays his employees fairly and well. His wife confided to me once that it's not unusual for Mike to slip a $100 bill to an employee (or employees) around Christmas or at other times of the year. When we go out to eat with this couple, the wait staff go out of their way to please Mike. He's generous with his business, with his compliments, and with his tips.

The employers in today's text stood in direct opposition to our friend. They neglected to consider the one who watches how we handle our money. It's been said that in the Gospel accounts, Jesus talks more about money than any other topic. God knows what consumes much of our attention and thought.

Whether or not we're employers, the Lord Almighty holds us accountable for our money management. How will you and I manage our finances this week?

Father, keep me from hoarding what You've given me. I pray to be above reproach in money matters. And may I give joyfully and share liberally. Give me a willingness to sacrificially help others less fortunate than I am. I pray in Jesus' holy name. Amen.

Another Tale of Two Trees

Like a cedar of Lebanon he will send down his roots; his young shoots will grow. His splendor will be like an olive tree, his fragrance like a cedar of Lebanon (Hosea 14:5, 6).

Scripture: Hosea 14:1-7
Song: "I Shall Not Be Moved"

From our lakeside cottage, we watched helplessly as a powerful storm uprooted a mammoth shade tree at the water's edge. The tree looked strong, but its roots didn't go deep. In slow motion and with a creaking groan, the stately tree toppled to the ground.

When Hosea wrote about the future blessings of a repentant Israel, his thoughts turned to the cedars of Lebanon. Although those trees don't grow to phenomenal heights, they often spread out over 30 to 50 feet on every side. They can live for over a thousand years when their roots bore down deeply into the soil.

The name *cedar*, borrowed from an Arabic word, means "power." Resistant to insects and fungus, strong and aromatic, the cedars of Lebanon provide a picture of beauty, strength, and resilience. Little wonder that Lebanon's national flag has a cedar tree at its center.

Our lakeside tree had a good source of water, but the water's easy access made the tree vulnerable. When the storm came, down went the tree.

Lord God, I want to be like a deep-rooted cedar of Lebanon, not a waterside weakling. I want my life to be a sweet aroma to You with roots secure in the life source— Jesus Christ. Forgive me for the times when I think I can do anything of worth on my own. In your powerful name, amen.

On a Leash of Love

He will teach us his ways, so that we may walk in his paths (Micah 4:2).

Scripture: Micah 4:1-5
Song: "O Master, Let Me Walk with Thee"

Mattie, a chocolate Labrador retriever, doesn't much enjoy baseball games. Even if her young master is on the ball field playing and his team is winning, after a few innings Mattie starts tugging impatiently at the leash. She wants an early and prolonged seventh inning stretch.

Marty, the ballplayer's father, knows Mattie will stay close. He doesn't want to miss a minute of the action, so he lets go of Mattie's leash with a simple command: "Go take yourself for a walk."

Mattie picks up the other end of the leash in her mouth and trots off to inspect the area under the bleachers. She keeps the end of the leash in her mouth while she noses about. She's out on her own, contentedly taking herself for a walk.

The prophet Micah anticipated the day when all his people would "walk in the name of the Lord our God for ever and ever" (v. 5). The Lord Jesus makes it clear that we don't have to wait for that future day to walk with Him. Even now, whoever follows Him will "never walk in darkness" (see John 8:12). Unlike Mattie, we don't ever have to take ourselves for a lone walk. The invisible leash in God's hand is love.

O God, the king of glory, help me today to walk in Your ways. May I show myself a reliable friend, a helpful neighbor, and a dependable worker. Help me to walk as You walked. I pray in the name of Jesus. Amen.

Lost with a GPS

Thomas said to him, "Lord, we don't know where you are going, so how can we know the way?" (John 14:5).

Scripture: John 14:1-7
Song: "All the Way My Savior Leads Me"

GPS systems in our cars get their information from orbiting satellites. But for some reason they don't always give us the correct information. My brother-in-law assumed he'd have no trouble finding the hotel where we were all staying the night before our daughter's wedding in Annapolis, Maryland. With his wife by his side, the grandmas in the backseat, and his GPS device on the dashboard, he drove right by the hotel. They ended up in New Jersey.

We've had similar experiences. Our GPS can't get us to the gate of our county fairgrounds. If we follow its directions, we find ourselves not only in the wrong county, but in the wrong state. I can't explain these aberrations.

Thankfully, with the directions the Lord gives us in His Word, we won't get lost or separated from Him. He tells us both the way to walk through life and that He himself *is* that Way.

We may make an occasional misstep, but He who is the way never faltered, tripped, or got off the course that the Father set out for Him. As we follow in His steps, He will consistently set our feet on the right path. He'll guide us through this life and into the next.

Father, I'm so thankful that You've made the way into your presence clear. I know it's only through Jesus that I have access to You by Your Spirit. In the name of Jesus, who lives and reigns with You and the Holy Spirit, one God, now and forever, amen.

A Sneak Peak Back

They deliberately forget that long ago by God's word the heavens came into being and the earth was formed out of water and by water (2 Peter 3:5).

Scripture: 2 Peter 3: 3-15a, 18
Song: "Arky, Arky Song"

"Forget this ever happened."
"Forgive and forget."
"Forget I ever said that."
Ever tried to forget something; just deliberately tried to forget it? I have no trouble forgetting things I want to remember. Forgetting things I *don't* want to remember doesn't come so easily. Frankly, it's impossible. I can't will myself to forget an unkind deed or cutting remark. Can you?

Peter tells us in his short, second letter that some folks deliberately forget memorable key facts that are recorded to teach us—things that teach men and women to live holy lives. He cites the worldwide flood of Noah's day.

We seldom try to remember God's judgment and wrath. But when we avoid those lessons, we miss powerful truths that can change the direction of our lives. By looking back, we gain wisdom in the daily practice of godliness for the future. In other words, we learn from what's come before to gain insight into what's ahead. Then we can "grow in the grace and knowledge of our Lord and Savior Jesus Christ" (v. 18).

Want a sneak peak of what's ahead? Take a long look back.

Father, teach me through my own hard lessons so that I mature in the faith. And remind me: I'm to be holy because You are holy. Through Christ, amen.

From Generation to Generation

Uzziah was sixteen years old when he became king, and he reigned in Jerusalem fifty-two years. . . . He did what was right in the eyes of the LORD, just as his father Amaziah had done (2 Chronicles 26:3, 4).

Scripture: 2 Chronicles 26:1-5
Song: "My Father's Eyes"

The minister died, and his young son was asked to lead the congregation. The young man had been faithful to his father and the teachings of the church as he ministered in the music department. He took the leadership position and followed in his father's footsteps. As he served in wisdom, the congregation grew and was fruitful.

One generation teaches the next generation by its actions and words. When we have good mentors and let ourselves learn from them, it is a blessing. We have often told our children: "Please just throw out the things we should have done differently as parents; take the positive attributes and make them better."

I adhere to certain principles handed down to me from my own loving parents. My parents were encouragers, and I love to encourage others as well. The things we do in life are important, not from other people's perspectives, but from our Father's viewpoint alone.

Almighty and most merciful God, let me be mindful of Your approval for the things I do and say. And even when others mistake my intentions, remind me that it is through Your eyes I seek approval. Through Christ, amen.

May 27–31. **Beverly LaHote Schwind** is active in jail ministry, rehab teaching, and nursing at a homeless shelter. She lives in Tennessee.

I Can Do It Myself

After Uzziah became powerful, his pride led to his downfall. He was unfaithful to the LORD his God, and entered the temple of the LORD to burn incense on the altar of incense (2 Chronicles 26:16).

Scripture: 2 Chronicles 26:16-21
Song: "Pass Me Not, O Gentle Savior"

"Look what I can do," my 6-year-old granddaughter shouted as she peddled her bike without the training wheels. Her father had run up and down the path with her and then let her sail by as she propelled the bike with her feet. We stood and watched, happy for her achievement. Her thoughts weren't on what her father had done to help her, but only what *she* had done.

A child's pride and boasting may be normal, but some adults who become successful also forget the people who've helped them along the way.

Pride can bring out the worst in people. It entertains greed and fear. It leads to unbelief in anyone but self. It says, "I don't need God, I don't need you; I can do it myself."

Jesus told a parable about a man with so much pride that he thanked God he was not like other men (see Luke 18:9-14). The humble man in the parable asked God to forgive him, as he was a sinner.

Bottom line: Let our "boasting" be only in the Lord. After all, according to Jesus, the first shall be last, and the last first.

Dear Lord, You had no pride when You went to the cross. You died a lonely and terrible death for the sins of the world—including my sins. Let my prayer echo that of the tax collector: be merciful to me, a sinner. In Jesus' name, amen.

Trash in the Basement

The high places, however, were not removed; the people continued to offer sacrifices and burn incense there. Jotham rebuilt the Upper Gate of the temple of the LORD (2 Kings 15:35).

Scripture: 2 Kings: 15:32-38
Song: "Search Me, O God"

The church's building committee toured the bowling alley that was for sale. They all agreed it would be a good building to house their growing congregation.

The sale was made, and the people were eager to begin the cleanup and remodeling. But the group was unaware of a room in the basement that hadn't been emptied of trash for many years.

As the congregation rejoiced at the beauty of the remodeled building, the trash remained in the basement. When the minister became aware of the situation, he ordered all the trash removed before it caused a problem. Trash can clutter our homes and our minds.

I work at keeping my "inner temple" clean, but then I find something trashy creeping back into my life. It can be a bad habit that returns, or an unworthy attitude I cherish. I need to check out the "basement" of my life to see what might be lying neglected there. Is a cleaning necessary?

O Eternal Lord God, I thank You for making me aware of the things I need to throw out of my life. Help me not to compromise my boundaries or become complacent. Daily I need to check and see if there is trash building up in me that needs to be removed. Give me the courage to do it. In Jesus' name, amen.

Spreading Seeds

Though a tenth remains in the land, it will again be laid waste. But as the terebinth and oak leave stumps when they are cut down, so the holy seed will be the stump in the land (Isaiah 6:13).

Scripture: Isaiah 6:9-13
Song: "Take Me into the Holy of Holies"

Teaching in a rehabilitation center and at a jail, I am aware that the Word often falls on barren ground. Yet we watch the changes in the women in rehab as they become more and more prepared to receive what God is saying to them. Their facial expressions change. Their eyes show comprehension, and smiles break out on their faces. The program is set up for 8–12 months, and the success rate is good: lives are changed for the better.

In the story of *The Hugging Tree*, two trees grew as one. The trees partially fell and were cut down; the trunks were all that remained. The next year two sturdy sprouts came forth from the trunks.

Jesus told the parable of the sower and the seed. The seed went out over all the ground, but only the seed that landed on the prepared soil grew. The more we are in the Word, the more we become tuned in to what God is saying.

The Bible tells us in James to be doers of the word and not hearers only (James 1:22). Spreading the seeds of the gospel to all is what we are commanded to do.

Lord, I want to prepare my heart so that Your Word finds a place to grow there. I want to know Your voice and be fruitful in the kingdom. When I hear Your voice, I want to do Your will and not just listen to it. Through Christ I pray. Amen.

Choices with Instructions

"Now then," said Joshua, "throw away the foreign gods that are among you and yield your hearts to the LORD, the God of Israel" (Joshua 24:23).

Scripture: Joshua 24:14-24
Song: "Stand Up, Stand Up for Jesus"

The leader on our mission trip to Guatemala told us what we needed to take with us and what we would be doing each day. "I am getting up at 5 a.m. and having prayer; if you want to join me, come and bring a Bible."

The leader took his stand and declared what he was going to do, and we respected him. We received our instructions from him, and we would have to decide what we wanted to do. The choices were up to us, but if we were to be with him in prayer, we would have to get up and bring our Bibles.

My father would announce that he was going fishing early in the morning, and if we wanted to go along we needed to be up at a certain hour. We loved being a part of this plan. My brother and I were up and ready, waiting for Dad.

The people in Joshua's camp had to make a decision, and they chose to go along with Joshua and gave their hearts to God. Of course, that meant they'd have to get rid of the idols among them.

Is there anything I need to throw out of my life before I can yield my whole heart to God?

O Lord, I thank You for the instruction of Your Word. I want to take a strong stand for You and tell Your message to others. Grant me boldness to testify to the grace and mercy of Your unconditional love. I pray in Jesus' holy name. Amen.

DEVOTIONS®

JUNE

The promise is for you and your children and for all who are far off — for all whom the Lord our God will call.

—*Acts 2:39*

Gary Wilde, Editor | **Margaret Williams,** Project Editor Photo by Thinkstock | Comstock | Thinkstock®

DEVOTIONS® is published quarterly by Standard Publishing, Cincinnati, Ohio, www.standardpub.com. © 2012 by Standard Publishing. All rights reserved. Topics based on the Home Daily Bible Readings, International Sunday School Lessons. © 2009 by the Committee on the Uniform Series. Printed in the U.S.A. All Scripture quotations, unless otherwise indicated, are taken from the *HOLY BIBLE, NEW INTERNATIONAL VERSION®. NIV®.* Copyright © 2011 by Biblica, Inc.™ Used by permission of Zondervan. All rights reserved. *New American Standard Bible (NASB),* © The Lockman Foundation, 1960, 1962, 1963, 1968, 1971, 1972, 1973, 1975, 1977, 1995. *King James Version (KJV),* public domain.

Just a Small Reflection

Who is this King of glory? The LORD of hosts, He is the King of glory (Psalm 24:10, *New American Standard Bible*).

Scripture: Psalm 24
Song: "Our God Is an Awesome God"

It was cold and dark at the bottom of the canyon, but I could hear a bird in the distance singing a song of the morning. As I looked up to search for the bird, I saw a sliver of yellow peek over the edge of the canyon's rim. Soon an orange glow appeared, rising higher into the sky, and I watched flashes of amber begin their descent slowly down the canyon walls.

Within minutes light filled the entire canyon. Gone was the cold dampness of the night; a whole new world had opened up. As the radiance flooded down the wall, I glimpsed a spark of my glorious Creator. The river rushing past me was no longer black and forbidding. I saw the green and turquoise ribbon racing over the rocks and swirling around the massive tree roots on the river bank.

Suddenly a silvery spray of water burst out from between the rocks and reached heavenward like a handful of tiny diamonds tossed into the glistening sunlight. It seemed as if God whispered to me, "This is just a small reflection of my glory."

O King of Glory, let every gateway in my life be opened up, that You may freely enter in. Help me be a better reflection of Your character, Lord, in all I do and say today—for Your glory. I pray this prayer in the name of Jesus, my merciful Savior and Lord. Amen.

June 1, 2. **Marty Prudhomme** is a Bible study teacher and freelance writer. She serves on the Louisiana State Leadership Team of Aglow, International, a ministry of prayer and evangelism.

The Weight of His Glory

Woe is me, for I am ruined! Because I am a man of unclean lips, and I live among a people of unclean lips; for my eyes have seen the King, the LORD of hosts (Isaiah 6:5, *New American Standard Bible*).

Scripture: Isaiah 6:1-8
Song: "The Great I Am"

Music swelled as 6,000 women from around the world sang praises to the Lord. I stood in awe as the music swept over me. Is this a little foretaste of what the living creatures around the throne of God sound like? (See Revelation 4:8, 9.)

Then I saw the flutter of a flag as a woman in her national dress began to walk around the room. Others followed, with their flags, all dressed in native attire. Each wore a banner proclaiming the name of her country, from Afghanistan to Zimbabwe. Scores of flag bearers paraded around the conference hall. It was breathtaking. It seemed that I could hear Heaven applaud, as I became suddenly aware of God's love for the nations.

In that moment I felt the weight of His glory. As I realized how small I was, with all my many faults, I wondered, *How can God love me?* I bowed my head and cried. As the glory of God filled the conference hall, I was totally undone in the presence of a holy God, Lord of the nations. That day I saw the Lord high and lifted up. I realized my unworthiness and His great compassion for the peoples of the earth . . . and for me.

Lord, You are King of kings, the great ruler over all the earth. I am humble before You and totally helpless without You. Please, never let me take You for granted or treat Your holiness with disrespect. I pray in Jesus' name. Amen.

Morning and Night

It is good to praise the LORD and make music to your name, O Most High, proclaiming your love in the morning and your faithfulness at night (Psalm 92:1, 2).

Scripture: Psalm 92:1-8
Song: "Praise the Name of Jesus"

During my teenage years, most of my friends played musical instruments or sang in the church choir. Although I envied them, they also inspired me. I wanted to make music too—not just playing records or tapes, but live music, something I created myself. Seeing my determination, a friend lent me her guitar for practicing. I learned a few chords first and then added a few Bible verses for lyrics. Even with a raspy voice and unconventional strumming, I loved putting the Scripture to music.

I composed little tunes about God's goodness and used them during my morning prayer times. Sometimes I took the guitar to work and sang my simple songs during lunch break. And at night, before bed, I'd practice strumming, adding more chords to my repertoire. I loved to worship the Lord in this fashion. I felt close to Him during those times . . . and I still do.

Today's verse encourages us to praise God daily and make music to His name. Before the day dawns or the evening ends, let us remember to worship Him. At any skill level, our musical efforts and joyful singing are sweet sounds to His ears.

Lord, I offer You the joy of my heart in word and melody. Because of You, I have purpose today and hope for tomorrow. In Christ's name, I sing and pray. Amen.

June 3–9. **Charles E. Harrel** had been a minister for more than 30 years before stepping aside to pursue writing. He enjoys digital photography, playing the guitar, and teaching Scripture.

The People of His Pasture

Come, let us bow down in worship, let us kneel before the LORD our Maker; for he is our God and we are the people of his pasture, the flock under his care (Psalm 95:6, 7).

Scripture: Psalm 95:1-7
Song: "The Lord's My Shepherd"

Our Chevy station wagon slowed to a stop. Ahead, I could see an old man standing in the middle of the road, wearing a heavy brown coat, woolen mittens, and a hoodlike covering over his head. As traffic waited on both sides of the highway, he carefully escorted his flock of sheep across the road. Two black and white collies followed his every command, helping to redirect any wayward sheep.

The flock moved slowly while the shepherd kept a watchful eye on us and other cars in the distance. As I looked out the side window, I could see their new destination: a pasture on the left, with a small meandering creek and several large shade trees. After the last sheep crossed over, the man smiled at us, nodded, and then rushed off to catch up with his flock.

Having lived most of my life in a large city, I had never seen such a sight. That day, our family's drive in the country was revelatory: I will never forget how this man cared for his flock.

Our Lord is much like that shepherd. He loves us, protects us, and leads us past the uncertainties in this life. As the people of His pasture, we can always depend on Him for guidance.

Precious Shepherd, thank You for saving me and leading me to Your pasture. I find safety there. My doubts and fears melt away, and every time I feel Your touch upon my life, I know You are watching over me. In Christ's name, amen.

Stop, Look, Listen

Remember the wonders he has done, his miracles, and the judgments he pronounced (1 Chronicles 16:12).

Scripture: 1 Chronicles 16:8-13
Song: "Where Shall My Wondering Soul Begin?"

While growing up, I lived near Oceanview Boulevard, a busy thoroughfare in the foothills of La Cañada, California. Cars and trucks rushed by with little regard for children crossing the street on their way home from school. Thankfully, my parents gave me some lifesaving advice, which I'm sure other parents have passed on to their children too: "Remember to stop, look, and listen, before you cross the street."

Our verse today comes from a psalm written by David. Similar to the advice my parents gave me, this passage lists three things to remember (about God): His wonders, miracles, and judgments. As we travel the crossroads of life, it's easy to get distracted and forget our priorities. However, when we *stop* for a moment and recall the wonders of God, we realize His divine power is eternal, never in short supply. Therefore, we can still *look* for His miracles today. Impossible situations become possible when believers put their faith in Him.

Most of all, we should *listen* for the voice of the Spirit when we read our Bibles, as we will hear comfort, encouragement, and instruction coming through to us. Stop, Look, Listen: they remind us to take God's Word seriously.

Lord God, with so much to remember these days, help me place priority on the things of the kingdom. As King David pointed out, only certain things are truly important and of lasting value. I pray in Jesus' name. Amen.

If You Build It

LORD our God, all this abundance that we have provided for building you a temple for your Holy Name comes from your hand, and all of it belongs to you (1 Chronicles 29:16).

Scripture: 1 Chronicles 29:10-18
Song: "We Dedicate This Temple"

No one thought we could do it, but we did. Our little congregation finished a half-million dollar church addition without borrowing money. The new structure included modern offices, spacious classrooms, upstairs restrooms, and a large foyer with a beautiful stained-glass window. Our local community loved the improvements, and so did the church members.

Some members, however, took on a "see what we have done" attitude. Thankfully, during Sunday's dedication service, the guest speaker reminded us that our wonderful building did not come from us. Even the funds for the project weren't ours. They were given as sacrificial offerings and therefore belonged to God. Likewise, the workers, whether compensated or not, were called and sent to us under God's watchful eye. What a reality check for us all!

Christians have accomplished amazing things over the years. They have evangelized far and wide, built great churches, and established marvelous ministries. Yet, all the praise for such efforts belongs to God. King David's benediction is a good reminder: Even if you build it, the work is still His.

Heavenly Father, with the passage of time, I seem to forget that every good and perfect gift comes from You. Please remind me to give credit where credit is due. For indeed, my life is in Your hands. In Jesus' name, amen.

Watch Out for Counterfeits!

The Spirit clearly says that in later times some will abandon the faith and follow deceiving spirits and things taught by demons (1 Timothy 4:1).

Scripture: 1 Timothy 4:1-5
Song: "Near the Cross"

I'd just returned home from a ministry assignment of many months, and I looked forward to catching up with family and friends. Steve, a high school classmate, heard I was in town and wanted to see me. He invited me to a Bible study to hear a man whose teachings had significantly influenced his life. Finally, after much urging, he got me to accompany him.

Halfway into the teaching, I began to feel uneasy. At first, this man's message sounded right. But the more I listened, the more twisted it became. He told the group that everyone goes to Heaven—to just keep believing and doing good things, that our goodness outweighs any bad. Nothing was mentioned about repentance, forgiveness, baptism, or the cross of Christ. Before the service ended, I headed for the door like a rushing linebacker. (They tried to stop me—but, thankfully, my former football training came in handy that day!)

Deception will abound in the latter times . . . and those times seem to be here. So stick to the truth found in the gospel, not just what sounds good. When we allow the Spirit of truth to guide us, demonic lies will not prevail (see John 14:17).

Master Teacher, I often hear people discussing their beliefs, and sometimes it's hard to know which ideas to embrace. Speak to my heart through Your Word, confirm the truths of the gospel, and give me discernment in all things. Through Christ, amen.

All Out of Thanks?

Jesus asked, "Were not all ten cleansed? Where are the other nine? Has no one returned to give praise to God except this foreigner?" (Luke 17:17, 18).

Scripture: Luke 17:11-19
Song: "Ten Thousand Thanks to Jesus"

My wife, Laura, teaches a kindergarten class at a Christian school in Portland, Oregon. Before serving lunch, she always invites her students to say grace with her. To prepare, she asks them to bow their heads and fold their hands. One day, one of her more curious students kept looking around, watching others in the class as they bowed their heads. Laura waited for Jade to bow too, but she didn't. Finally, Laura said, "Jade, it's time to pray."

"What for?" she asked.

"We are going to thank the Lord for our food now. Aren't you thankful?"

"Oh, no," Jade replied. "I'm all out of that!"

Apparently, 9 of the 10 healed from leprosy were found lacking in gratitude as well. Only one man returned to praise God and give thanks to Jesus.

Have you ever run short on thankfulness? Taking a few minutes to show appreciation or to bless someone who has helped us can be much more than an afterthought; rather, we can make it our constant first response. Thankfulness is big in the kingdom of God. Hopefully, we will never be "all out of that."

Lord, Your gift of eternal life has saved me from death and darkness. Your hand of mercy holds my whole life. Thank You, in Jesus' name. Amen.

The Lord Himself

Surely God is my salvation; I will trust and not be afraid. The LORD, the LORD himself, is my strength and my defense; he has become my salvation (Isaiah 12:2).

Scripture: Isaiah 12
Song: "A Mighty Fortress Is Our God"

Nations who can afford the costs will spend billions of dollars on defense systems. Using space-age technology and early warning devices, some countries can track an incoming warhead, giving them time to deploy countermeasures in hopes of destroying it.

In the news we often hear national leaders boasting of their attack and defense capabilities. Certain nations put much faith in their nuclear deterrents, some rely on their superior air power, and others trust in the strength of their armored divisions. Yet if actual war does break out, any such defenses could fall short in providing the necessary protection.

Many people do something quite similar—trusting in their retirement accounts, various insurance policies, and other job-related securities—to "defend" against life's insecurities. There is nothing wrong with such safeguards, of course. Still, Isaiah foresaw a better surety, an eternal one: Not only does the Lord *provide* salvation, He *is* our salvation. In all matters of safety and ultimate security, God is all we need. We have no reason to fear with the Lord himself on our side.

Dear Lord, I face struggles on many fronts, and most of them are spiritual battles. Since You alone have the power to rescue me, I will place my trust in You. Thank You for being my deliverer and my fortress of safety. In Your name I pray. Amen.

Going Through the Motions?

Stop bringing meaningless offerings! . . . I cannot bear your worthless assemblies (Isaiah 1:13).

Scripture: Isaiah 1:10-17
Song: "The Heart of Worship"

All of us regret some of the things we did in our youth. I have more such memories than I care to admit, and one of my bigger regrets is a particular high school dating relationship.

I allowed myself to be "fixed up" with a girl. She was a friend, but I knew from the outset that this couldn't develop into a romantic relationship. I should have said as much, but I succumbed to the pressure of friends who thought we would be "so cute together."

The result? A long-term relationship in which I was simply going through the motions. My heart wasn't in it, and I hurt this girl when I finally admitted the truth. Even though nearly 20 years have passed, I still regret my actions.

There is nothing worse than a fake relationship, the height of hypocrisy. And yet is that how we sometimes approach our relationship with God? It is frighteningly easy to go through the motions of worship and prayer.

Surely our Lord isn't interested in heartless worship, distracted prayer, or ministry done begrudgingly. Thankfully, the Holy Spirit constantly calls us to a deeper, heartfelt love.

O God, forgive me when I approach You with anything less than sincere joy, heartfelt gratitude, and genuine love. There is nothing fake in You! In Jesus' name, amen.

June 10–16. **Mike Edmisten** is the senior minister of the Amelia Church of Christ in Amelia, Ohio. He and his wife, Nicki, have two sons.

How Would You Do It?

Their land is full of silver and gold; there is no end to their treasures. Their land is full of horses; there is no end to their chariots (Isaiah 2:7).

Scripture: Isaiah 2:5-17
Song: "Give Us Clean Hands"

If I were God, I would do some things differently. That sounds almost sacrilegious, but it's true. If you're honest, I bet you would admit that you would do some things differently too.

One of the things I'd do is draw a clear line between blessing and cursing. If someone is godly, they would be blessed. If someone rejected the Lord, they would be cursed. Simple, right?

But that's not always how God works. In Isaiah 2, we see fabulously wealthy people who had completely walked away from God. In fact, Isaiah said that there was no end to their wealth. There was also no end to their sinfulness.

It doesn't seem right from our perspective. But if we could see things from the Lord's perspective, would we come to a radically different conclusion? For example, we might remember that just because someone isn't suffering doesn't automatically mean that God is blessing. And just because judgment is delayed doesn't mean that judgment will never come.

Bottom line: I need to be careful that I don't see my own material possessions as proof that God is pleased with me. Those possessions may, in fact, blind me from the truth.

God, our culture abounds with idolatry. It's easy to put our hopes in money and possessions—but help us reject these idols and worship You alone. In Christ, amen.

Don't Major in the Minors

Is not this the kind of fasting I have chosen: to loose the chains of injustice and untie the cords of the yoke, to set the oppressed free and break every yoke? (Isaiah 58:6).

Scripture: Isaiah 58:1-7
Song: "Rescue the Perishing"

"How did we get here?" That's a question I often hear from my boys. They fall asleep on a long drive, only to wake up and find that we have arrived at our destination. They missed the entire drive—hence the question.

It's a good question for the church. I love the church. Jesus died for the church. The church is the hope of the world. Nevertheless, the church is far from perfect.

How did we get here? How did we go from caring for the poor to hosting potlucks in the fellowship hall? How did we go from releasing the oppressed to youth-group pizza parties?

I'm not down on these "fellowship events," but let us remember that a world is dying while we are feasting. Or, as the witty late preacher Vance Havner put it, "Too many Christians are stuffing themselves with gospel blessings while millions have never had a taste."

I'm not trying to make us feel guilty for enjoying our blessings. I'm simply reminding us of our mission: it is too important for us to major in the minors and minor in the majors. As long as someone is poor, oppressed, or lost, our mission is incomplete.

Almighty and everlasting God, You came to seek and to save what was lost. That was the totality of Your mission. Help me recapture Your urgency and Your passion. In the precious name of Jesus I pray. Amen.

Making Him Famous

"For as a belt is bound around the waist, so I bound all the people of Israel and all the people of Judah to me," declares the LORD, "to be my people for my renown and praise and honor. But they have not listened" (Jeremiah 13:11).

Scripture: Jeremiah 13:1-11
Song: "Famous One"

Most people have dreamed of becoming famous. At various stages of my life, I have imagined being a famous baseball player, rock star, bull rider, mime (it's embarrassing, but this was a short-lived dream of mine), country singer, preacher, talk radio host, writer . . . and the list goes on.

As I have matured, I have discovered that all of these dreams of fame were rooted in the same source: my basic insecurity. If I became famous, the accolades of my fans would be the cure that I needed for my shaky self-image.

Talk about a pointless pursuit! Even if I were to become a great celebrity, it wouldn't cure the brokenness inside me. That kind of healing is found always and only in Jesus.

And in our Scripture today, God speaks of His own renown. In other words, the job of His people is to make the Lord himself famous.

My own fame is worthless. It does nothing for me, and it doesn't help anyone else. But when Jesus becomes famous, I am healed. And so is anyone else who accepts Him.

Lord, I exist for Your renown—to make You famous. If everyone comes to know Your name without ever knowing my name, that would be the fulfillment of my highest calling. In the precious name of Jesus I pray. Amen.

Am I Listening?

"When I called, they did not listen; so when they called, I would not listen," says the LORD **Almighty** (Zechariah 7:13).

Scripture: Zechariah 7:8-14
Song: "Word of God, Speak"

Any parent knows what it's like when a child just won't listen. I remember an old Looney Tunes cartoon where Foghorn Leghorn told a youngster, "Pay attention to me, boy! I'm not talkin' just to hear my head roar!"

Parentally speaking, I've been there, done that. I have felt that kind of frustration. But it doesn't just stop at frustration. When one of my boys doesn't listen to me, there are consequences. Our heavenly Father acts in much the same way. When we refuse to listen to Him, there are consequences. In some cases, the consequences are simple: people won't listen to Him, so He won't listen to them, as our Scripture today tells us.

God abounds in grace and compassion, but that doesn't negate His judgment and discipline. If my prayer seems to be constantly unanswered, could it be that God is choosing not to listen to me because I have stubbornly turned a deaf ear to Him?

What is God saying to you and me today? He *is* speaking. It is very likely that He is speaking directly to an area of brokenness or disobedience in our lives. What is He saying? (Maybe an even better question is: Am I listening?)

O God, I will take this moment to be still and to listen for Your wisdom and guidance. You've heard enough from me, but I cannot hear enough from You. Fill me with a fresh sense of Your presence, a clearer idea of Your will, and a renewed determination to please You. I pray these things in the name of Jesus. Amen.

A Simple Equation

The seed on good soil stands for those with a noble and good heart, who hear the word, retain it, and by persevering produce a crop (Luke 8:15).

Scripture: Luke 8:9-15
Song: "Thy Word Is Like a Garden, Lord."

I am terrible at math. The only reason I'm not broke or in jail is because my wife balances our checkbook. But in this passage, Jesus gives us an equation that even I can understand: A + B + C = Living a God-Honoring Life.

"A" is *hearing* the Word of God. We need to hear the Word each week from a minister who passionately and lovingly preaches the truth.

"B" is *retaining* the Word. We must remember it. Scripture memorization may seem like an antiquated spiritual discipline, but it is still relevant (because Jesus said it is still relevant).

"C" is *persevering* through the Word. There will be times when the difficulties of our lives seem at odds with the truths of Scripture. One preacher described it as "seasons when life and truth collide." In other words, can we still persevere in God's truth when everything else in our life seems to tell us to walk away? In the moment of testing, can we stand strong in the faith?

I love this simple equation from our Scripture today. Add these three together—hearing, retaining, persevering—and we'll find the fruitful life that God has designed for us.

Dear Heavenly Father, thank You for the gift of Your Word. It is fresh, no matter how much we hear it. It is precious, so we will remember it. And it is true, so help us persevere in it. In Christ I pray. Amen.

Who Is Really in Charge?

You turn things upside down, as if the potter were thought to be like the clay! Shall what is formed say to the one who formed it, "You did not make me"? Can the pot say to the potter, "You know nothing"? (Isaiah 29:16).

Scripture: Isaiah 29:9-16
Song: "You Are God Alone"

I was watching one of those reality police shows the other day, and it made me laugh out loud. A police officer was arresting a man, and this guy had the audacity to start barking out orders to the officer! The officer not-so-gently reminded him, "I have the badge, therefore I give the orders."

I haven't had many run-ins with the law in my life. On the few occasions where I have been confronted by a police officer, I immediately submitted to his authority. He's in charge; I'm not.

However, even though I easily recognize the authority of a human police officer, I sometimes try to switch places with the Lord of the universe! My prayers become a laundry list of things that I want Him to do for me. I bark out orders as if He were my willing servant.

Why do we become so expert at turning things upside down, as Isaiah describes in our text? For the Israelites, it brought a heavenly reminder about who is actually in charge.

God is consumed with His own honor and glory. That's not egotistical. It is simply because He is God, and we are not.

Lord God, the height of arrogance is to place myself on Your level. Do whatever it takes to break down my walls of pride, soften my heart, and remind me that I serve and worship You—not the other way around. In the name of Jesus I pray. Amen.

Look . . . and See

They have no speech, they use no words; no sound is heard from them. Yet their voice goes out into all the earth (Psalm 19:3, 4).

Scripture: Psalm 19:1-6
Song: "Creation's Lord, We Give Thee Thanks"

Viktor Frankl, Jewish psychiatrist and holocaust survivor, writes in his classic work, *Man's Search for Meaning*, the story of a young woman about to die. Her lonely time in a concentration camp cell was coming to an end, and Frankl was able to talk with her in the hours before her death.

She was grateful for her life experiences, she told him. She pointed to her one tiny window that gave her the view of a chestnut tree's branch each day. She said that the tree, that one branch, had become her cherished friend. She had come to view it as a link to eternal life, soon to begin for her.

This young woman found deep meaning in two tiny blossoms budding and then opening a little more each day. God's creation—the tiny bit she could see—spoke to her spirit about the reality of her mighty Creator, magnificent in power, and at the same time tender in creativity.

How clearly are God's eternal power and divine nature shown through our natural world (see Romans 1:20)! When we look, may we truly see.

O God, give me eyes to see Your glory this day. As I look at Your creation may I gain courage and strength to live my days in service to You. Through Christ, amen.

June 17–23. **Jan Pierce** lives in Vancouver, Washington. She writes devotional and family life material and spends several months each year in India.

What Makes You Happy?

The precepts of the LORD are right, giving joy to the heart. The commands of the LORD are radiant, giving light to the eyes (Psalm 19:8).

Scripture: Psalm 19:7-14
Song: "Joyful, Joyful, We Adore Thee"

If you were to ask your friends and family the following question, what answer do you think you'd hear? The question: "What makes you happy?"

My guess is you'd hear a variety of answers from "Chocolate" or "My morning coffee," to more serious responses such as, "My wife and children" or "My career." You might get answers such as "A walk on the beach," "My favorite music" or "Time in my garden." And it's true that all of these can bring pleasure into our days.

However, the psalmist reminds us that a bedrock happiness springs from a right relationship with God, who created every good thing in our lives. There is joy in our hearts when our lives align with God's will—when we follow His ways.

There's not only safety and well-being in following God's "good rules." If we know His love for us, we'll recognize that our deepest joy comes from willing obedience to God's precepts. They lead us straight to Him.

Gracious Father, I thank You for Your Word that helps me make choices each day. You teach me by Your commands and by Your example. In You I discover purity and righteousness. When I follow You I am safe, content, and, best of all, able to please You. In the name of Jesus, who lives and reigns with You and the Holy Spirit, one God, now and forever, amen.

What's the Good News?

No one will be declared righteous in God's sight by the works of the law; rather, through the law we become conscious of our sin (Romans 3:20).

Scripture: Romans 3:9-20
Song: "Beneath the Cross of Jesus"

A favorite "good news, bad news" joke for ministers goes like this: The church board tells their minister, "There's good news and there's bad news. The good news is that attendance has been much higher these past three weeks. The bad news: you've been on vacation!"

In his letter to the Romans, Paul had news for the Jews. The good news was they had distinct advantages over the Gentiles. They'd been entrusted with God's commandments and were the keepers of the covenants He made with them. Their greatest leaders had walked closely with God throughout history.

Then Paul had to burst their bubble by giving them the bad news: Following the rules and basking in their special relationship with God wasn't going to save them. That was shocking news and didn't make Paul their favorite preacher. There is news here for us, as well. Bad news first: none of us will get to Heaven by following rules. "What's the good news?" you ask. It's the fact that we recognize our need of Jesus when we measure our behavior against the law. And then that remarkable exchange of His life for ours ushers us right into the throne room of the Father. Good news indeed!

Lord, thank You for grafting me into Your tree of life. Help me recognize my sin so I can repent and once again walk in the light of Your love. Through Christ, amen.

What Do I Get?

God demonstrates his own love for us in this: While we were still sinners, Christ died for us (Romans 5:8).

Scripture: Romans 5:6-14
Song: "Amazing Love"

If you've ever been a parent or a teacher, you'll know that children often raise this burning question: "What do we get?" It seems they're programmed to expect some sort of reward for good behavior. Sadly, in our culture, they even expect rewards when they *fail* to do anything positive. I've been known to answer their question with, "You get a nice, warm smile," or "You get the honor of my presence."

We adults aren't so very different in our expectations. When we work hard or strive to follow God's commandments, we may expect good things to follow. And sometimes we don't show much patience with those who break the rules and aren't making the same efforts to live good, upright lives. (Surely they don't *deserve* any rewards!)

Then we're stopped in our tracks by the verse above that tells us Christ died for us—gave up His life for us, while we were still sinners. He didn't tell us to get our behavior in line and then He'd think about it. Instead, He poured out unconditional love while all of us were absolutely filthy in our sin. Amazing love—that, friends, is what we get.

I stand before You, **Lord,** humbly contemplating the amazing love You have shown to me. While I was dead in my sin, You loved me and chose to give me Your very life. My only response in light of such sacrifice is to serve You all of my days. In the name of Jesus I pray. Amen.

Alive

I am the Lord; that is my name! I will not yield my glory to another or my praise to idols (Isaiah 42:8).

Scripture: Isaiah 42:1-9
Song: "He Lives"

The scantily-clad man sits in the dust, his head bent to his work. In his hands he holds a primitive knife and a piece of wood. He spends his days carving an image that will sit in a prominent place in some Hindu home: Shiva or Ganesha or one of the other myriad gods. The sale of these idols provides food for his family.

The idol will grace a shelf or sit in a stone niche. Flowers will adorn the area, hymns will be sung, and promises made. Perhaps a portion of the family's income will be offered, or part of the harvest. In any case, worship flows to these pieces of metal and wood, though fear often lurks in the worshippers' hearts. You see, many of these gods are believed to be capricious and evil; even devoted followers have cause to fear them.

The Bible says that those who worship false gods will become like them, lifeless and empty (see Psalm 115:7, 8). But our God is alive. He refuses to give His glory to anything or anyone. When we talk to Him, He hears us and He loves us with nothing but good plans for our lives. Yes, we serve a living God who does us only good (even when it can be painful for us). I choose to worship Him. I choose life.

Most holy God, I praise You above all else. There is no other God but You. Thank You for all You do for me daily and for the good plans You have for my life. I will give You thanks forever. In the name Your Son, Jesus, I pray. Amen.

Someday

He who was seated on the throne said, "I am making everything new!" . . . "It is done. I am the Alpha and the Omega, the Beginning and the End" (Revelation 21:5, 6).

Scripture: Revelation 21:1-7
Song: "I Will See Jesus"

I've had conversations with believers lately about the end times. Some people are tracking each biblical prophecy in the march of time toward eternity. It's true that no one but the Father knows the day and time of the coming of our Lord, but we are to watch carefully for His return.

Is the whole world watching? Consider the newscasts these days—they're filled with stories of natural calamities around the world. There are earthquakes, floods, tornadoes, to say nothing of wars that continually spring up all around the globe. We all observe these dangerous times and try to interpret them.

How then are we to spend our days? Do we tremble in fear at the possibility of devastations in our own neighborhoods? Do we fall into despair at the ungodly trends in our own country? Do we worry over the decadence of despots around the world?

No, we don't. Instead, we remember what the Lord has told us. He's on His throne, making everything new. His words are trustworthy and true. The battle with spiritual death is already won, and He's preparing to quench our thirst for Him with the free gift of the water of life. Meanwhile, we live for Him.

O God, my King, I know Your words to me are trustworthy and true. My desire is to live each day in service to You and Your people. I choose not to live in fear, but instead to trust in You for my salvation. In Jesus' name, amen.

Between Alpha and Omega

See, I will create new heavens and a new earth. The former things will not be remembered, nor will they come to mind (Isaiah 65:17).

Scripture: Isaiah 65:17-25
Song: "Coming for Me"

It was Sunday evening and time for one of our church families to present a teaching or a skit. The Martins rose and did a reading in which they spoke of particular human circumstances followed by the phrase, "The kingdom of Heaven is now." They were a talented family, musically and dramatically, and their lives were encouraging to me as a new believer. I listened carefully as they spoke their powerful lines.

"A young mother is holding her stillborn child" . . . *The kingdom of Heaven is now.* "The accident occurred when a semi-truck crossed the center line" . . . *The kingdom of Heaven is now.* "He's serving 10 years for armed robbery" . . . *The kingdom of Heaven is now.* I was listening, but I didn't understand. Shouldn't the kingdom of God be good and beautiful and filled with joy?

I watched that performance over 30 years ago, and I still remember it vividly, because it took some years of maturing in Christ to begin understanding the kingdom of God. I'm still learning. One thing I do know: the kingdom *began* when Christ came and it will *end* in perfection, when He comes again. For now, we're between Alpha and Omega, and there's still some difficult living to do before the lion lies down with the lamb.

Dear Lord, show me how to live in these days before You return. May Your kingdom come on earth, and may I be useful to You in it. Through Christ I pray. Amen.

For Our Peace

O Jerusalem, Jerusalem, thou that killest the prophets, and stonest them which are sent unto thee, how often would I have gathered thy children together, even as a hen gathereth her chickens under her wings, and ye would not! (Matthew 23:37, *King James Version*).

Scripture: Matthew 23:29-39
Song: "Awesome in This Place"

Jesus didn't mince words. He called the day's religious leaders hypocrites and snakes. But though He knew the evil in their hearts He still loved them, having longed to gather them as a hen gathers her chicks. Yet He could not help them, because they wouldn't acknowledge Him as Messiah.

I wonder what emotions Jesus experienced in this scene. Did He tremble with anger over their pride? draw a ragged sigh of exasperation over their stubbornness? weep in sorrow over their fate? (And was there perhaps a very human panic at what was soon to happen to Him at their hands?)

I think of Jesus' feelings now, as I face a difficult day. In spite of today's hypocrisy and deception, in spite of our part in His suffering, Jesus longs to gather us under His "wings" of salvation, comfort, and protection. We can rest in Him, with a deep peace, for the price of our redemption was paid soon after that long-ago scene.

Lord, You entered the world as one of us—fully human, fully God. Thank You for understanding all we encounter in life. Carry us through! In Jesus' name, amen.

June 24–30. **Phyllis Beveridge Nissila** is a wife and mother of two grown daughters. Working as a writer, she is also an instructor at Lane Community College in Eugene, Oregon.

The Way Home

Behold, the days come, saith the LORD, that it shall no more be called Tophet, nor the valley of the son of Hinnom, but the valley of slaughter (Jeremiah 7:32, *King James Version*).

Scripture: Jeremiah 7:30–8:3
Song: "Lord, I Lift Your Name on High"

From flower to flame, delight to desolation, garden to Gehenna: this passage of Scripture is the story of how a king's retreat became a valley of slaughter.

Idol worship and child sacrifice by fire devastated this once lovely tract of land near Jerusalem and destroyed its people. Even the bones of the dead were unearthed by conquerors and scattered to become "dung upon the face of the earth" (Jeremiah 8:2, *KJV*). It would be many years before descendants of its exiled inhabitants came home.

Sin is like that: innocence destroyed; paradise lost. And we know better. Yet, as former congressional chaplain Peter Marshall once said: "Most of us know perfectly well what we ought to do; our trouble is that we do not *want* to do it."

But God had a plan: Jesus, who left Heaven for earth, showed the way back to God, appealing to the hearts of the most stubborn sinners. And in another tract of land near Jerusalem, this marvelous Messiah, blood-stained, sacrificed himself for the sins of all time. Now all who respond to His invitation can follow Him, through the waters of baptism, to their eternal home.

Into Your forgiving arms, **Lord,** I come. You have conquered the rebellious impulse in my heart and opened my life to the real life, eternal life. Thank You for Your incomparable mercy and grace! Through Christ my Lord I pray. Amen.

Now the Blessings Flow

He did that which was evil in the sight of the LORD, according to all that his father had done (2 Kings 24:9, *King James Version*).

Scripture: 2 Kings 24:1-12
Song: "Father, I Adore You"

"Like father, like son." Whether due to nature or nurture (or both), the child often mimics the parent. Where the example is evil, damage spreads; where good, blessings will flow.

The duo in today's passage, King Jehoiakim and his son, King Jehoiachin, resembled each other in rebellion against God. Their disobedience caused Jerusalem to be invaded and eventually conquered, its inhabitants forced into captivity. Thus the sins of the father were repeated in the son, and many people paid the price.

Thankfully, for them and for us, there is another Father/Son partnership here for good, not evil; for salvation, not destruction.

Jesus said He did what He saw His Father do (see John 5:19). He healed the sick, made the blind see, and delivered the demon-possessed from their torment. And because He knew of His Father's great love for mankind, Jesus himself paid the price for people then and now to be set free of sin's captivity—generation after generation after generation.

And therefore the blessings flow.

Thank You, **Father,** for the life and work of Your Son. Give me His heart of compassion for the people in my world today. May I somehow convey the character and concern of His Spirit who indwells me. In the name of Jesus I pray. Amen.

Lost Treasures

All the articles of the house of God, great and small . . . he brought them all to Babylon (2 Chronicles 36:18, *New American Standard Bible*).

Scripture: 2 Chronicles 36:15-21
Song: "Holy Spirit, Thou Art Welcome"

When I imagine the pillage of the temple referenced in this Scripture passage, I picture cartload after cartload of glittering artifacts creaking and groaning through the dusty byways of the holy city as they rumble toward Babylon. I picture people peering out from behind doorposts, mourning over the destruction of what was once the jewel of the promised land and is now the conqueror's loot.

I hear moans of regret over the worship of false gods. Creating those idols exposed the people of the true God to such destruction, in spite of repeated warnings.

The treasures of the Most High are no longer made of silver and gold to grace chambers of cedar and brass. They are gifts of the Spirit. The Lord no longer dwells in the Holy of Holies, but in the hearts of believers.

But still the destroyer comes. The prince of darkness steals faith, ransacks hope, and plunders love for God and each other, every time we bow to his lies. But as one ancient proverb tells us: "By bravely enduring it, an evil which cannot be avoided is overcome." Yes, we overcome by the overcomer: our victorious Lord Christ.

Holy Lord, teach me, correct me, and guide me. May I this day depend on You alone, every time temptation comes. Through Christ I pray. Amen.

No Better Deal

The LORD, the God of heaven, has given me all the kingdoms of the earth and he has appointed me to build a temple for him at Jerusalem in Judah. Any of his people among you may go up to Jerusalem in Judah and build the temple of the LORD . . . and may their God be with them. (Ezra 1:2, 3).

Scripture: Ezra 1:1-8
Song: "The Redeemed of the Lord Shall Return"

It was the deal of the century. Not only could the captives return to Jerusalem after 70 long years in captivity, they could leave with the king's blessing.

Not only could they take all of their possessions back home with them, but King Cyrus encouraged their neighbors to give them money, supplies, and cattle—along with a freewill offering for God's house. In addition to all of that, Cyrus gave back the treasures that his predecessor had stolen from the temple.

It was an offer God's people could hardly refuse! But there is an even better offer today. Jesus, the King of all kings, frees sin-captives, provides us with the Holy Spirit to guide us on our spiritual journey, and forever blesses those who accept His offer.

Yes, you and I, by the grace of God, enjoy the priceless treasures of salvation: faith, hope, love, and eternal life in the new Jerusalem. It's the deal of *all* centuries.

Father, help me spread the good news—You have graciously offered fellowship with You through the person of Your Son, Jesus. Today may I recall this privilege and take advantage of it through moments of quiet prayer. In the name of Jesus, amen.

God in the Details

The whole company numbered 42,360, besides their 7,337 male and female slaves; and they also had 200 male and female singers. They had 736 horses, 245 mules, 435 camels and 6,720 donkeys (Ezra 2:64-67).

Scripture: Ezra 2:64-70
Song: "His Eye Is on the Sparrow"

Recently, one of my brothers announced he had found, online, the exact location of the grave of our littlest sister, Dorothy, who died in February, 1971, shortly after she was born. While Mom was still recovering, Dad, two of my brothers, aged 4 and 6, and the minister laid the baby to rest in a local cemetery. A small tin sign marked her grave.

Through the years, none of the family has remembered the exact site—until my brother's discovery. Though we never "met" Dorothy, somehow, knowing now that her tiny body was buried in space 14, section C, lot 900 in the cemetery on Crest Drive makes her brief life more real, more precious.

The facts and figures recorded in today's Scripture show us the returnees from the Babylonian exile: the people—and the animals. Such data help us see faces and hear songs of celebration. And the stomping and braying of camels, mules, donkeys, and horses brings it all down to earth in real history. And to me, the information even makes God, who orchestrated the homecoming of thousands of His people, seem more real too.

Heavenly Father, thank You for Your intimate knowledge of—and care for—me. You are more than a mere concept; You are the ever-living God of history and the Lord beyond all time. Praise to You, through Christ my Savior! Amen.

First Things First

On the first day of the seventh month they began to offer burnt offerings to the LORD, though the foundation of the LORD's temple had not yet been laid (Ezra 3:6).

Scripture: Ezra 3:1-7
Song: "You're My Glory"

There was much to be done to restore the glory of the temple in Jerusalem. But before the rebuilding of the gates, terraces, and tunnels and before the reconstruction of the courts, corridors, and chambers, the people "built the altar on its foundation" (v. 3) and offered sacrifices of prayer and praise to God.

For believers, who are temples of God's Spirit today, our restoration follows a similar pattern. On the altar of the sacrifice of God's own Lamb, Jesus, we lay our sin-damaged lives. Then as we yield to the Holy Spirit, whom Jesus promised would lead and guide us into all truth, our lives are transformed into the image of Jesus himself. How can we help but praise Him for His transforming power in us? And there's a great benefit too, as Congressman George M. Adams once said: "To praise is an investment in happiness."

From rubble to glory in Jerusalem; from death to life in Christ. Amidst all such gracious acts of God, let us begin and end with offerings of heartfelt thanksgiving.

God the Father, Son, and Holy Spirit, I praise You for renewing and restoring me. Help me always remember that I can never claim to be a "self-made" person. You were there at the beginning of my earthly days, and I will stand before You at the end of them. Keep me in Your loving care until that day. In Jesus' name, amen.

My Prayer Notes

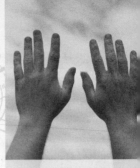

DEVOTIONS®

JULY

Show mercy to me according to your great love.

—Nehemiah 13:22

Gary Wilde, Editor　　　**Margaret Williams,** Project Editor　　Photo by Getty Images | Photos.com | Thinkstock®

DEVOTIONS® is published quarterly by Standard Publishing, Cincinnati, Ohio, www.standardpub.com.
© 2012 by Standard Publishing. All rights reserved. Topics based on the Home Daily Bible Readings,
International Sunday School Lessons. © 2009 by the Committee on the Uniform Series. Printed in
the U.S.A. All Scripture quotations, unless otherwise indicated, are taken from the *HOLY BIBLE,
NEW INTERNATIONAL VERSION®. NIV®.* Copyright © 2011 by Biblica, Inc.™ Used by permission
of Zondervan. All rights reserved. Scripture quotations marked (*NKJV*) are taken from the *New
King James Version®.* Copyright © 1982 by Thomas Nelson, Inc. Used by permission. All rights
reserved.

Only the Best!

The temple I am going to build will be great, because our God is greater than all other gods (2 Chronicles 2:5).

Scripture: 2 Chronicles 2:1-9
Song: "Great God, We Give Thee Praise"

Once a year our high school youth group transforms the foyer of our church into the "Northland Café" for an evening of fine dining. With some deft decorating touches, mood lighting, and soft music in the background, patrons are treated to an evening many call the highlight of their Valentine's weekend.

Newcomers to the dinner find it hard to believe that our teens, along with a few sponsors, can pull off such a feat. But our youth have determined that this evening is dedicated to God and that He is worthy of the best they can offer.

"Only the best" could have been Solomon's motto as well. He gathered skilled craftsmen, precious metals, and the finest materials to build a magnificent temple for the Lord. He spared no expense, and no detail was to be overlooked. As Solomon put it, "The temple . . . will be great, because our God is greater than all other gods."

We serve a great God who deserves our best. Whatever talents or skills you may possess, whatever tasks you undertake, whatever opportunities come your way, give God what He deserves: nothing less than your best!

Lord, You are the great God of all creation. Whatever I set my hands to do in Your service, may I, like Solomon, strive to give only my best. Through Christ, amen.

July 1–7. **Dan Nicksich** is the senior minister of the Northland Church of Christ in Grant, Michigan. He and his wife, Donna, are still adjusting to the empty nest.

Change of Plans

**The LORD said to my father David, "You did well to have it
in your heart to build a temple for my Name"** (1 Kings 8:18).

Scripture: 1 Kings 8:14-21
Song: "I'll Go Where You Want Me to Go"

A young man and his wife were turned down for the mission
field due to his wife's fragile health. Disappointed, the young
man turned to his father's business: producing grape juice as an
alternative to wine for communion services in local churches.

Under Charles Welch's leadership, the company grew tre-
mendously, and the disappointed would-be missionary was able
to give extensively to support mission works around the world.
What seemed at first to be a great burden turned instead into a
tremendous blessing.

David wanted to honor God by building a great temple for
His glory. How disappointing it must have been to hear God
say no. The Lord was pleased with David's desire, but the plan
wasn't what God had envisioned.

Your best-laid plans to honor God may not be what God has
in mind. But don't worry; He still has great things in mind for
you. Remember David's example. And remember another man
of God who wanted to serve on the mission field but was redi-
rected to serve in a different fashion. His original dream was
shattered, but he ended up doing far more for mission work
than he had ever dreamed.

Lord, I often end up running ahead of You. Direct my paths, and slow me down that
I may hear and discern Your voice. Help me to follow, even if Your path may be a
different one than I envisioned. In Jesus' name I pray. Amen.

The Temple: Us

Don't you know that you yourselves are God's temple and that God's Spirit dwells in your midst? (1 Corinthians 3:16).

Scripture: 1 Kings 8:22-30
Song: "Spirit of the Living God"

Most people would cringe at the thought of loaning their car to a college student, but Dean had dedicated his new car to God's service. He was a campus minister who shared his life — and at times, his car — with students in need.

When a distraught student called to apologize to Dean after another driver had smashed into Dean's car, the young minister simply said, "It's not my car; it's God's car." Then, when he went out to view his obviously totaled vehicle, Dean lifted up a simple prayer: "Lord, here's your car. I'm not sure what You're going to do with it now, but here it is."

Solomon dedicated the temple he had built, knowing full well that it could never contain God. And it wasn't that God *needed* a temple. Rather, a temple would serve God's people as a place for worship, sacrifice, and instruction. The temple would be a constant reminder of God's presence and power.

Your car, your house, your life. Dedicate it all to His service. It's not that God needs anything from you or me. Rather, through offering all we are — and have — to God, we can be a constant witness to His presence and power. In other words, it's not surprising that God now says *we* are His temple.

Dear Lord, I welcome Your Holy Spirit. May He fill me that I might be Your witness. Help me never allow attachment to the things of this world to cloud my witness. Do let Christ be seen through me. In His name I pray. Amen.

Smarter Than a 5th Grader?

When the chief priests and the teachers of the law saw the wonderful things he did and the children shouting in the temple courts, "Hosanna to the Son of David," they were indignant (Matthew 21:15).

Scripture: Matthew 21:10-16
Song: "Jesus Loves the Little Children"

I don't know if Jesus would have liked the television show *Are You Smarter Than a 5th Grader?* But I know some people who would fail that test (I'm a good candidate).

As Jesus approached Jerusalem, the children cried out to praise Him. The chief priests and teachers of the law objected, thinking it unseemly, verging on blasphemy. In this case, the children proved smarter than the religious leaders.

I wonder how people would react if Jesus were coming into town today. I picture children flocking to Him. I wonder how the adults would respond. Would we be as smart as 5th graders?

Have you ever noticed how we schedule our times to praise Jesus? It's as if we can't praise Him unless it's Sunday morning, with appropriate instrumental accompaniment. Wouldn't it be great to be stirred to spontaneous praise by a fresh encounter with Jesus daily?

How often does the Lord inspire you to spontaneously speak of His goodness, His grace, His mercy? In other words, how often are you and I as smart as a group of children who gathered to praise Jesus one day, as He entered Jerusalem?

Father, today I lift my praise to You! Through Jesus You have cleansed me, saved me, and made me whole. All honor and praise I lift to You. In Jesus' name, amen.

Worthy of Our Praise—Whenever!

You brought us into prison and laid burdens on our backs (Psalm 66:11).

Scripture: Psalm 66:1-12
Song: "Let's Just Praise the Lord"

I might have been 6-years-old when I watched for the first time, Cecil B. DeMille's classic movie, *The Ten Commandments*. I was mesmerized at his portrayal of the Red Sea crossing. I felt as if I were right there as an eyewitness.

I love watching that scene. It never gets old. And David must have felt the same way, for in his catalog of reasons to praise God, "turned the sea into dry land"(v. 6) is right up there with the rest.

I like to think of the Psalms as lessons in praise. We see God's people praising Him in any and all circumstances with the constant affirmation that their Lord is worthy. "You brought us into prison" (v. 11). Yes, even amidst imprisonment, the psalmist affirms that God is worthy of our praise.

It's obvious that in our "me first" culture, it's all about us. We fail to see God in the same light as those who penned these great works of praise. They understood that when God opens the door for a time of suffering, He is still working to refine us, to focus us, to make sure that we don't lose sight of things eternal.

Are you in prison today? suffering? struggling? God still has a plan for you—and He is worthy of praise wherever you are.

Lord, we all go through times of suffering in this world. But our circumstances do not diminish Your worthiness or our need to lift up Your name in praise. Remind me of this truth whenever I encounter difficult times. In Jesus' name, amen.

Open Graves

Not a word from their mouth can be trusted; their heart is filled with malice. Their throat is an open grave; with their tongues they tell lies (Psalm 5:9).

Scripture: Psalm 5
Song: "Sing, My Tongue, the Savior's Glory"

The dentist's epitaph reads, "Stranger, approach this spot with gravity; Dr. John Brown is filling his last cavity." From the appropriately named Tombstone, Arizona, comes this gem: "Here lies Lester Moore. Four slugs from a .44, no Les, no more." Finally the one that I'm guessing is a husband's revenge: "Beneath this stone, a lump of clay lies Arabella Young, who on the 21st of May began to hold her tongue."

What gets more attention than a wagging tongue? What causes more grief than gossip? What causes more distress than deceit? With our words we sever friendships. With our words, we destroy marriages and business relationships. With little more than words, parents and children part ways, siblings separate from siblings.

David speaks of those whose throats are like open graves. They destroy others while charting their own course of self-destruction. In other words, with our tongues we can destroy ourselves and others—or with our tongues we can proclaim our joy and trust. Clearly, what we say speaks volumes about the one in whom we have placed our trust.

O Lord God, let my throat be a fountain of praise for You. Take my voice and let me sing of Your goodness; take my lips and let them be filled with eternal gratitude for Your mercy. In the name of Jesus I pray. Amen.

Weeping Despite the Joy

Many of the older priests and Levites and family heads, who had seen the former temple, wept aloud when they saw the foundation of this temple being laid, while many others shouted for joy (Ezra 3:12).

Scripture: Ezra 3:8-13
Song: "Rejoice in the Lord Always"

Some were shouting praise but some were angered. Jesus rode into Jerusalem, and everyone was stirred.

Some were gloating and some were weeping. Jesus was led to Calvary for crucifixion, and everyone was stirred.

Some shouted, others wept. The foundation of the temple was being laid. Those who remembered the glory of Solomon's temple wept aloud at this scaled down version, but others cried out in great joy.

The same event can stir radically different reactions. Some are easily sidetracked from the things of God. Some saw an enemy instead of the Messiah. Some saw a building rather than God's temple. It may not have been as magnificent as Solomon's opulence demanded, but was it worth weeping over?

I sense that many of us today are similarly sidetracked. It may be the new building, the new style of worship, or some other issue. Is it worth the anguish we invest? Is it worth the turmoil and dissent?

Lord, I want to focus on eternity, to seek first the kingdom, to rejoice in the things worth rejoicing over, and never allow the troubles of this world to blind me to things above. As I see Jesus and concentrate on building His kingdom, let me go forth in joy and set aside all that causes unwarranted distress. In the name of Christ, amen.

On Our Own

You have no part with us in building a temple to our God. We alone will build it for the LORD (Ezra 4:3).

Scripture: Ezra 4:1-5
Song: "In Christ Alone"

A ministry dedicated to restoring the lives of youth on Pittsburgh's north side was about to receive funding from the government. The offer was tempting—the substantial funds could mean more resources, a bigger building, and even the ability to reach more kids.

But there was a catch. The government gave the group one condition: *Do not preach the gospel of Jesus Christ.*

They refused the funding. Yet now the Urban Impact Foundation is changing lives "one person, one family, one block at a time." The message of Christ, of His promise of salvation, full and free, is at the heart of this ministry. The organization continues to thrive, thanks to private donations from churches and individuals across western Pennsylvania. It depends solely on God and the obedience of His people for its success.

Sometimes there's work that God wants us to do—as individuals, as a church, or as a Christian community. Allowing anyone or anything to take over—compromising the gospel message—renders our kingdom work ineffective. Only God's people can bear spiritual fruit on earth.

Lord, thank You for having a plan for my life. Help me to follow the plan in obedience to Your command. In Jesus' name, amen.

July 8–14. **Lisa Earl** teaches online writing classes from her home in western Pennsylvania. She enjoys spending time with her husband and son.

Foundations of Faith

They are restoring the walls and repairing the foundations (Ezra 4:12).

Scripture: Ezra 4:11-16
Song: "We Rest on Thee"

My husband and I live in a growing suburb. Every week it seems as if a new shopping plaza or housing development has suddenly appeared. The telltale signs of new construction are always the same: a once grassy or tree-covered area stripped to dirt, muddy tire tracks leading to rows of cinder block foundations. Once the foundations are laid, the buildings spring up.

Isn't faith like that? It, too, requires a firm foundation. The basic materials are always the same: prayer, Bible study, fellowship, and service. Once the foundation is laid, we're equipped to do "flashier" things like evangelizing, teaching, and preaching.

The Israelites began repairing the temple by fixing its foundation. They didn't start with the glitz and glitter we often associate with the temple: juniper, cedar and olive wood, gold-encrusted cherubim, and carved palm trees (see 1 Kings 6). They started with the basics—strong walls and a firm base.

As believers, we are the temple of the Holy Spirit. We too are being "built" in the faith, and we also require maintenance. Our "foundations" must be restored day after day, sometimes moment by moment. Although these spiritual basics aren't showy, they assure an ever growing, maturing faith.

Lord, please renew and strengthen my spiritual foundations. Reveal to me the areas of my life that need to be repaired, and heal those areas today. Forgive me for neglecting spiritual basics in pursuit of flashier achievements. In Jesus' name, amen.

Never Still

Thus the work on the house of God in Jerusalem came to a standstill until the second year of the reign of Darius king of Persia (Ezra 4:24).

Scripture: Ezra 4:17-24
Song: "O Courage, My Soul"

A few years ago, a series of difficulties stopped me in my tracks. My husband was laid off, my work environment was becoming increasingly negative, and we faced conflict with our relatives. Furthermore, our employment situation forced us to delay having children.

Church life was no better. Our small group dissolved, and the church's membership dwindled. Eventually we reached a breaking point and left the congregation as well.

I allowed these trials to stop me from growing in my faith—or so I thought. Yes, we left our church. But, as believers in Christ, it was impossible for us to leave the body of Christ. That is, God's work on His temple—each of us Christian believers—never comes to a standstill. Even in the midst of conflict, His will is being done.

My husband now has a full-time job. We are part of a growing church and a thriving small group. We have a beautiful son. Our relationships are being restored, left and right.

I don't know what my future holds, but I know that God keeps working, even when we lay down our spiritual tools. We may give up, but God doesn't give up on us.

Father, I thank You for never giving up on me. Thank You for working in my life, even amidst the most trying times. I bless Your name, through Christ my Lord. Amen.

Essential Spiritual Support

The prophets of God were with them, supporting them (Ezra 5:2).

Scripture: Ezra 5:1-5
Song: "Courage, Brother, Do Not Stumble"

I can picture their faces now—warm, smiling, familiar. Gray-haired, they were sometimes clapping, sometimes chatting with the people next to them, sometimes watching intently.

My parents and grandparents attended every school and church event I participated in as a kid. They didn't seem to do anything—they were just there. While I was the one who had to learn how to play the piano, ice skate, or memorize lines for the school play, their jobs were equally important. Without their support, I wouldn't have had the confidence to perform.

When God's people restored the temple, the prophets Haggai and Zechariah were with them. The Scripture says they "supported" the workers. While it doesn't specify exactly *how* they supported them, it's clear that they provided essential encouragement.

As believers, we are called to build Christ's church. Sometimes we might need to be in the center of the action, while at other times we must stay on the sidelines, offering our encouragement. At those times, let us understand that our support, our encouragement—and sometimes just our presence—are absolutely essential to the success of the work.

So . . . who can you cheer on today?

Lord, grow in me the gift of encouragement. Place people in my life who need support, and give me the words to encourage them today. In the name of Christ, amen.

Not Yet Finished

So this Sheshbazzar came and laid the foundations of the house of God in Jerusalem. From that day to the present it has been under construction but is not yet finished (Ezra 5:16).

Scripture: Ezra 5:6-17
Song: "Unto Thy Temple, Lord, We Come"

When my husband and I bought our house, we gutted it and remodeled it. Then we were all set for the next 20 years or so, right? Wrong. Needed repairs continued to pop up.

A house requires constant maintenance. Sometimes it needs major things like a new roof or siding. Other times it's the little things that need to be taken care of. And if the little things are neglected, they can become big problems. My husband spent an entire summer scraping off layers of old paint before he could even begin to restore the trim on the outside of the house. The overgrown shrubs had to be pulled out, roots and all, before new ones could be planted.

Our spiritual journeys are the same. Sometimes we're struggling with "major" sins—obvious things like addiction, infidelity, or financial irresponsibility. At other times, our sin is less obvious. Jealousy creeps in, eventually straining relationships. An innocent conversation somehow becomes malicious gossip, wounding those around us. Pride inches its way into our thought life, manifesting itself as arrogance. The "little" things take root, and then we're in need of serious repair work.

Lord, reveal to me the sin in my life. Please forgive me for glossing over "small" sins and allowing them to fester. Weed them out, I pray, in Christ's name. Amen.

Spiritual Rubble

I decree that if anyone defies this edict, a beam is to be pulled from their house and they are to be impaled on it. And for this crime their house is to be made a pile of rubble (Ezra 6:11).

Scripture: Ezra 6:1-12
Song: "The Old Rugged Cross"

Everything surrounding the temple involved rules: rules about how the temple should be built; rules about who could enter, and when; rules about what should be sacrificed, who could offer them, and when they could be offered. And broken rules brought swift punishment.

The punishment in today's Scripture seems "over the top" to modern minds. It only makes sense in light of how important the temple was in the Old Testament. The temple represented God's presence on earth; dishonoring it was dishonoring God.

Reconciliation with God always requires sacrifice or punishment. Thankfully, we have access to the all-sufficient sacrifice—Jesus Christ, through whom we have the privilege of being God's temple. In order to build the new temple, Christ was crucified on a beam—the cross.

The practical application in all of this is to remember that our lives are "rubble" without Christ—spiritual, emotional, and sometimes physical rubble. Let us trust in the Christ of the cross to rebuild us in His glorious image (see Philippians 3:20, 21).

O God, the King of glory, thank You for taking the punishment for my sin in the incarnate Christ. Thank You for building Your temple, the church, even though I am not worthy, in myself, to be one of the small stones. In the name of Jesus, amen.

A Feast for the Exiles

The Levites slaughtered the Passover lamb for all the exiles (Ezra 6:20).

Scripture: Ezra 6:13-22
Song: "Lamb of God, We Fall Before Thee"

When our church celebrates Communion, the view from the back of the sanctuary is breathtaking. Believers walk down the aisles on their way to the table, some praying, some singing, some simply staring straight ahead, waiting to kneel before God. The weaving pattern of people approaching, kneeling, and then returning to their seats symbolizes our spiritual journey.

We're like exiles coming forward. As we approach the altar of God, none of us is worthy. We have all sinned and fallen short of God's glory (see Romans 3:23). In the Old Testament, the Levites, or priests, had to sacrifice animals for the sins of the people. In today's passage, God's people celebrated with joy after the Levites sacrificed the Passover lamb.

Now, in the era of the church, Jesus Christ is our *agnus dei*, the Lamb of God. And His sacrifice is eternal, covering all of our sins for all time—it never needs to be repeated. When we receive Communion, we celebrate His all-sufficient sacrifice.

When we receive the bread and the cup, let us remember that we were all exiles, separated from God. Through the blood of Christ, we've been restored—and we can celebrate our restoration with joy.

Heavenly Father, thank You for being present with me when I come to remember the eternal sacrifice of Your Son. Thank You for inviting me—an exile—to Your table despite my sin. In the name of Jesus, precious Lamb of God, I pray. Amen.

God's Temple

The temple of God is holy, which temple you are (1 Corinthians 3:17, *New King James Version*).

Scripture: 2 Chronicles 7:12-18
Song: "To Thy Temple Holy"

Five-year-old David, my grandson, had snuck the hose into the garden area, run the water, and enjoyed a mud-puddle hour. Now I was scrubbing the dirt from his chubby hands, legs, and feet. His grubby clothes were in a pile on the floor.

"Oh, David," I sighed, as I helped him clean up. "I do love you, and you are a sweetheart. But today I'm afraid you are a dirty sweetheart."

"Yup. I know," David said with a serious face. "Sometimes things get out of hand, don't they?"

Sometimes things get out of hand in my life too. I overindulge in food (like chocolate). Or I pass along some nasty gossip.

Sadly, I have trouble forgiving and loving someone who has hurt my family. I believe God loves me, but He has said, "You are my temple." His temple is supposed to be holy. It should be kept clean, holding pure thoughts and being filled with love. When I let things get out of hand, a dirty shabbiness sneaks in.

I really do want to be God's holy temple. But there's just one way: Second Chronicles plainly says I must humble myself, pray, seek God's face, and turn from my wicked ways.

Holy God, if I am Your temple, then I too need to be holy. But I need Your help; I cannot do it alone. I pray for this in the name of Jesus. Amen.

July 15–21. **Elizabeth Van Liere,** who lives in Montrose, Colorado, has been writing for many years. But at age 87, in the spring of 2011, she published her first book.

Come and Rescue Me

Hear me, O LORD, for Your lovingkindness is good; Turn to me according to the multitude of Your tender mercies (Psalm 69:16, *New King James Version*).

Scripture: Psalm 69:9-18
Song: "Does Jesus Care?"

An ugly lump was removed from my friend's leg, and a scary report came back: cancer. Dark days followed that included radiation, hair loss, chemo, and nausea. And just when she thought it was over, the doctor prescribed another set of chemo treatments, which led to more nausea, more weakness, more cloudy skies.

Through it all, Susan kept her eyes on God. She wrote poems, telling of God holding her hand. She sent me a picture of herself wearing a knitted hat made by a friend, with yarn curls swinging down, framing her smiling face.

Did she have moments of despair? Yes. Were there times of fearing pain? Yes. But like David, the psalm writer, she cried out to God. Each time she took a harder grip on His loving hands.

Her husband, her family, and her friends rallied around her, kept her in prayer. It was Susan, however, who brought the rest of us closer to our helper by her steady hope in the Lord. Now, three years later, her poem, "With Praise and Thanksgiving," testify to God's sustaining power.

Almighty and most merciful God, thank You that I can come to You with my troubles. Help me grow through them and be a light to others so they can have hope, even in the midst of great difficulty. In the name of the Father, the Son, and the Holy Spirit, I pray. Amen.

Lesson from the Servant of All

On this one will I look: On him who is poor and of a contrite spirit, and who trembles at My word (Isaiah 66:2, *New King James Version*).

Scripture: Isaiah 66:1-4
Song: "Keep Me Wholly Thine"

In the days of Jesus, a good host would have a servant wash the feet of a visitor. The host himself wouldn't stoop to do that; it was understood to be a servant's job. Yet, at the last Passover, our Lord, after eating with His disciples, became their servant. He humbled himself, lowered himself to His knees, and washed their feet.

Earlier, as recorded in John 8:31-36, Jesus spoke about truth, slavery, and freedom. It made me wonder: I know about freedom, but do I really know about being a slave? Am I perhaps a slave to myself?

I do treat myself as though I am royalty. I get and give to me whatever suits my ego: food, drink, clothes, a house and all that goes with it. Do I ever lower myself to wash someone's feet? In other words, do I ever let go of all I have in order to help someone?

If not, then this is the truth: If I always put myself first, I will continue to be a slave to self, unable to live with Jesus. And freedom? True freedom comes when I take the lesson Jesus taught His disciples: have a servant's heart.

Dear Father, help me keep my eyes on Your kneeling Son. Please grant me a servant's heart so I will be willing to serve others, loving them in a deeper sense than I have known—even deeper than I love myself. In Christ's precious name, amen.

The Secret Servant

Your Father who sees in secret will Himself reward you openly (Matthew 6:4, *New King James Version*).

Scripture: Matthew 6:16-18
Song: "Alone with God"

Several times in the book of Matthew we find Jesus telling the people, in effect: "Don't be a show-off. Pray, give, and help others in secret." For instance, in Matthew 23 He pointed at the teachers of the law and the Pharisees, saying: "Don't be like them. Everything they do is for show. They want everyone to see how good they are. That is their reward."

A show-off is like a peacock, spreading his feathers, trying to get the attention of a young miss, getting her to see how beautiful he is. Only the male has these beautiful feathers, which equal more than 60% of his total length. He likes to strut around with the finery fanned across his back, touching the ground on either side. And when the female responds, he has his reward.

So it is with those who make sure to let others know about their goodness. They are viewed with admiration, put on a pedestal, honored with the respect they feel is their due. They have received their reward.

Sadly, the reward turns to dust. Jesus calls us to fast, pray, and do good in secret. If we humble ourselves, God sees, and His reward will last forever.

Heavenly Father, I need Your help to keep from becoming a show-off. I admit, I like receiving compliments for something well done. But God, let me do it in silence, for Your glory, and in Your name. Human praises are momentary, but a reward from You will last for eternity. In the name of Jesus, amen.

To Seek and to Do

Ezra had prepared his heart to seek the Law of the LORD, and to do it, and to teach statutes and ordinances in Israel (Ezra 7:10, *New King James Version*).

Scripture: Ezra 7:1-10
Song: "I Love to Tell the Story"

One of our young missionaries, Andrew, once told us he had been taught in college not to use the long lists of biblical names in his preaching. They would put his listeners to sleep. But he disagreed and read us the genealogy of Joseph, Matthew 1:1-16, and of Mary, Luke 3:23-38. No one fell asleep as Andrew told about the people that came before Joseph and Mary.

In the same way, today's Scripture gives us a look at Ezra's lineage. We find mostly strange, unfamiliar names until we come to the last name listed: Aaron, the brother of Moses. Then in Ezra 7:6 we read that Ezra was a skilled scribe in the law of Moses.

What does this mean for us beyond the fact that he *sought* God's laws? He *did* them. And he taught what he learned to the Israelites. Did he just make all this up out of thin air? No. This was handed down through the ages, resulting in a person who was God's man.

What have our ancestors given to us? We can hand down to our children, grandchildren, and their children what we've been taught about Jesus, about salvation through Him. By His grace, we can pass on His love to the world.

Lord, I have been blessed to know You from childhood. Let me now proclaim Your goodness to my family, to my friends, to my neighbors. Through Christ, amen.

Follow the Leader

They continued steadfastly in the apostles' doctrine and fellowship, in the breaking of bread, and in prayers (Acts 2:41, 42, *New King James Version*).

Scripture: Ezra 8:15-20
Song: "Guide Me, O Thou Great Jehovah"

I've heard quite a few declarations like these over the years . . . "I'm going hiking; I can worship God outdoors just as well as in any church."

"I like to play golf on Sunday mornings. It's the one time I can relax. Besides, I can worship God on the course."

"I usually take a long drive by myself on Sundays. I see wild life and mountains and beautiful valleys—that's my church."

Ezra thought about God in a different way. Some 1,500 men and their families had volunteered to go with Ezra to rebuild the temple. However, Ezra realized there were no Levites who could serve God in the temple. So the call went out, and 258 Levites were found.

Why was it so necessary to have the Levites along? In addition to having the responsibility to serve in the temple and assist the priests, the Levites had talent and training in singing and playing musical instruments. Ezra wanted them there to help lead the people in praising God in the temple.

It's easy to say God is in the outdoors and that I can worship Him there. But is it enough just to see the beauty of the world? Do we carry our Bibles with us and read His Word when we're hiking, playing golf, or driving?

Great Jehovah, be my guide through life, I pray. Thank You for those leaders who help show me the way, the way to You. In the name of Jesus, amen.

He Has Your Best in Mind

The hand of our God is upon all those for good who seek Him (Ezra 8:22, *New King James Version*).

Scripture: Ezra 8:21-23
Song: "Cast Thy Burden upon the Lord"

My grandson, Matt, stormed out of his dorm. The phone call he had been waiting for had hit like lightning. The caller had said, "Sorry, but we don't need you right now."

Matt ran down the campus path, mumbling a prayer. "I am so angry and confused, God. When I saw their ad, I knew I was supposed to work for them. Sure, they promised to put me at the top of their list for future web designers, but I need work right now, while I'm paying for college."

He stepped off the walkway and leaned up against a tree. Hands clenched, he said, "God! I believed You led me to come to this college. I believed You led me to apply for this job. But the door has shut in my face. What's going on, Lord?"

Slowly, he relaxed. He sighed, then said, "God, I'm laying it at Your feet."

Those words filled Matt with peace. As he headed back to his room, starting down the hall, his roommate barreled out the door. He had some "interesting" news for Matt about a job.

God knows our desires, hears our prayers, and always responds with our spiritual growth in mind. Yes, He always answers: sometimes it's Yes; sometimes it's No; sometimes it's Wait.

Almighty and everlasting God, I fear making Your way the only way for my life. May I always pray as Jesus did, "Not my will, but Yours, Father" (see Luke 22:42). In His precious name I pray, amen.

Once for All

By one sacrifice he has made perfect forever those who are being made holy (Hebrews 10:14).

Scripture: Hebrews 10:1-14
Song: "Forgiven"

I know of a woman who lived her entire adult life consumed with guilt. She blamed herself for the death of her child, yet, in reality, she was not to blame. When she became a Christian, she spent hours poring over Scripture and books on the topic of forgiveness. Yet, to the end of her life, she still suffered from the emotional anguish of false guilt.

What would drive a person to insist on holding on to guilt, deserved or undeserved? Answers to that question would probably fill a psychology textbook. But, for the sake of illustration, let's imagine it was, indeed, this woman's fault that her child died. Would that be too big for God to forgive?

Today's Scripture tells us we are made holy through the sacrifice of the body of Jesus Christ, once for all (see v. 10). Jesus Christ died, one time, to cover all sin for all people. Did this woman repent of both her imagined and real sin? Yes, many times. However, unlike the Old Testament priests who offered sacrifices again and again, because of the blood of Jesus, she would have only needed to do it once.

Father God, I pray for all anguished souls held in bondage to feelings of guilt. Help us to receive, and cling to, the freedom of Your mercy, through Christ. Amen.

July 22–28. **Brenda J. Garver** of Farwell, Mississippi, is a Christian writer in addition to serving God in the capacities of wife and mother, teacher and encourager, caregiver and nurturer.

Bowing, Like a Bulrush

Everyone who was willing and whose heart moved them came and brought an offering to the LORD for the work on the tent of meeting, for all its service, and for the sacred garments (Exodus 35:21).

Scripture: Exodus 35:20-29
Song: "Yesterday, Today, Forever"

In our Scripture passage today, the word *willing*, or some variation of it, appears five times. And whenever a word is used repeatedly in Scripture, it benefits the reader to take note. The Hebrew word underlying our English translation is *abah*, which has several meanings, but the one most intriguing is also the most unlikely: it refers to a bulrush. What could a waterside plant, known for the supple strength of its stem, have to do with the willingness of God's people?

Dr. Al Novak in his timeless word study book, *Hebrew Honey*, explains: "A bulrush bows its head in the wind (see Isaiah 58:5, *KJV*). This is what God wants of His child, whether in the whirlwind of troubles or in the gentle breeze of the Spirit's leading."

When it comes to willingness to give, let's take a lesson from the Israelites of the Exodus, who were like the bulrush. They were a strong, yet yielding people, willing to bend to the will of God with joy in their hearts.

O God, the King of glory, thank You for the beautiful imagery of the willingness of God's people found in the humble bulrush. Whether blown about in the storms of life or tossed about from obedience to Your will help me to be strong enough—and flexible enough—to bow before You with joy in my heart. In Jesus' name, amen.

For Him, the Best

The LORD said to Moses, "Accept these [offerings] from them, that they may be used in the work" (Numbers 7:4, 5).

Scripture: Numbers 7:1-6
Song: "Give of Your Best to the Master"

Once a year, the church holds a "dessert auction" as a fund raiser to help send kids to summer camp. Before the auction begins, myriad baked goods are spread out on tables for bidders to examine. Then, a hushed stillness descends on the crowd as the auctioneer picks up a luscious looking blueberry pie, holds it up, and proceeds to list its delicious attributes: a flaky, melt-in-your-mouth crust and a filling chock full of plump, juicy berries.

With the mouthwatering pie twirling beneath the noses of hungry bidders, the price goes up to almost $50. Cinnamon rolls at $35 a dozen fly off the auction table. Even the humble no-bake cookie brings in a goodly sum. At prices such as these, it's likely the cooks were quaking in their boots. *Did I put enough sugar in that pie? I hope those cinnamon rolls aren't burnt on the bottom!*

Hopefully, knowing the potential value of their offerings, each cook did his or her best—making the very best cheesecake ever, the finest pie, the most tender and delicious cinnamon roll.

Was that the attitude of those tribal leaders of Israel who brought gifts to be used in God's service? No doubt they gave their best oxen, their finest carts. And we can follow such an example: When we offer anything of our life and labor to Him, may it be our very best.

Father God, may all I offer to You be my best, remembering that what I give and do in Your name has eternal significance. Through Christ, amen.

Poured Out and Overflowing!

As soon as the order went out, the Israelites generously gave (2 Chronicles 31:5).

Scripture: 2 Chronicles 31:2-10
Song: "We Are So Blessed"

A church congregation discovered that one of its members lived in a house that was falling down, literally. Winter was fast approaching, and there was no heat in the house. Upon inspection, it was found the house needed a new roof, new siding, several new sidewalls, new plumbing and electrical fixtures, a furnace, a bathroom, a kitchen, and the list went on. Basically, the house needed to be gutted and started over.

With a small membership, there was no money in the church's budget for house rebuilding. How could such a feat be accomplished?

Like the Israelites in our Scripture today, when the people in the church learned of the needed work, the floodgates opened, and God's people gave. But not just money; in fact, very little money was involved. Rather, brothers and sisters in Christ gave what they had—their time, their skills, and their minds and muscles. Their giving, in turn, began a tidal wave that swept over the entire community until other people, including a government agency, became involved and gave as well. In time, the man's house was completely rebuilt.

My Lord God, You are awesome—the extreme gift giver. What a privilege it is to be in partnership with You in the work of Your kingdom! How wonderful to know that when we give to You—You give back far more than we can imagine. Thank You, Father, in the precious name of Your Son, Jesus. Amen.

A Universe of Love

Love the Lord your God with all your heart and with all your soul and with all your mind and with all your strength (Mark 12:30).

Scripture: Mark 12:28-34
Song: "Beautiful One"

After visiting the planetarium at Kentucky's Creation Museum, I came away thinking, *I'll never look at the night sky the same again.*

What an experience it was! Visitors file into a smallish room and sit in reclining chairs. Suddenly, the room darkens as a dome shaped screen comes into view above—and now we are no longer visitors, but travelers. As the vast, starry universe unfolds before our eyes, we rush past planets, then solar systems, then galaxies and beyond. Like brilliant jewels in a crown, nebulae form colorful clouds of shimmering space dust. Gargantuan galaxies spin in ponderous beauty, their tails light years in length. All is vast, limitless. I am in total awe at the expanse of the universe and the God who created it all.

Then my thoughts begin to pull backwards, turning inwards, getting smaller and smaller, until I come to only me. Myself. One soul among billions, living in one galaxy among trillions, floating within one solar system among quadrillions, on one planet among quintillions. Then my heart, soul, and mind bow humbly in the knowledge of God's love for me—a love as great and endless as the universe itself.

Father God, that You should love me so personally absolutely floors me. The words "thank You" are woefully inadequate, but You see my heart. In Jesus' name, amen.

The Big and the Small

Calling his disciples to him, Jesus said, "Truly I tell you, this poor widow has put more into the treasury than all the others. They all gave out of their wealth; but she, out of her poverty, put in everything—all she had to live on" (Mark 12:43, 44).

Scripture: Mark 12:38-44
Song: "Near to the Heart of God"

Who could forget the 2010 oil spill in the Gulf of Mexico? The disaster affected not only the people living along the Gulf coast, but, in a ripple effect, changed the lives of countless others, including Carl-Henric Svanberg.

Mr. Svanberg is chairman of British Petroleum, the company responsible for the spill. Several months into the spill, during an interview, the beleaguered man sought to show the company's concern for human suffering by making a statement that drew upon a Swedish phrase for "the common man." In English, his words were (unfortunately) translated: "We care about the small people . . ." A furor erupted as people considered the implications: We're big; you're small. We're important; you're not.

Jesus had a lot to say about the big and small people. Many of His harshest words were for the Pharisees, the big shots of His time. Based on that, I think I would much rather be like the poor widow—"small" in importance to the world, but "big" in the eyes of Jesus.

Dear Father in Heaven, may this always be my heartfelt cry: keep me ever, and only, near to Your heart. Show me what it means to give out of my poverty, and give me the courage to follow through in obedience. In Jesus' name, amen.

Warning: Shield Down!

The hand of our God was on us, and he protected us from enemies and bandits along the way (Ezra 8:31).

Scripture: Ezra 8:24-35
Song: "Protect and Save Me, O My God"

While reregistering for virus protection on my computer, I inadvertently left the virus shields down, leaving my computer unprotected and vulnerable to all kinds of problems. Thankfully, the mistake was caught quickly, and my computer remained safe. But anyone who makes a living via their computer knows the angst I felt at the thought of imminent cyber-disaster.

Christians need protection too. Our enemies aren't viruses or hackers, but someone far worse—Satan himself. A friend recently expressed concern to me that her son, a believer newly returned to the faith, was trying to live the Christian life without reading God's Word. We both agreed that he was leaving himself vulnerable to attack. He didn't have his armor on.

Ezra knew that God protected him and his caravan as the people traveled back to their land. That protection was absolutely essential, if their mission was to succeed.

Similarly, the armor of God found in Ephesians 6 is an absolute necessity to us as we launch into life's battles. To be walking about, living and breathing in enemy territory, without the armor of God? It's even more foolish than leaving the virus shields down on a perfectly innocent computer.

Father God, thank You for giving me Your armor to keep me safe from sneak attack. Without it, I'm like a computer without virus protection. Remind me that putting on my spiritual armor must be part of my daily routine. In Jesus' name, amen.

Rest, Sweet Rest

Six days do your work, but on the seventh day do not work, so that your ox and your donkey may rest, and so that the slave born in your household and the foreigner living among you may be refreshed (Exodus 23:12).

Scripture: Exodus 23:12-17
Song: "Now the Day Is Over"

As I looked out over the majestic, tree-covered mountains, I breathed in deeply and felt stress and anxiety slide from my shoulders and float across the treetops. But it wasn't only the glory of Creation that eased my spirit. I was captivated by the knowledge that for three days I had no schedule. No plans. No appointments. No demands. My husband and I were here for pure rest and relaxation.

Do you feel guilty when you take some time off from your daily demands, whether for three days or three hours? If so, remember that God himself rested from His creative work and instructed His people to do so as well. He even gave them two day's worth of food on the day before their Sabbath.

Rest was important to God and still is—not just rest for His people but for those who *serve* His people. When I was a child, stores weren't open on Sundays; we planned ahead to have a day of rest. But now, in our constant activity, have we lost something essential to our creaturehood?

God, even You rested from the labors of creation, and I know You want me to rest too. Help me, as a sacred duty, to carve out such times. In Jesus' name, amen.

July 29–31. **Lanita Bradley Boyd** is a teacher, writer, speaker, wife, mother, grandmother, and friend who lives in Fort Thomas, Kentucky. She especially enjoys mentoring young women.

Giving My Firstfruits

Speak to the Israelites and say to them: "When you enter the land I am going to give you and you reap its harvest, bring to the priest a sheaf of the first grain you harvest" (Leviticus 23:9, 10).

Scripture: Leviticus 23:9-14
Song: "Harvest Time"

My little boy with his chubby hands came toddling to me, holding out the first dandelion of spring. His eyes gleamed with delight as he presented the flower to me. I took it gladly, knowing that it was important to him, and that to him it wasn't just a weed but a beautiful gift.

In the same way, we can delightedly bring gifts to God. From His perspective, our gifts may not amount to much, but He knows our hearts and knows when we're eager to please Him.

What gifts can I present? The children of Israel had crops to offer; most of us do not. But I do have the firstfruits of my daily labor. My firstfruits may be a generous part of my paycheck, or it may be warm bread from my oven, shared with a lonely neighbor.

Firstfruits for God may be giving my time to care for the children of a single mom while she enjoys some time alone. My firstfruits may be reading to a shut-in who is no longer able to read for himself. Today I look within myself to determine what good gift I can give to God and to those whom He loves.

Kind and righteous heavenly Father, I come to You with a humble heart, wanting to sacrifice to You the firstfruits of my daily labor. Help me to see the needs around me and share with an open and loving heart. In Jesus' name, amen.

Rejoicing in the Good Things

Then you and the Levites and the foreigners residing among you shall rejoice in all the good things the LORD your God has given to you (Deuteronomy 26:11).

Scripture: Deuteronomy 26:1-11
Song: "We Gather Together"

Various family members worked in the kitchen, cooking the plump turkey and dressing, fruits, salads, sweet potatoes, corn, beans, and other tasty dishes for our feast. Four Malaysians visited for the special meal, and we welcomed them to sit among us and get acquainted. "This is so special—for you to have us here for this wonderful banquet!" SuSu said with excitement. "I have never eaten these foods in Malaysia."

We explained which items were traditional foods and which were new recipes we were trying. Talk and laughter continued throughout the meal. "We welcome you to our home," Josh said to the 20 people at the long tables. "When we were in Malaysia, we enjoyed the hospitality of some of your family members, and now we rejoice that you can share a meal with us, as well. We welcome you, praising God for blessing us that we can be together today. We always pray before each meal, and today we give thanks for our friends as well as this food."

With our international visitors, we enjoyed a feast of both food and friendship. Together we rejoiced at the good things God had given us.

Father, when friends and family gather for a meal, I am deeply aware of Your bountiful blessings. Thank You for providing our daily needs of food, shelter, and clothing. And a special thanks for friends and family. In Your Son's name I pray. Amen.

DEVOTIONS®

AUGUST

You alone are the LORD. . . . You are a gracious and merciful God.

—Nehemiah 9:6, 31

Gary Wilde, Editor | **Margaret Williams,** Project Editor | Photo © iStockphoto.com

DEVOTIONS® is published quarterly by Standard Publishing, Cincinnati, Ohio, www.standardpub.com.
© 2012 by Standard Publishing. All rights reserved. Topics based on the Home Daily Bible Readings,
International Sunday School Lessons. © 2009 by the Committee on the Uniform Series. Printed in
the U.S.A. All Scripture quotations, unless otherwise indicated, are taken from the *HOLY BIBLE,
NEW INTERNATIONAL VERSION®. NIV®.* Copyright © 2011 by Biblica, Inc.™ Used by permission
of Zondervan. All rights reserved. Scripture quotations marked (*NASB*) are taken from the *New
American Standard Bible®.* Copyright © 1960, 1962, 1963, 1968, 1971, 1972, 1973, 1975, 1977,
1995 by The Lockman Foundation. Used by permission. (www.Lockman.org) All rights reserved.

For the Future Generations

This is to be a lasting ordinance for the generations to come (Leviticus 23:41.)

Scripture: Leviticus 23:33-44
Song: "Great Is Thy Faithfulness"

Our family had been pummeled by grief—the deaths of our dear mother and aunt—and snow kept some family members from attending their funerals. We decided to gather, months later, to celebrate their lives and the fruits of their labors.

Over 40 of us, ages 1 to 93, assembled in the ancestral home on the appointed summer day. We met children we'd never seen before; we reestablished relationships with relatives we'd known only in childhood. We worshipped together, singing familiar hymns that were a part of our family heritage. We even celebrated communion together.

After a bountiful meal of foods that my mother and aunt had excelled in, we again assembled to talk about their lives and influence. In-laws and step-grandchildren told of how they'd been welcomed into the family by these two women of God.

We had a heritage to celebrate, as did the ancient Israelites. We celebrated and reviewed how God had worked in our lives, as did they. We imitated what our ancestors had done, as they did. And—thanks be to God!—every week all Christians have a special gathering to honor God.

Father, You are magnificent in Your care for me, and I thank You and praise Your name. Guide me as I meet with other believers to honor You. In Jesus' name, amen.

August 1–4. **Lanita Bradley Boyd** is a teacher, writer, speaker, wife, mother, grandmother, and friend who lives in Fort Thomas, Kentucky. She especially enjoys mentoring young women.

Praise in the Pines

Ezra opened the book. All the people could see him because he was standing above them; and as he opened it, the people all stood up (Nehemiah 8:5).

Scripture: Nehemiah 7:73–8:6
Song: "We Have a Sure Prophetic Word"

The early morning sun beat down on our heads as we walked a path through tall grasses to the distant grove of trees. There we met our fellow campers at Yosemite National Park for praise and worship. When we reached the shade of the towering pines, others were streaming in from various campsites, greeting each other. Then everyone became quiet as a tall, thin man rose, his open Bible in his hand.

"Let us stand for the reading of God's Word," he said, and we all stood. As we listened to the majestic words from the Psalms, my heart overflowed with joy.

Remembering that moment helps me recall something quite significant about the Israelites of Nehemiah's day: the only way for them to know the words of God would be to hear them read aloud. We are truly blessed to have God's Word in print, so we can read it anytime, anywhere. And is there a more inspirational way to hear God's Word than to listen outside on a sunny morning, with warm breezes rustling the trees?

At the end of the reading, we all added heartfelt "Amens." We were strengthened and inspired to go out and live the words we had heard.

Dear Lord, I am so grateful that I have Your inspired Word to read for myself. May I relish that Word as my daily bread. In the name of Jesus, amen.

Embracing Joy

Go and enjoy choice food and sweet drinks, and send some to those who have nothing prepared. This day is holy to our Lord. Do not grieve, for the joy of the LORD is your strength (Nehemiah 8:10).

Scripture: Nehemiah 8:7-12
Song: "The Joy of the Lord"

Anna grew up in a God-fearing but judgmental household. Any infraction was not only punished but brought up again and again. "How could you be so stupid? I thought you'd learned your lesson when you had that same problem at your grandmother's house last year!" her father would shout.

Anna lived with immense guilt. As a middle-aged woman, she obsessed over her sins from her early adult life. She continued to live for Jesus, even to the point of bringing her husband to Christ, and then their three sons. But though she was outwardly an exemplary Christian woman, Anna constantly condemned herself.

Then she found a loving congregation of God's people who focused on grace and acceptance rather than past sins. Anna marveled at the joy she saw, even in people whose lives were far less than perfect. Finally, Anna asked for the prayers of these godly people and they embraced her in spite of her shortcomings. Now she joyfully believes the words in Psalm 103:12: "As far as the east is from the west, so far has he removed our transgressions from us."

Heavenly Father, You know my every sin. Thank You for Your forgiveness and for Your forgetfulness. In the name of Jesus, my Savior, I pray. Amen.

Joy in Suffering

The whole company that had returned from exile built temporary shelters and lived in them. From the days of Joshua son of Nun until that day, the Israelites had not celebrated it like this. And their joy was very great (Nehemiah 8:17).

Scripture: Nehemiah 8:13-18
Song: "Sunshine in My Soul"

In 1995, Idris Miah of Bangladesh went with a group of Muslim men to condemn Abu Bakkar, a Muslim man who had been baptized into Christ. As they approached his house, they heard him praying for the village and for the very men who had come to threaten him with death if he remained a Christian. They tried to enter the house but could not.

Back at his home, Idris Miah couldn't put from his mind the prayer of Abu Bakkar. Abu had a bad reputation, and yet he was praying for Idris and his village. Intrigued, Idris went back in the middle of the night to learn more about the Jesus that meant so much to Abu.

After hours of studying together, Idris also gave his life to Christ. He went home and told his wife and children and they believed. The book *Extreme Devotion: The Voice of the Martyrs* tells how Idris and his family suffered greatly from the rejection of their village, losing his job and having his children ejected from school. Yet he held firm in his faith, saying, "I have the joy of Jesus in my heart. I give my life and my family to Jesus. I hope this gift is acceptable to my Lord."

Dearest Father, You are truly my joy-giver. You help me see beyond the trials and temptations of today to the triumphs of life with You eternally. Through Christ, amen.

Ignorance Is No Excuse

Now, fellow Israelites, I know that you acted in ignorance, as did your leaders. . . . Repent, then, and turn to God (Acts 3:17, 19).

Scripture: Acts 3:17-26
Song: "I Want a Principle Within"

My granddaughter drops a spoon to the floor. As soon as I pick it up, she drops it again and again. She continues until she's proven the law of gravity.

By the time a child can talk, she already knows many laws of nature that can't be broken without consequences. And even as adults, we continue to learn by trial and error. I tried several different routes from my house to the office until I found the shortest, at 7.4 miles. But I've learned to look for lowered speed zones when my highway goes through the center of town. Why? Because the court won't accept ignorance of the law as an acceptable excuse.

In the same way, breaking spiritual laws also carries predictable consequences. Ignorance is not an excuse. As Paul so eloquently stated in his letter to the Romans: "The wages of sin is death" (Romans 6:23).

Praise God, He provides a way out for us: "Repent . . . and turn to God." Once we're forgiven, we can move forward, ever learning from our mistakes.

Father, You long to prevent me from making mistakes that will hurt me. Thank You that You forgive sins, even those done in ignorance. In Jesus' name, amen.

August 5–11. Award-winning author and speaker **Darlene Franklin** lives near her family in Oklahoma City, Oklahoma. She recently signed a contract for her 17th book.

A Tale of Two Siblings

Which of the two did what his father wanted? (Matthew 21:31).

Scripture: Matthew 21:28-32
Song: "Wherever He Leads I'll Go"

As a child, my son hated to say no. And with his tendency to schedule 10 minutes for a 20-minute task, he frequently promised more than he could accomplish.

Picture me, with only the trash standing between me and a clean house, asking my son, "Would you take the bags to the trash bin?"

"Sure." (I don't think he ever said "No.") He returned his attention to the CD he was listening to.

Relieved, I waited, my eyes straying from the clean house to the full trash bags waiting by the door. Five minutes ticked by . . . ten . . . I repeated my request.

Again, he promised. Again, I waited.

On the other hand, "No" was my daughter's favorite word. She found it easy to deny requests for help, too focused on the task at hand to let me interrupt her. I'd ask again, she'd refuse, again. The funny thing is, when she finished whatever she was doing, she'd see the trash, heave a sigh, and carry it outside.

God looks at the actions of our hands and feet—not merely the promises of our mouths.

Dear Father in Heaven, sometimes I promise to do something, like praying for a friend in need, and start well. But I confess that often, after a good beginning, I fail to carry through. Forgive me. Teach me the discipline of fulfilling my promises. I pray this prayer in the name of Jesus, my Savior and Lord. Amen.

God's Questions

You said, "Listen now, and I will speak; I will question you, and you shall answer me" (Job 42:4).

Scripture: Job 42:1-6
Song: "God Moves in a Mysterious Way"

"When God asks a question," said the preacher, "I've learned I better pay attention." The biblical writers asked God lots of questions. But I had rarely paid attention to the questions God asked them—and through them, the questions He asked me.

In the Bible study following the sermon, I learned that God asks more than 500 questions in the Bible, starting with "Where are you?" (Genesis 3:9).

Where was I? I was facing an empty nest after my daughter graduated from high school, and debating about whether or not to change to part-time hours so that I could write more.

What did I want? (Matthew 20:21). It wasn't enough to cry "Pay attention to me over here!" I had God's attention, and He wanted me to spell out what I longed for. I wanted to write more. Now, five years later, I'm writing full time.

How could He comfort me? (Lamentations 2:13). That question told me God cared and longed to comfort me, when my daughter died three years ago.

God answered Job's long outburst by peppering him with questions. Maybe when we need an answer from God, we should listen to His questions.

Father God, You began the dialogue with Adam in the garden, and You still want to talk with Your children. You desire one-on-one time with me, so teach me the blessing of two-way conversation in prayer. Through Christ, amen.

Kayla's Blessing

First go and be reconciled to them; then come and offer your gift (Matthew 5:24).

Scripture: Matthew 5:21-26
Song: "Blessed Be the Tie That Binds"

Both of us had daughters with life-altering disabilities, but the similarities ended there. Kayla's physical ailment brought national attention and help. My daughter Jolene's mental illness came with misunderstanding and rejection. Kayla's mother sold a book she had written with her daughter at about the same time my daughter died. Resentment flared red hot in my heart.

Three years later, I found myself at a retreat with the mother and daughter. The Lord tapped me on the shoulder. "It's time to make this right." I joined them at a dinner table and apologized for my earlier neglect.

After a time of worship, I went to the piano, which has so often been my source of comfort. Before I had sung one hymn, Kayla joined me. We sang several hymns together and ended with "O Little Town of Bethlehem."

Like Kayla, Jolene loved hymns. During that hour at the piano, I felt as though Jolene stood at my shoulder. God used the child I had envied to bring comfort and healing.

When I decided to make things right with my Christian sisters, I never expected the gift they—and God—would give me in return. Reconciliation flowers into true worship.

God, I confess that I ignored Your command to reconcile with my sister for too long. How much richer might my worship have been if I had obeyed quickly? The next time someone offends me, may I run to make things right. In Jesus' name, amen.

The Prisoner's Tale

But the tax collector stood at a distance. He would not even look up to heaven, but beat his breast and said, "God, have mercy on me, a sinner" (Luke 18:13).

Scripture: Luke 18:9-14
Song: "Mercy Is Boundless and Free"

One Sunday, before singing a solo during the worship service, I commented on the week's Scripture about judging others. I listed several things that didn't bother me—and then I stuck my foot in my mouth. "But I think I would have a problem accepting a released prisoner as my brother in Christ."

What God knew—and I didn't—was that an ex-convict sat on the back pew of the church that day. When I discovered that fact, I fell under immediate "conviction" myself! God's sense of humor—and His desire to transform me into His likeness— next led me to a new church made up almost entirely of ex-cons saved by God's grace.

So deep into captivity to drugs that she lost her children and went to jail multiple times, Sally testified to God's mercy at every opportunity.

Doug and Carla and their two children seemed like a picture-perfect family—and they were, after God's transforming grace.

Diana wrote song after song testifying to God's mercy.

In my fellow servants I met the tax collector of Jesus' parable. Each of them had cried out to God, "Have mercy on me."

Father, today I stand before You, head bowed, my heart crying "Have mercy on me, a sinner." For I have sinned and I continue to sin. I thank You for Your mercy, and I trust Your grace to teach me to walk in obedience today. In Jesus' name, amen.

Family Reunion

I tell you that in the same way there will be more rejoicing in heaven over one sinner who repents than over ninety-nine righteous persons who do not need to repent (Luke 15:7).

Scripture: Luke 15:1-10
Song: "The Ninety and Nine"

When I accepted Barbara's friendship invitation on Facebook, I didn't know what lay in store. We shared the same maiden name, but I didn't pay that much attention.

An avid genealogist, Barbara told me she believed that we were related through my great-grandfather. As soon as she confirmed my father's identity, she peppered me with questions. Who was my mother? When and where did she marry my father? How sad that my father had died a few years ago.

Talk about information overload! Since my parents were divorced and lived a thousand miles apart, I had minimal contact with my father's family. I didn't even know he had died.

Barbara wasted no time before she broadcast the news that she had tracked down yet another member of the far-flung Sparks clan. She introduced me to a host of distant cousins. They in turn welcomed me with open arms. I met politicians, musicians, teachers—but all of them people who loved the Lord.

In the Sparks family tree, I was the single sheep for whom the shepherd, Barbara, went in search. The family overflowed with rejoicing when I was found.

God, You can trace my family tree back to Adam and Eve. You knew me in my mother's womb, You had called me before the world began. And yet all of Heaven rejoiced on the day I acknowledged my need of You. Through Christ, amen.

When Bad Things Happen

Now therefore, our God, the great God, mighty and awesome, who keeps his covenant of love, do not let all this hardship seem trifling in your eyes (Nehemiah 9:32).

Scripture: Nehemiah 9:2, 6, 7, 9, 10, 30-36
Song: "Blessed Be Your Name"

God is great, mighty, awesome, bound to His people by a covenant of love. And His people endure hardship.

Those two statements have puzzled plenty of better minds than mine. They strike at the heart of the perennial question, "Why do bad things happen to good people?"

The question changed from academic to personal for me one hot July day. Not that I thought of myself as "good" when both my children were taken from my custody. I could only ask forgiveness, begin the long road back to mental and emotional health, and trust God's love to make things right in His time.

Day by day, God revealed himself to me through His Word. I heard a preacher say, "God's heart was the first to break," and I knew God didn't regard my hardship as trifling. His might and love proved themselves to me in the midst of my trials.

Whatever hardships lie ahead of me, I know none of them will be trifling in God's eyes—because He loves me unconditionally. He proves His covenant in the midst of those hardships and is forming me through them. As the great preacher Henry Ward Beecher put it: "We are always on the anvil; by trials God is shaping us for higher things."

God, open my eyes to all You are, and all You wish me to be, during every hard time that comes my way. Your covenant of love is everlasting. In Jesus' name, amen.

Joyful Song

Come, let us sing for joy to the LORD; let us shout aloud to the Rock of our salvation (Psalm 95:1).

Scripture: Psalm 96:1-9
Song: "O for a Thousand Tongues to Sing"

More than a half-century has passed, but the image remains crystal clear. George was the minister of the small congregation where I worshipped each Sunday, and how he loved to sing. He was fond of those old gospel songs, and he sang them with no thought of how loudly he proclaimed their message. I'd see his face redden and the veins in his neck stand out prominently. The problem was that George couldn't carry a tune.

Every Sunday, the people gathered to give God the worship He deserves. Every Sunday, their minister opened his hymnal and sang mightily—and off key. His joy was evident.

Last week, I attended a hymn festival at a large church. It was glorious—the organ, the orchestra, the adult and children's choir, the thousand voices joined in song, and the man beside me who discordantly lifted his voice in praise with each hymn.

I thought of George as I stood by my companion in worship. How they both must love God. But, then, so do I. So, I began to sing a little louder, the music flowed through me, and I praised the Lord in joyful sounds.

Most Holy Lord, help me to give You the praise and worship of my life, for You deserve all honor and worship. May my joyful sounds please You because they come from my heart. In the name of Jesus, amen.

August 12–18. **Drexel C. Rankin** served as an ordained minister for more than 35 years. In retirement he regularly works in a food pantry and delivers weekly Meals on Wheels with his wife, Patty.

Sovereign God

Say among the nations, "The LORD reigns." The world is firmly established, it cannot be moved; he will judge the peoples with equity (Psalm 96:10).

Scripture: Psalm 96:10-13
Song: "Jesus Shall Reign"

I sat down with my cup of coffee and morning paper, and I faced disturbing headlines: flooding and tornados that had caused millions of dollars in damages and an earthquake that had caused more than a hundred deaths. Then there was another fatal shooting on the west side of town, followed by tales of homelessness, layoffs, foreclosures, and epidemic disease. Reading the news reminds me that I have little control over much of life. I am not God.

But the psalmist affirms a God who causes the heavens to rejoice. This God knows the number of hairs on my head. He knows my comings and goings. He formed me in my mother's womb and knows more about me than I can possibly imagine. He knows my yesterdays, my today, and my tomorrows. This God tells me, "I know the plans I have for you."

So, I read my morning paper with a fresh perspective. Even amidst all the bad news, I can praise and trust this God. I can find the glimmers of hope and signs of good news in the reported events. I affirm that this God works on my behalf, loves me, and loves this whole world of His creation.

Sovereign Lord of the Universe, You are my strength and hope in all of life. Help me to trust You, even when I do not understand Your ways. I pray this prayer in the name of Jesus, my Savior and Lord. Amen.

Seek the Lord

You are to seek the place the LORD your God will choose (Deuteronomy 12:5).

Scripture: Deuteronomy 12:2-7
Song: "Seek Ye First the Kingdom of God"

My high school teacher persistently declared: "The wise person is not the one who knows all the answers to life, but is the one who knows where to go to *find* the answers to life." That maxim is deeply ingrained in my spirit.

In this age of knowledge, the click of a computer mouse allows me to access almost any piece of information I might desire. I can determine a location, find a friend, or educate myself about even the most obscure data. I can discover just about anything.

But I know that clicking the computer mouse is not the way to seek the Lord or to determine God's will for my life. To be wise in the Lord, I am to seek Him daily for direction and insight. And this entails more than simply praying longer, louder, and faster.

The good news is that God loves to reveal His secrets to those who seek Him. I know what makes me vitally sensitive to God's revelation in my life. I also know what dulls me and blinds me and makes me not want to seek Him.

What must I move away from today in order to seek the place where God is calling me? How will I draw closer to Him today?

Ever-loving Lord, help me to discover those matters in my life that keep me from drawing closer to You. Help me realize those points of my life that draw me nearer to You. In all things, may I seek Your will and bring glory to Your name. I pray in Jesus' holy name. Amen.

A Better Way

The LORD is good, a refuge in times of trouble. He cares for those who trust in him (Nahum 1:7).

Scripture: Nahum 1:6-15
Song: "There's a Wideness in God's Mercy"

I was incredibly angry with him. I had supported him when others called for his firing. I offered him opportunities to rectify the situations he faced in his personal and corporate life. In the vernacular, "I had his back."

When I realized that he had lied to me, my justice was swift and unyielding. There was no dialogue.

As I look back, I am displeased with myself when I recall dealing unkindly with those who've upset me—a friend who disappointed me, a child who disobeyed, an associate who failed to follow through on a promise. I was not God-like in some of those situations.

Thankfully, God does not deal with me according to my sins. I am reminded again and again that God is merciful, caring, and good. He holds no grudges. He is a refuge in times of pain, grief, or cascading difficulties.

How can I be gentler in dealing with the faults of others? How do I dialogue with one who has not kept a promise? How do I cope lovingly with one who has disappointed me?

God's way of dealing with people who disappoint Him doesn't come naturally to me. It's a harder way. Also a far better way.

Almighty and most merciful God, teach me to be merciful, caring, gentle, and abounding in love. May I be more like You when I deal with those who disappoint me. In the name of Christ I pray. Amen.

God in My Future

This is what the LORD says: "I will restore the fortunes of Jacob's tents and have compassion on his dwellings; the city will be rebuilt on her ruins, and the palace will stand in its proper place" (Jeremiah 30:18).

Scripture: Jeremiah 30:18-22
Song: "God of Our Life"

Albert Einstein once quipped, "I never think of the future; it comes soon enough." Unlike Einstein, I probably consider the future more than I should.

In business, we do strategic planning. In churches, we meet in long-range planning committees. Planning for the future requires that we guess at what the future might hold, and we are often wrong.

I need to be reminded that my future dreaming should be not shaped only by my ability to describe and imagine. I need to be willing to be quiet and listen for the voice of God.

God, also, is at work dreaming of a liberating future for me and for the world. God knows my future, and He sees things about me that no one else realizes. As His child, I need to attend to what God is saying to me whether through Scripture, the community of faith, or the still small voice within me.

I am still a work in progress. God is still coaxing me into His eventuality. So I need to be more patient as God moves me into my future. After all, I can see only the beginning, while God sees the expected end—and it is good.

God of all my years, lead me in my coming days that I may live into the future that You want for my life. In Jesus' name, amen.

Comfort My People

As a mother comforts her child, so will I comfort you (Isaiah 66:13).

Scripture: Isaiah 66:10-14
Song: "There Is a Balm in Gilead"

I was having a rough morning. The computer was running slowly, the weather had turned drizzly, and my lawn mower was still in the repair shop. Then my wife read to me the list of church members and friends who are facing the most difficult of times—the imminence of death.

David is in the final stages of cancer and has just had a visit from his out-of-town daughter. Likely, it is their final visit.

Fred, 92-years-old, entered the hospital with congestive heart failure two months ago and has lingered in rehabilitation for the past month. He says that he simply wants to go home, sit in his chair in the yard, and talk with his neighbors. He knows his time is limited.

Rachel's father is slowly dying in another state. Poor health limits her ability to travel and be with him.

And the list went on.

I was simply inconvenienced. Others were facing the finality of their own lives or the lives of those they loved. These were people in deep need of comfort.

Comfort! That is what God wants for His children. It is what God calls me to offer to another, in His name.

God of comfort and peace, may I always be aware of those around me whose lives need the comforting I can provide in Your name. Help me to comfort others with the comfort that I have received from You. Through Christ, amen.

Joy Is Contagious

The singers also were brought together from the region around Jerusalem. . . . The sound of rejoicing in Jerusalem could be heard far away (Nehemiah 12:28, 43).

Scripture: Nehemiah 12:27-36, 38, 43
Song: "The River Is Here"

Some mornings I just don't want to show up at the gym. Yet, even on those mornings, I somehow drag myself into the locker room, lace up the shoes, and make my way onto the treadmill.

Then a strange thing happens. Energy begins to pulse through my body, my pace quickens, and I am invigorated. No longer is this drudgery. Something has happened; I'm feeling alive.

And here's the key: The people who surround me in that room have affected my attitude. Their energy invigorates me—refreshes me.

People do profoundly influence each other. Joy is passed from person to person, and we often actually determine our mood by the company we choose to keep. For example, when I spend time around people filled with God's joy, I am graced with a feeling of joy that floods through me.

Discover the wonder that is in every moment. Look for people in your life today who help you to celebrate God's presence and God's gifts. Without those people in my life, I miss those joyful and happy moments that surround me.

Dear God, I know that You want more for me, something better than my imagination could envision. You want my life filled with absolute joy. Forgive me for forgetting that I have so much to celebrate because of Your mercy. Teach me to celebrate with joy all You have done for me. I pray in Jesus' holy name. Amen.

The Bread of Life

When the sons of Israel saw it, they said to one another, "What is it?" For they did not know what it was. And Moses said to them, "It is the bread which the LORD has given you to eat" (Exodus 16:15, *New American Standard Bible*).

Scripture: Exodus 16:13-26
Song: "Satisfied"

If I had been among the Israelites and woke up to see white flakes spread across the desert floor, would I have said, "What is it?" I may have thought about my journey thus far, or whether this man called Moses was truly following God's instructions. I might have believed that God was the giver of all blessings, but if I'd heard Moses say, "It is the bread which the Lord has given you to eat," would I have accepted the idea that God was indeed providing for my needs?

God has always cared for His people. For example, amidst our weekly work He's told us to put aside our labors on the Sabbath and rest. Like the Israelites, some of us regularly observe that day of rest (and worship)—the Lord's Day—and are blessed with God's provision of spiritual nourishment.

Early in our marriage, we struggled financially. After arriving home from Sunday service one afternoon, we discovered $250 in cash tucked under our front door. Tears filled our eyes as we thanked God. He had fulfilled our needs, once again.

Lord, thank You for the daily bread I need. Sorry that sometimes it takes me a while to see it's Your hand that supplies. In Jesus' name, amen.

August 19–25. **Shirley Reynolds** is a freelance writer living in a rural community in the mountains of Idaho. Besides writing, one of her passions is riding her 4-wheeler through the back country.

Signs to Follow

It is a sign between Me and the sons of Israel forever; for in six days the LORD made heaven and earth, but on the seventh day He ceased from labor, and was refreshed (Exodus 31:17, *New American Standard Bible*).

Scripture: Exodus 31:12-18
Song: "Sweet Hour of Prayer"

Living in a rural community has not only supplied me with scenic beauty. My lifestyle in remote Idaho has also brought its own share of deprivations, such as no streetlights. But after years of traveling the county highways, I have become accustomed to the myriad road signs and landmarks, usually still visible on the darkest nights. I've learned to recognize the curves, houses, and small towns as they pass by in my headlights. Now, I know the way by heart.

God left a sign for the Israelites to adopt and follow forever. He set aside the Sabbath Day, and it has been a sign to my own family throughout the generations, like the old landmarks on the roadside.

Our neighbors have become aware that we attend church on Sundays. This has allowed them to see that worship on this set-aside day has been, and always will be, a tradition in our family. After the chores of the week have ended, our hearts and minds turn to the day of rest. We need it, for, as one quipster put it: "If we don't come apart (to be with the Lord) . . . we'll come apart."

Dear Lord, may I always keep the first day of the week for worship and rest. Help all of us show our families and friends the meaning of God's gift of rest by the way we balance our work and our leisure. Through Christ, amen.

Hearing the Voice of God

"Thus says the Lord who made the earth, . . . "Call to Me and I will answer you, and I will tell you great and mighty things, which you do not know" (Jeremiah 33:2, 3, *New American Standard Bible*).

Scripture: Isaiah 58:9-14
Song: "His Yoke Is Easy"

I watched a man take the bits from the horses' mouths. The animals stood still as if frozen. Their eyes observed the cowboy's every move, while their bodies quivered. The yoke binding the two large Percherons was finally detached. As soon as the last item of control was taken off, the man said, "You're free!"

With a whinny and a toss of their heads, the horses galloped across the field. I stood by the fence and watched the joyfulness in their freedom. I asked the ranch hand, "How can those horses stand being under the yoke and pulling a wagon for more than two hours?"

"Oh, they know what's coming," he said. "They know they'll have their rest and food when it's over."

When we've labored under the yoke of daily problems, it sometimes seems as if it's hard to keep a close relationship to God. But when we've cried to the Lord during those troublesome times, we can be assured of His voice saying, "Here I am." What an awesome thought!

Dear Lord, please alert me to times when I've allowed myself to become so busy with life that I don't hear Your voice. Help me to free my mind of worldly things and come before You every day for renewal. Teach me how to rest in You. I pray this prayer in the name of Jesus, my merciful Savior and Lord. Amen.

Too Busy?

Jesus said to them, "The Sabbath was made for man, and not man for the Sabbath" (Mark 2:27, *New American Standard Bible*).

Scripture: Mark 2:23-27
Song: "Fill My Cup, Lord"

My working day began at 5 a.m. and ended at 9 p.m. I moved robot-like from my Pop-Tart® breakfast, to riding the metro bus, to checking my in-basket, to placing headphones on my head, to moving my fingers on the keyboard, to taking the metro home again, and falling into bed—only to repeat the process the following morning.

But when Sunday arrived, I reveled in the music, cried over stories the minister told, and prayed. Now, I can't imagine not dedicating the Sabbath—Sunday for Christians, the first day of the week—as a day of worship.

In those days, because of the rush of my life, Sunday became a welcome day of reflection, a time to please God. It was a time to slow down and praise the Lord. At times, I was worn out and tended to focus on my needs, but it was then I knew that adjustments were needed if I wanted to ensure that my physical and spiritual well-being were under the Lord's direction. When Jesus said, "The Sabbath was made for man," it came to my attention that I have an awesome responsibility to worship Him.

Dear Lord, You have reminded me of the importance of worship and being with fellow believers in a church service. Teach me how to trust You more, knowing that You hold my life in Your hands. Show me how to treat the day of rest as a gift from the Creator. In Jesus' name, amen.

Withered Spirits

They were watching Him to see if He would heal him on the Sabbath, so that they might accuse Him. He said to the man with the withered hand, "Get up and come forward!" (Mark 3:2, 3, *New American Standard Bible*).

Scripture: Mark 3:1-6
Song: "Heal Me, O My Savior"

While working with teens at our church, I traveled to Los Angeles for a work and witness trip to the homeless. Our minister told us, "Don't miss an opportunity to share God!" Every morning, we prayed and talked about opportunities. We prayed for boldness, as Jesus was bold when He said to the man with the withered hand, "Get up and come forward!"

We approached each day emboldened and prepared for the ways God might lead us. I thought, if we are to "be Jesus to our world," then we needed to be alert and watchful. We came upon a woman sitting on a curb, shivering from the cold. She said, "Come over here!"

We stopped and prayed with her right there on the streets of Los Angeles. Then, when we asked what she needed, she said, "I just want a large-print Bible!" Knowing we had one Bible left from the ones we had passed out that day, I looked and saw it was a large-print edition. I knelt down, placed the Bible in her hands, and said, "It's a miracle. This one's from the Lord!"

Lord God Almighty, please clear my mind of anything and everything that would deter me from hearing Your voice. Help me to spend my life for You with an attitude of worship, so others may see Your light through me. In the name of the Father, the Son, and the Holy Spirit, I pray. Amen.

Tithes and Hard Times

I reprimanded the officials and said, "Why is the house of God forsaken?" Then I gathered them together and restored them to their posts (Nehemiah 13:11, *New American Standard Bible*).

Scripture: Nehemiah 13:4-14
Song: "Bring Your Vessels"

My father told a story of how our church had fallen on hard times; how people hadn't given their tithes, due to their own hardships. Some families had broken up because of sin in their lives. It came to the attention of the church board that since there wasn't enough money to pay wages to the staff, the minister needed to bring the problem to the congregation.

They prayed for revival, and revival came. Our choir director, with a family of 12, started working three jobs in order to contribute more. Others held round-the-clock prayer meetings. Other families mortgaged their homes. People's lives were restored, and they placed their trust in God. The church was not forsaken—and that church is alive and well today.

I've heard our minister say, "Don't forsake the house of God!" When finances became tight, he was honest and brought the issue to the people. When God's people have gathered together on Sundays and allowed that day to be a day of restoration, God's family has survived.

Dear Lord, when the burdens of life weigh us down and we don't feel as if we have anything to give, please help us to see that our faith must ultimately rest in You alone. Help us to give when we don't feel we can. Help us to be like the saints of old, who "pushed through" in Your service. In Jesus' name I pray. Amen.

On a Treadmill

In those days I saw in Judah some who were treading wine presses on the sabbath, and bringing in sacks of grain and loading them on donkeys. . . . So I admonished them on the day they sold food (Nehemiah 13:15, *New American Standard Bible*).

Scripture: Nehemiah 13:15-22
Song: "Cleanse Me"

My husband retired from the railroad about two years ago. In the final months of his employment, he was on-call, where he worked around the clock. Many Sundays came and went, when I attended worship services alone.

When I asked him if he could transfer to another shift and attend church, he said it was impossible to change. However, the hours spent away from his family wore on his mind. He lacked sleep, proper nutrition, and focused only on the next call-out. And as the months passed, he realized that his job was becoming more important than the Lord's Day. He knew he needed Sundays for his growth in Christ: to receive instruction, to enjoy fellowship, to offer to God the worship He deserves.

He opted for a shift with less pay, but he was home with his family and able to worship. Now, when I sit in church with my hand in his on a Sunday morning, I feel truly blessed that he made that decision to be available on the Lord's Day.

Almighty and everlasting God, thank You for the privilege of Sunday's worship and rest. Help me to keep this day sacred in my life, that it might be a great joy to me and a witness to others of Your goodness. I pray this prayer in the name of Jesus, my Savior and Lord. Amen.

Look at the Birds

Look at the birds of the air; they do not sow or reap or store away in barns, and yet your heavenly Father feeds them. Are you not much more valuable than they? (Matthew 6:27).

Scripture: Matthew 6:25-34
Song: "This Is My Father's World"

I am not overly enthusiastic about birds, but they grab my attention when they fly into my backyard. Their colors are amazing. How does God mix such bright tones? And the way they land and take off from my lawn fascinates me. Why did God design them that way?

A few minutes later, the birds leave, and I head back to my study. Sometimes the awe of that moment lingers in my mind as I get started with my day, but I usually get wrapped up in my work, and the scene fades away.

I hate to admit it, but sometimes worry also enters my world, and I start to focus solely on my problems. Jesus says to look at the birds when we start to worry. It's not enough to read the passage in Matthew 6. We actually need to *look at the birds* and notice how God provides for them.

Of course, we all know we shouldn't worry. We just need more practice in saying "No" to those fearful thoughts that seem so natural. I'm sure it can help to stop and look at the birds occasionally. Just as He cares for them, He cares for us.

Lord, thank You for birds—and all the amazing creatures in Your world. May they all remind me today of Your watchful care. In the name of Jesus, amen.

August 26–31. **Tait Berge,** of Colorado Springs, is the Church Relations Director at Mephibosheth Ministry. He has a bachelor's degree in Leadership and Ethics and has written two books.

I Raise My Hands

Praise the LORD, my soul. LORD my God, you are very great; you are clothed with splendor and majesty (Psalm 104:1).

Scripture: Psalm 104:1-4
Song: "Lift Up Your Hearts"

It was a long time before I felt comfortable raising my hands in worship. I grew up learning that church was a quiet, respectful place. You wore your Sunday best, and children were to be seen and not heard. You stood when everyone else stood, bowed your head and folded your hands during times of prayer, and sang hymns to organ accompaniment.

I also went to that kind of church as an adult. I wore a suit every Sunday. I bowed my head during prayer time and sang those old hymns. Then I switched churches. Everyone dressed casually. The music was upbeat and—here's the kicker—people actually enjoyed singing! With their hands up, they displayed a love for the Lord that I had never seen before. It took me time to join in, but now I'm the first one to raise my hands.

Don't get me wrong. I'm not saying this style of worship is for everyone. Some of us are certainly more inward and feel the "flow of the Spirit" in the highest liturgies and grandest chorales. But in my own journey of faith, something in my soul needed to be freed. And that is the key: the psalmist tells us his *soul* was praising God. That can happen every Sunday—in cathedral-like contemplation or in meeting-house jubilation.

Lord, I love to worship You. Thank You for giving me an inner freedom to praise You with unrestrained joy—putting my whole self into it! Through Christ, amen.

Not an Instinct, but a Choice

He waters the mountains from his upper chambers; the land is satisfied by the fruit of his work (Psalm 104:13).

Scripture: Psalm 104:10-18.
Song: "All Nature's Works His Praise Declare"

When I read Psalm 104, I am reminded of the glories of nature. I see rain falling on a mountain and flowing down to a river. I see the green grass and flowers blowing in the wind. I listen to night sounds echoing through the air. God's creation doesn't have a care in the world, even though it functions in large part by means of cycles and instincts and a certain brutality among the species. It is at peace, though, in the sense that it exists under God's sovereign design and rule.

Previously we looked at why we shouldn't worry. Jesus reminded us that the birds and the flowers don't worry because God knows what they need. Today we read of how He meets that need. He waters the mountains. He makes grass grow for cattle and wild beasts. The land is satisfied and is at rest.

What's on your schedule today? meeting an important deadline? keeping a doctor's appointment? accompanying your child to her first day of school? Is your anxiety level up? Take a minute and focus on Psalm 104. Watch God water the mountains. See how that water turns into refreshment for the creatures of the earth. Remember you're a part of all that—but with so much more than mere instinct. You and I have a will that we can align with God's will. That is the place of ultimate peace.

Lord, thank You for taking such good care of all of Your creation, including me. In the holy name of Jesus, my Lord and Savior, I pray. Amen.

A Refreshing Week

He made the moon to mark the seasons, and the sun knows when to go down (Psalm 104:19).

Scripture: Psalm 104:19-23
Song: "Creator of the Earth and Sky"

This summer I spent a few relaxing days at a Christian camp near a beautiful Minnesota lake. I thoroughly enjoyed the teaching, fellowship, and worship that filled so many of my hours there; however, just being outside and enjoying God's awesome north-woods creation seemed to nurture me more than anything else. My soul needed it.

Feeling the warm sun on my face, I knew God was with me. Hearing the wind rustling through leaves spoke to my heart as if God were whispering my name. And watching the waves splashing up on the lakeshore reminded me: God is constantly moving in my life.

When the sun set for another day—painting the western horizon with such brilliant hues of pink and gold—I once again felt God's love for me.

He created all of this for His beloved creatures, that they might lift their hearts to Him in thanks and praise.

Yes, God used His creation that week to draw me closer to Him. I am thankful, and I am moved to respond just as the psalmist did at the end of his beautiful poem: "I will sing to the Lord all my life; I will sing praise to my God as long as I live" (v. 33).

Lord God of all creation, thank You for my senses through which I can know You and love You. I am more than a mind, and You are more than a concept! Most of all, I praise You for the incarnation of Your Son, Jesus, in whose name I pray. Amen.

It's Still the Living Word

The LORD reigns, let the earth be glad; let the distant shores rejoice (Psalm 97:1).

Scripture: Psalm 97:1-9
Song: "The Lord Reigns"

I knew I'd heard the 97th Psalm recently. It wasn't from reading the Bible or a responsive reading at church. But where had I heard it? I couldn't put my figure on it until a contemporary worship song came up on my play list. "That's it!" I thought. "That's the 97th Psalm!"

Contemporary Christian music has a special meaning in my life. I listen to it every day. Sometimes my eyes are too heavy to read my Bible, and my body has had it for the day. Then, listening to music is the only thing I can do. My soul is begging for spiritual care, and I nurture it by focusing on the music. As I listen, I find peace, and the Holy Spirit "shows up" to do what only He can do—minister to my soul.

Isn't it interesting that God can take something that was written a long time ago and add a contemporary "feel" to it? Maybe that's why we call it the *living* Word. It's still relevant.

Psalm 97 is so much more than an ancient worship song, written by ancient people, preserved in a book. It's a song in God's Word that is as fresh today as it was on the day it was penned. Whether chanted in a monastery or blasted from my stereo, it lives because it witnesses to the living Word: our supreme Lord Jesus Christ.

God, thank You for Your Word, written in the Bible and incarnate in Jesus Christ. May Your Word always be alive in the hearts of every generation. Through Christ, amen.

My Meditation Before the Lord

I will sing to the LORD all my life; I will sing praise to my God as long as I live. May my meditation be pleasing to him, as I rejoice in the LORD (Psalm 104:33, 34).

Scripture: Psalm 104:31-35
Song: "With Joy We Meditate the Grace"

I spend hours in my wheelchair. I eat, work, and play in this metal contraption, and it can become tiring to be in this thing day in and day out. But I have no choice. It's just the way it is.

One thing that is never tiring about it, however, is my time with the Lord. Yes, I spend way too much time watching television and playing on the computer, but when I decide to turn off those things and pick up my Bible, I'm a changed person.

During my quiet times, I remember that I was made to worship God, and it's my pleasure to do so. It's what I was meant to do. As I study my Bible, read a devotional, or pray, I rejoice and enjoy my time with Him. My meditations before the Lord are the highlight of my day. I hope they please Him.

You may not be in a wheelchair, but you have the same choices. You could watch television, play on the computer, or read that romance novel. Or you can spend time with the Lord, before all else.

And is it a mark of maturity to do that? I like the way Albert Einstein once put it: "Live in that solitude which is painful in youth, but delicious in the years of maturity." As we grow older in Christ, let us learn better to please Him in our quietness.

Lord, sometimes I'm afraid to be in solitude, but help me courageously enter those quiet times, ready to listen for Your voice of love and wisdom. Through Christ, amen.

DEVOTIONS®

September

I will sing to the LORD all my life; I will sing praise to my God as long as I live.

—Psalm 104:33

Gary Wilde, Editor   **Margaret Williams,** Project Editor   Photo © Kmitu | Dreamstime.com

DEVOTIONS® is published quarterly by Standard Publishing, Cincinnati, Ohio, www.ctandardpub.com.
© 2012 by Standard Publishing. All rights reserved. Topics based on the Home Daily Bible Readings,
International Sunday School Lessons. © 2010 by the Committee on the Uniform Series. Printed in
the U.S.A. All Scripture quotations, unless otherwise indicated, are taken from the *HOLY BIBLE,
NEW INTERNATIONAL VERSION®. NIV®.* Copyright © 2011 by Biblica, Inc.™ Used by permission
of Zondervan. All rights reserved. The *New American Standard Bible®* (*NASB*). Copyright © 1960,
1962, 1963, 1968, 1971, 1972, 1973, 1975, 1977, 1995 by The Lockman Foundation. Used by permission. (www.Lockman.org). All rights reserved. The Holy Bible, *New Living Translation* (*NLT*).
Copyright © 1996, 2004. Used by permission of Tyndale House Publishers, Inc., Wheaton, Illinois
60189. All rights reserved. *The Contemporary English Version* (*CEV*) Copyright © 1991, 1992,
1995 by American Bible Society. Used by permission. All rights reserved..

Dinner Time

All creatures look to you to give them their food at the proper time (Psalm 104:27).

Scripture: Psalm 104:5-9, 24-30
Song: "God Sees the Little Sparrow Fall"

Five o'clock is dinner time, and my dog, Santana, knows it. Whether he's outside or waiting by his dish, he's always eager to chow down. He comes running at full speed into the kitchen as soon as he hears food hitting the bowl and waits until I give him the OK to eat. He isn't picky. He is finished by the time I get back to my living room, and he is satisfied.

Psalm 104 describes how creation works. As Santana looks to me for food and care, the entire creation looks to God to take care of its needs. That's how He made it. In His wisdom, God designed the fish in the sea, the birds of the air, and other living things to roam the earth. He saw to it that every creature had the proper environment to live in, complete with food to eat and water to drink.

The Lord is truly masterful in administering His creation! Look around today and see how great our God is. Listen to the birds and hear their praise for life. Feel the wind and be reminded that the Spirit of God is near. Be aware of His creation today and know that you too are in His care.

Lord, how wonderful is Your work! As I go about my day, help me to remember that You take care of all of Your creation with perfect and infinite care—including me. All praise to You, through Christ my Lord. Amen.

September 1. **Tait Berge** is the church relations director at Mephibosheth Ministry. He lives in Colorado Springs and, when not working, enjoys hockey and golf.

Order Out of Chaos

God made . . . all the creatures . . . And God saw that it was good (Genesis 1:25).

Scripture: Genesis 1:20-25
Song: "Be Still and Know"

I glanced at my watch as I slid behind the wheel. As the minutes fled, I realized Tiffany waited at school and was late for her rehearsal. Furthermore, I had missed Troy's game—and choir practice was in one hour! Disorder blew around me like confetti in the wind. How could I escape this chaos? Was this hectic pace really God's plan for my life?

This morning I watch the quaking aspen tree outside my window; its leaves flash as they quiver in the still air. An industrious robin tends her brood. At this moment, I know God is the author of order. He divided chaos into night and day and separated animals into categories, each category their own kind. In God's plan, life became organized and structured. He set a system in place and saw that it was good.

When I choose too many activities to fill a single day, I introduce chaos. My mind shuts down, and only "erratic flight" characterizes my thinking processes. But I can decide to go to God—and this time stay long enough to listen. He changes the tempo and brings order when I let Him create my day.

O God, author of peace, I know You wait patiently for me every day, but I so often run past You. Create structure for me and give me a quiet heart that seeks You first. Thank You, through Christ my Savior. Amen.

September 2–8. **Barbara Durnil** is a retired medical worker and freelance writer in Southern Idaho. Writing for God is her joy and passion.

Marvelously Made

God saw all that He had made, and behold, it was very good. And there was evening and there was morning, the sixth day (Genesis 1:31, *New American Standard Bible*).

Scripture: Genesis 1:26-31
Song: "I Am Loved"

I drove away from the luncheon feeling depressed. Sharon had it all. Her physical perfection radiated with blinding annoyance. She had a loving husband and two darling children. Their classic two-story home stood in an upscale neighborhood and included a pool off the patio, with a BMW in the driveway.

What had happened to me? I lived alone, drove an old Ford truck, and every day was a bad-hair-day. My self-esteem hit the floor with a sorry thud.

"Why so downcast, O my soul?" What's that you say? The words repeat themselves in my mind. I remember that God is my Creator, and He has set me apart from all creation as a unique personality. God made me in His image.

Here's a thought: If I begin to measure myself by human standards, isn't it degrading to the Lord himself? After all, I reflect God's character through the Holy Spirit in me. Possessions and money matter not to God. It is my life in Him that carries infinite value. As I put my hope in God and praise Him, my self-worth comes into perspective. When I see my life through His eyes—behold, it is very good.

Creator God, open my heart that I may know how precious I am to You. When I realize Your love for me, useless comparisons leave me. Your hand formed me, and Your breath gives me life. In You, I find my worth. Through Christ, amen.

It Is Finished

By the seventh day God completed His work which He had done, and He rested on the seventh day from all His work which He had done (Genesis 2:2, *New American Standard Bible*).

Scripture: Genesis 2:1-9
Song: "I Heard the Voice of Jesus Say"

Ouch! My pinched finger throbbed as I dropped the steel fence post into the truck. I turned for the roll of wire, and my back complained as I heaved its weight up to the tailgate. I really disliked building a fence! It was exhausting. The road ended at the trees, and I gathered a load of posts. But beyond the big cedar, I stopped short.

What in the world was that? There on the line stood a new wire fence. The completed work glistened through the trees, and I had not driven a single one of those posts. I plucked the taught wire and tested the rock-solid posts. The work was perfect, and I could rest.

A breeze touched my face as I sank to the forest floor. This gift lifted my heart, and my body relaxed. *What a great neighbor I have!*

In the same way, God gives me rest from my work to earn His favor. He himself rested, not from fatigue, but because He finished creation. He asks me to rest now in the completion of His redemptive work. There is no labor needed to improve *that* gift or to make it mine, other than trust Him and accept His grace.

Father, my salvation is complete because the work of Jesus on the cross is finished for eternity. I now put my energy into trusting You, instead of trusting my efforts to earn Your favor. Hold me now, as I rest in Your arms. In Jesus' name, amen.

See That Special Image

When Adam had lived one hundred and thirty years, he became the father of a son in his own likeness, according to his image, and named him Seth (Genesis 5:3, *New American Standard Bible*).

Scripture: Genesis 5:1-5
Song: "I Love You with the Love of the Lord"

"Whose child are you, and where did you come from?" Have you ever heard that from a frustrated parent? I have said it myself a few times. Then there is the standard, "You get that from your father." Inherited traits range from curly hair to athletic prowess; some are negative, many positive. (So I tend to take *selective* credit for the various traits of my children.)

I wonder if Eve looked at Seth and saw Adam. She must have, for there were no grandparents to cloud the reflection of the child. As he grew, did he become the astonishing image of his father? Did he act and speak like Adam?

But wait—he was made in *whose* image? Adam was created in God's image, and Seth according to that image too. It seems that grandpa's nose doesn't matter so much, because it is God's image that is supremely important. When I forget the physical genetics and look for God revealed in my children—and in people around me—I begin to see great potential and purpose. It's the image of God in us that gives value and significance to every life.

O Creator God, the prophet Samuel saw the physical image of David, but You saw the heart and soul. Help me see my children and others with Your eyes—eyes that pierce the outer crust and see the value and potential that lies within. Amen.

Voice of Triumph

Through the praise of children and infants you have established a stronghold against your enemies, to silence the foe and the avenger (Psalm 8:2).

Scripture: Psalm 8
Song: "Clap Your Hands All You People"

"Mama, don't be sad, Jesus will take care of you. Look, see the flower, the stem is all bent over, but Jesus keeps the flower beautiful!" Her big blue eyes reflected the innocence of her heart. Absolute trust and open love for God hung in the air, and I gathered Jenna in my arms.

Her simple praise had broken my fear. That morning, when I received medical test results calling for a biopsy, a battle began. Cancer ran in my family—but I was too young for this attack! Fear instantly gripped me, and I began to plan my strategy for the months ahead. How quickly my prayers became bargains and pleas with personal motives and agendas attached. I lost my stronghold.

Children sing "Jesus Loves Me" because they know He does. There is no labor to earn it, no bargain to make; their praise bubbles up from simple honesty. And when I lay down my battle plans and pick up a childlike trust, then my praise becomes pure, and strongholds are set against the enemy. My praise becomes a shout to God with a voice of triumph.

Almighty God and Father, help me simply to know that You are my eternal stronghold. Strengthen my belief and unreserved trust in You so that my praise will be as pure and innocent as a child's. It is that praise that brings my victory. Through Christ, amen.

The Better Way

That you be renewed in the spirit of your mind, and put on the new self, which in the likeness of God has been created in righteousness and holiness of the truth (Ephesians 4:23, 24, *New American Standard Bible*).

Scripture: Ephesians 4:17-24
Song: "Create in Me a Clean Heart"

My feet hit the floor with new resolve. This was a new day, and I planned to change my attitude. I would greet each customer with a smile and a gracious spirit. And when the complaints and harsh words came at me, I would be compassionate and understanding.

I could do this. My determination was high . . . until the first stoplight . . . and the impatient driver behind me honked the instant the light turned green. At the store, a customer pushed past me as I unlocked the door. I checked my watch: it was four minutes before the hour, and my spirit took another dive. *O God, what is wrong with me? Why can't I love as you love?*

That, in fact, is the problem. I can't. My decision to do so doesn't make it happen. David cried, "God, give me a clean heart and steadfast spirit." He had it right, didn't he? God must give me a new heart and new spirit, or I will continue to struggle.

God doing the work, however, liberates me! I become free from my own effort and ultimate failure. I can indeed get up each morning and ask God to create the heart that will carry me through the day.

O God, thank You for freeing me from the labor, and the guilt, when I fail. Create Your heart in me today and renew my spirit with Yours. In the name of Jesus, I pray. Amen.

People Who Need People . . .

It is not good for the man to be alone. I will make a helper suitable for him (Genesis 2:18).

Scripture: Genesis 2:18-25
Song: "Bind Us Together"

I am a solitary person. When I have a choice, I avoid crowds and large parties. In fact, I've been known to remain in seclusion for days at a time, coming out only to forage for food.

Horses, dogs, and barnyard animals make great companions. I discovered several years after widowhood, however, that being a mild recluse just wasn't God's plan for me. As I "dug in" on my property and withdrew, it became apparent that it wasn't working. I needed someone to hold me responsible and to help me grow. I needed incentive and mental stimulation. I also needed to give part of myself to others. My animals were companions, but there was no kinship. I needed *people*.

God found no partner for Adam in animals; instead, He duplicated His image from Adam's flesh. God placed people together so they could uphold each other, which resulted in blessing.

The body of Christ is made up of people. That body stimulates love and good deeds and brings cheer by speaking the wonders of God. Need enrichment? Come before Him with thanks, speak to one another "through psalms, hymns, and songs from the Spirit, singing to God with gratitude in your hearts" (see Colossians 3:16).

Precious Lord, never let me grow complacent about my position in Your body. It is there I find support, and there that I offer support to others. Though You dwell in my heart, remind me that Your gifts are to be used in Your church. In Jesus' name, amen.

From Utah to . . . God

You yourselves have seen what I did to Egypt, and how I carried you on eagles' wings and brought you to myself (Exodus 19:4).

Scripture: Exodus 19:3-8
Song: "Keep on Praying"

Moving day, 4:30 a.m., and the house is empty except for the sleeping bag I lie in. With great excitement I anticipate my 17-hour drive from Utah to my new home in Colorado.

At dawn, while I was driving on a deserted mountain road, a large doe ran in front of my SUV. I was going too fast to just slam on the breaks. *Smash!*

I pulled the car off the road and cried hysterically. The front of the car was bent so the front right tire couldn't move, the radiator was cracked, and the deer was dead. And no one was around to help. All I could do was pray.

Soon, out of nowhere, a tow truck driver going home from his night shift arrived and pulled out the car's damaged bumper so I could drive. He explained that the car could still make it to Colorado.

In a desperate moment, God heard my prayer—I hadn't been in a church for years. Once settled into my new home, my neighbor invited me to dinner and then to church. God brought me from Utah back to Him.

Lord, thanks for being with me when scary things happen. Though I hadn't been close to You, You never left me. You heard my call for help. In Jesus' name, amen.

September 9–15. **Dee Martz** lives in Louisville, Colorado. She is an office manager, technical writer, and editor. She walks dogs for the Humane Society.

Obedient Blessings

See, I am setting before you today a blessing and a curse—the blessing if you obey the commands of the LORD your God that I am giving you today (Deuteronomy 11:26, 27).

Scripture: Deuteronomy 11:26-32
Song: "Sweet Peace, the Gift of God's Love"

At the medical office where I work, I opened the receptionist window to help a patient. "Where's the doctor? I've been waiting for 45 minutes. I need to be somewhere in an hour," she yelled in my face. I was caught off guard as her anger flared.

My heart pounded. I couldn't yell back, or I'd lose my job. *What's the professional response to this?* More importantly, how would God want me to respond? I knew I could reply with love . . . but how would that look? Her side: this lady clearly felt her needs weren't being met. My side: I felt verbally attacked for something over which I had no control.

Romans 12:18 says, "If it is possible, as far as it depends on you, live at peace with everyone." God's command to love one another was so applicable here. I could respond from a heart of love for hurting, broken people or yell back, ramping up the hatred in an already charged situation. How difficult it is sometimes to calm down and make the right choice.

When I've chosen to love, forgive, and try to understand another's feelings, I've always felt better. As it says in Proverbs 14:30, "A heart at peace gives life to the body." What a blessing for simply obeying His Word!

Thank You, **Lord,** for helping me remain calm when others are angry—and for blessing me with peace when I daily choose to obey You. Through Christ, amen.

From Destructive to Divine

See I set before you today life and prosperity, death and destruction. For I command you today to love the LORD your God, to walk in obedience to him (Deuteronomy 30:15, 16).

Scripture: Deuteronomy 30:11-20
Song: "It Is Well with My Soul"

It started with two airliners crashing into two skyscrapers, killing more than 2,600 people. Could anything have been more difficult for our country?

One minute, images of the good life on a clear, blue-sky September 11 morning amid the high-rise buildings of New York City; the next minute, death and destruction as the first airplane hit the World Trade Center, the beginning of an event now known as 9/11. Where were you when you heard the news?

In the aftermath, a two-ton, 20-foot-high, cross-shaped steel beam was found in the wreckage, perhaps a reminder that, no matter what, God hasn't deserted us. Even though this was the worst national tragedy many of us have known in our lifetimes, it provided an opportunity to turn to God. Many did.

For years since this devastating event, volunteers and professionals have worked to restore, rebuild, and protect this city and our country. Communities have created memorials and held fund-raisers, and many have donated to these organizations and continue to pray for the victims' families. Even amidst this great evil, God is working to bring redemption and new life.

O Lord, no matter how great the destruction, nothing is beyond Your repair when I choose to walk in Your ways. When I've created my own life's disasters, because of bad choices, You've rescued and restored me too. In the name of Jesus, amen.

How the Spirit Leads

We are witnesses of these things, and so is the Holy Spirit, whom God has given to those who obey him (Acts 5:32).

Scripture: Acts 5:27-42
Song: "Holy Spirit, Rain Down"

When you've chosen to share the gospel, didn't it seem as if everything just fell into place? My friend, Tammy, taught a church group in Singapore. Before the church meeting, she was reading 1 Corinthians 1:10-13 about divisions in the church. The importance of unity stuck in her mind.

At her meeting, a lady said she quit going to church years ago because of hurtful things that were said to her by other members in the congregation. Tammy shared this Scripture with her, and the woman decided to try church again.

When Tammy's family was deciding to leave Singapore to go back to the United States, she was torn between her ministry and preparing to move. At the most practical level, she dreaded the time-consuming planning for an overseas move. She prayed about it, and when reading John 21:15-17, where Jesus urged Simon Peter to "feed my sheep," she felt as if the Holy Spirit was directing her to keep feeding her own "sheep" in Singapore. The result: The move preparation went effortlessly, giving her time to continue leading her group for several more months.

Similarly, in Acts, the disciples' testimony was directed and confirmed by the Holy Spirit. Thankfully, this same Spirit of God is given to all who respond to Him with obedience.

Father, give me the courage to trust the guidance from the indwelling Holy Spirit in my life's decisions. And let my love for You lead others to You! Through Christ, amen.

Same Temptations Today

The woman said to the serpent, "We may eat fruit from the trees in the garden, but God did say, 'You must not eat fruit from the tree that is in the middle of the garden, and you must not touch it, or you will die'" (Genesis 3:2, 3).

Scripture: Genesis 3:1-7
Song: "Dear Lord, Thou Art the Tree of Life"

Feeding our bodies and souls is about choices and consequences. The Bible says God gave us plants, birds, and some animals to eat—not candy bars, cheese puffs, and soda pop! God wants us to make good choices . . . for our good. When we exercise and make wise food choices, we stay healthy and in shape.

Likewise, when we make choices that feed our souls, we will stay ready to serve God. And He gave us plenty to pick from His garden. The fruits of the Spirit are our food for the soul—"love, joy, peace, patience, kindness, goodness, faithfulness, gentleness and self-control" (see Galatians 5:22, 23).

Moderation in everything applies not only to the food we eat, but to what we feed our souls. If we don't nourish our souls in spending time with God, in reading His Word, and in praying, our love for others could wither and die.

Eve wasn't listening to God when she made her choice in the Garden of Eden. The enemy's subtle way of distorting and deceiving her made eating the forbidden fruit too tempting. Let us beware of the same kind of temptations that come to us on any day of the week.

Lord, thank You for providing so abundantly, giving me so many choices. Give me Your wisdom in my decision-making this day! In Jesus' name, amen.

You Still Have the Lord

By the sweat of your brow you will eat your food until you return to the ground, since from it you were taken; for dust you are and to dust you will return (Genesis 3:19).

Scripture: Genesis 3:18-24
Song: "To God Alone Be the Glory"

We'd already lost thousands of dollars overnight. "Do you think we should take half our 401(k) money, move it to cash, and sell the house?" I asked my husband as we sipped our morning coffee, while the stock market continued to drop several million dollars a second.

Our house was the home in the country I'd always wanted—a Cape-Cod style on three acres, abutting 80 acres with a panoramic view of the Rocky Mountains. Four months after buying it, my husband came home and announced, "There's going to be a downsizing at work tomorrow." He wouldn't be laid off, we decided. But the next morning, we found we were wrong. In the ensuing months, the stress of debt strained our marriage and brought us to the brink of divorce.

We work hard for a living—"by the sweat of your brow"—but it can all be taken away so quickly. And when we leave this earth, our material possessions won't go with us.

If you feel you have lost it all, you have not. You still have what's in your heart: the gift of God's indwelling Spirit to guide you through the toughest times. Thanks be to God!

Father, I know there are consequences for my actions and inactions. Please help me make my decisions guided by Your wisdom—and guide me to continue Your good works while I'm on earth. In Jesus' name I pray. Amen.

Passing the Blame

[God said]: "Have you eaten from the tree that I commanded you not to eat from?" The man said, "The woman you put here with me—she gave me some fruit from the tree, and I ate it" (Genesis 3:11, 12).

Scripture: Genesis 3:8-17
Song: "Come, Sinners, to the Gospel Feast"

I made a huge error at work. In the computer, I entered the eight-digit account number instead of the dollar amount of a customer's payment. I work with a team of six, and the system is set up so no one can tell who entered what. If I didn't say anything, no one would know the mistake was mine. But if I told my boss, I'd be in big trouble—I was close to losing my job from all the other mistakes I'd made lately. Should I take the blame and confess what I did . . . or do nothing?

My actions would affect many people adversely—the person whose account had the error, coworkers, and my supervisor. So I chose to admit my mistake. I took action to correct it, and the consequences for all concerned weren't as bad as they would have been had I kept silent. (And I kept my job.)

God wants all of us to do what's right and be honest. When Adam passed the blame to Eve, God confronted only them. Yet according to the apostle Paul, the whole human race still lives with the consequences of their choices (see Romans 5:12-21).

Lord God of Heaven and earth, You know what's best for me, yet every life experience offers me the opportunity to make good or bad decisions. Thank You for this freedom, but please remind me that no matter how difficult the trouble, following Your way is always the right way. Through the name of Jesus I pray. Amen.

A Window of Hope

Make a roof for it, leaving below the roof an opening one cubit high all around. Put a door in the side of the ark and make lower, middle and upper decks (Genesis 6:16).

Scripture: Genesis 6:11-22
Song: "Bury Thy Sorrow"

I sat on a plane with a young woman who'd graduated from college 15 months earlier. In spite of a 4.0 G.P.A. and great references, she'd been rejected by medical schools because of low medical test scores. Discouraged, she didn't know what to do. I urged her to pursue some other opportunities, reminding her: When God closes a door, He leaves open a window of hope.

Before Noah built the ark, God gave him specific instructions about its design. The length, height, and depth of the ark prevented it from capsizing in stormy seas.

In His construction plan, God provided windows all around, just below the roof. These contributed light, fresh air, and a most important element—hope. Through these openings, Noah and his family would be able to see when the rains stopped, when the sun began to shine, and when the first evidence of land appeared over the horizon.

When rejection and discouragement tumble into my life, it's easy to think things will never improve. That's when I remember Noah's windows and turn back to God with renewed hope.

Lord, when doors keep slamming shut, I get discouraged. Help me to press into Your will and into Your Word in order to keep moving forward. In Jesus' name, amen.

September 16–22. **Jinny Sherman** is a freelance writer who also mentors women. She loves hiking the hills of Southern Oregon with her husband, Rick. They have two adult children.

One Righteous Person

Go into the boat with all your family, for among all the people of the earth, I can see that you alone are righteous (Genesis 7:1, *New Living Translation*).

Scripture: Genesis 7:1-10
Song: "Rise Up, O Men of God"

Harriet Tubman had some things in common with Noah. They both lived lives that honored God. They stood firm against the evils of their day. They listened to Him and followed His leading, even though at times His instructions must have seemed odd. Noah obeyed, in spite of what was probably strong ridicule from his neighbors. (Who builds a huge boat in the desert?)

Harriet Tubman was born into slavery 40 years before the Civil War. From her birthplace in Maryland, she escaped to Pennsylvania, a free state, but soon returned to rescue members of her family. Over the years, she rescued more than 70 slaves, risking her life to transport them along the network of safe houses known as the Underground Railroad. A devout Christian, she depended on God to protect her and those with her. None of the slaves she guided to freedom were caught.

Let us never underestimate the influence of one godly person in a family or community. Noah and Harriet each made tough decisions and acted courageously. Their actions affected their families—and the whole of humanity—in a major way.

Lord, You know the fear that lurks in my heart. Help me draw courage from the lives of Noah and Harriet Tubman. They were everyday people committed to You, and You accomplished great things through them. I give myself to You this day. Please use me as You will. In Jesus' name, amen.

No Rudder

For forty days the floodwaters grew deeper, covering the ground and lifting the boat high above the earth. As the waters rose higher and higher above the ground, the boat floated safely on the surface (Genesis 7:17, 18, *New Living Translation*).

Scripture: Genesis 7:11-24
Song: "All the Way My Savior Leads Me"

The Coho Ferry in Port Angeles, Washington, is a magnificent seagoing vessel. It cruises in from Vancouver, British Columbia, and makes an arc around a long breakwater, then slides into port and sits awhile. Finally, it executes a quarter turn to connect with the dock, so the cars and passengers can exit from the rear. It takes a skilled captain to perform these maneuvers.

Noah wasn't exactly the captain of the ark. He and his family floated in a massive, barge-like boat without an oar, sail, or rudder. He had no way to steer!

Did he sometimes wish he did? (Or was he so thankful he and his family were safe that he didn't care where God took them?) The reality was that he had to completely trust God to guide them.

When life throws tough things at me—a relative with cancer, a lost job opportunity, back or neck pain that keep me awake at night—I can focus on a few marvelous facts: the Sovereign Lord is with me, and He knows where I am. He has plans for me that are for my good, and He will steer a wise course for me.

Gracious Lord, sometimes I get myself into awkward messes, and sometimes life blindsides me. But whatever the situation, You know a way out. When life is uncertain, help me trust that, if I will humble myself, You will guide me. In Christ, amen.

Snapshot of Encouragement

The waters continued to recede until the tenth month, and on the first day of the tenth month the tops of the mountains became visible (Genesis 8:5).

Scripture: Genesis 8:1-12
Song: "Trusting Jesus"

Our son, Joshua, was born 11 weeks early. Though I was excited to see him, fear knotted my muscles. Would he survive?

A few days later, Joshua lay on his side, a rubber glove hovering behind him. Every few seconds it inflated and thumped him on the back. I raised my eyebrows to the nurse.

"Joshua's breathing pattern is typical for premature babies. He takes a breath, waits, and forgets to breathe again, so his heart slows down. He'll grow out of it."

I certainly hoped so! Later, a doctor introduced herself and said, "I have your son's heart problem under control." Heart problem? She left, and my body began trembling. *O God, help!*

Next morning at church, I sidestepped to avoid a blond, blue-eyed youngster who whizzed past. I gasped. Joshua had the same coloring. Instantly, I imagined what he might look like as a healthy boy. That snapshot of encouragement buoyed me until we brought Joshua safely home.

After the rain stopped, Noah and his family remained in the ark for nine months without sight of land. Had God forgotten them? No, just one glimpse of land gave them hope—they would be out of the ark soon.

God of hope, I praise You! When everything around me looks bleak, give me the eyes of faith to wait for Your plan and Your timing. In Jesus' name, amen.

Switching Decades

Then Noah built an altar to the Lord, and there he sacrificed as burnt offerings the animals and birds that had been approved for that purpose (Genesis 8:20, *New Living Translation*).

Scripture: Genesis 8:13-22
Song: "Great Is Thy Faithfulness"

I'm about to switch decades. Birthdays with zeroes after them used to make me groan or sink into the blues, but I've chosen a new attitude. I've discovered that age transitions are easier for me when I have a party with my closest friends. With that to look forward to, I don't focus on my increasing age.

This year my prayer partners and confidantes will gather at a nearby lake for a barbecue picnic. We'll hike, talk, and laugh. But some time during the day, we'll sing "Great Is Thy Faithfulness" to thank God for the many ways He's helped us all during the 20 years we've known each other.

After Noah's long ordeal, he built an altar to worship the Lord, who had protected and provided. Noah built the ark out of *obedience*, but he created the altar out of *devotion*.

Each year, I recount in a journal what God has done and thank Him for the many answers to prayer, miracles for family and friends, and other blessings. From these recollections, I gain wisdom and courage to face today's challenges—and the faith to trust Him for tomorrow.

Great God, thank You for life, for friends and loved ones, and for years to enjoy them. Give me eyes to see all You do and a humble heart to praise You for Your mercies, which are new every morning. In Jesus' name, amen.

The Fruit of Blessing

God blessed Noah and his sons, saying to them, "Be fruitful and increase in number and fill the earth" (Genesis 9:1).

Scripture: Genesis 9:1-7
Song: "The Lord Bless Thee"

"The Lord bless you and keep you . . . and give you peace" (Numbers 6:24, 26). My husband and I gave that blessing to Josh and Anna every evening. We never knew when we started this tradition with our children what a vast influence it would have on them.

When Josh and Anna were teens, a woman approached me after Vacation Bible School and said, "This week there were two young people who worked hard, had good attitudes, and were always dependable."

"How nice," I said.

"Since they don't look alike, I didn't realize they were related." *Why is she telling me this?*

"Josh and Anna were great all week," the woman explained.

I blinked. My kids? Pictures of untidy rooms, bickering, and resistance to chores flashed through my mind. "Really?" I had no idea they were so cooperative with *other* adults!

"They were a great blessing."

"Thank you." I wanted to take the credit for raising such great kids. The character traits she mentioned were beyond what I had taught them. This fruit came from God's work in their lives.

Lord, Your blessing on Noah and his children enabled them to fulfill their task on earth. Thank You that You bless Your children. And thank You that when You assign me a task, You give me what I need to fulfill it. Through Christ I pray. Amen.

A Colorful Crescent

Whenever . . . the rainbow appears in the clouds, I will remember my covenant between me and you and all living creatures of every kind. Never again will the waters become a flood to destroy all life (Genesis 9:14, 15).

Scripture: Genesis 9:8-17
Song: "Blessed Be Your Name"

The first rainbow's brilliant hues arched over Noah's family to remind them of God's covenant and to bring them joy after their long ordeal. When I was 8-years-old, my dad was in a head-on freeway collision. Doctors told him he would never walk again. Sadness consumed me. Daddy, who loved to hike, bike, and swim—on crutches for the rest of his life?

I had no way of knowing then the important lessons I would learn because of this calamity. The first I learned by watching Dad's determination. He exercised his leg several times a day and eventually proved the doctors wrong. After physical therapy and several surgeries, he learned not only to walk but to run.

Second, I observed genuine love, as my parents stuck together to work for Dad's recovery. True friendship was illustrated as people from church brought delicious meals every evening.

Dad's accident turned our household upside down for six months. But the examples I witnessed—of perseverance, commitment, and friendship—have arched over my life like a rainbow, adding wisdom and beauty. They have also shaped my adult responses to tough situations.

Lord, when I'm in the thick of a frightening situation, I tend to shrink with fear. But You are able to do far more than I can imagine. Remind me! In the name of Jesus, amen.

Be a Man

Brace yourself like a man; I will question you, and you shall answer me (Job 38:3).

Scripture: Job 38:1-7
Song: "God of Wonders"

Life as the mother of three teenage boys can be baffling. Seth, the oldest, picked on the youngest, Sam. Sam retaliated. Seth blocked his swing and, in the process, inadvertently gave Sam a bloody nose. Sam ran to the bathroom, dealt with the blood, and returned to his brother. "I'm sorry," he said.

"You're the one with the bloody nose, Bud." Seth's voice was full of apology. Sam's reply? "I'd rather get a broken nose by you than anyone else." Male bonding makes no sense to me.

I felt the same when I read God's words to Job. Throughout the Bible we have many men whining to God, questioning Him. The psalmist, for example, tells us to pour our complaints out before God. Yet here's Job, who has suffered beyond comprehension, and God tells him to . . . *be a man*.

I would have brewed Job a cup of tea and pulled out the tissue box. But God told Job to buck up—and then systemically reminded him of how small he was compared to God's majesty. Later in Job 42:5, Job tells the Lord, "My ears had heard of you but now my eyes see you." That kind of bonding makes all the sense in the world!

Holy God, sometimes when I complain I'm forgetting who You are. Forgive my arrogance and receive my praise, through Christ my Lord. Amen.

September 23–29. **Paula Moldenhauer** longs to be close enough to God to breathe His fragrance. A freelance writer and mom of four, she and her husband live in Colorado.

Deep Places

Have you journeyed to the springs of the sea or walked in the recesses of the deep? . . . Have you comprehended the vast expanses of the earth? Tell me, if you know all this (Job 38:16, 18).

Scripture: Job 38:12-18
Song: "O the Deep, Deep Love of Jesus"

The tour guide leads through the recesses of a cave, commenting on the stalactites, then turns out the lights. The dark penetrates. Climbing a *fourteener* mountain is the opposite kind of experience. I break tree-line and push to the peak. There is nothing but light and sky above, expansive vistas below. And if I stand at ocean edge, I'm reminded some things are too vast—too deep and too wide—to comprehend. Each encounter leaves me breathless.

Then I think of God, and how creation proclaims His character. The view from the peak or at the edge of the ocean is farther than I can see, yet Scripture says my sins are removed from me as far is the east is from the west. God is more majestic than the mountains. He is the light that penetrates any darkness. His love is deeper than the ocean.

Preachers tell me to dive into the ocean of God. I want to. But the temptation is just to splash around in a little pond of intermittent devotion. Yet there is nothing to fear. As the old song says, "The deep, deep love of Jesus . . . rolling as a mighty ocean in its fullness over me."

Lord, no matter how deeply I dive or how far I walk, I can't grasp the measureless wonders of this earth—or the magnificence of Your love. Through Christ, amen.

Great God, Great Care

Do you send the lightning bolts on their way? Do they report to you, "Here we are"? (Job 38:35).

Scripture: Job 38:28-38
Song: "Indescribable"

Growing up in the foothills of the Ozarks, I understand the term gully-washer, am well-acquainted with razor-sharp jags of lightning, and have been startled awake by thunder rumbling like the throaty voice of a great giant. My children have less experience with such things. It storms in Colorado, but our home, sheltered by the Rockies, hasn't seen too many gully-washers. Yet this summer the heavens opened and unleashed floods of raging rivers down our neighborhood streets. Awed, the kids watched out the windows in fascination.

One thing my children have known is the wonder of snow. What delight to watch them as little ones, twirling in the softly falling white, mouths wide open—or standing stock still, eyes full of amazement as they studied a single, perfect, starlike flake captured on a finger.

Camping in the mountains, we see the white stars glisten like diamonds on black velvet, more than we can count. We're well aware of how small we are and how little we know. Yet it's a good thing to be "put in our place" as we marvel at God's creation, isn't it? Good to know that such a great God cares so greatly for you and for me.

Amazing Lord, only You understand all the intricacies of Your creation. Only You put the stars in place, send the lightning bolts, and make the snowflake. You are unfathomable, and so my heart swells with worship, in the name of Jesus. Amen.

Saved by His Mighty Arm

Do you have an arm like God's, and can your voice thunder like his? (Job 40:9).

Scripture: Job 40:6-14
Song: "Sheltered in the Arms of God"

What started out as a playful outing to watch a sea turtle turned into a brutal buffeting of waves. My husband and I swam around a jutting point of rock, hoping to enter the calmer Hawaiian bay on the other side of it. I fought not only the great Pacific Ocean, but the rising panic within. *Father, help me not be so afraid.*

Calm came over me. Then I was submerged, somersaulting, and pulled out to sea. Miraculously, I didn't fight. Completely relaxed, I was an underwater rag doll.

Suddenly I felt myself rising. As my head broke the surface I gasped for air and looked into the white face of my husband. He'd watched me being taken from him and, in a valiant effort, anchored himself by wrapping one strong arm around a coral reef while reaching for me with the other. He grabbed my swimsuit and, leveraging himself on the coral, pulled with all his might. His arm was a bloody mess . . . but I lived.

Jerry's strong arm (strengthened by God's) saved me. Though a good swimmer, I had been totally incapable of helping myself. If I'd tried, I would have fought against the arm reaching for me. Trapped in the undertow, I would have perished.

Mighty God, sometimes I think too much of myself, flexing puny muscles in Your face. Fighting too-big battles, I strive on my own, rejecting Your sovereign will. Forgive me. You are the only one adorned in glory. Praise to You, through Jesus. Amen.

What to Do?

The LORD must be furious . . . because our ancestors did not obey the laws written in this book. Go find out what the LORD wants us to do (2 Chronicles 34:21, *Contemporary English Version*).

Scripture: 2 Chronicles 34:14-21
Song: "Song of Confession"

The younger boys and I memorized Scripture about the attributes of God—one for each letter of the alphabet. The passage of the day focused on *M* for God's *mercy* and was found in Daniel 9:9, 10.

"The Lord our God is merciful and forgiving, even though we have rebelled against him; we have not obeyed the Lord our God or kept the laws he gave us." I don't remember what the altercation of the morning was. Sibling squabbles ended in unkind words and hurt feelings—and Mom's impatient response. A tired, home-schooling Momma, I cried out to God and asked what we should do to survive the morning's struggles.

We had a family powwow and, before long, had talked through the problems, forgiving each other. Then we prayed for God's forgiveness and empowerment to do better.

All of a sudden my youngest looked at me with eyes lit with understanding. "It's like that verse, Mom. We sinned against God by the way we acted—but He is merciful and forgives us!"

Heavenly Father, thanks to Your Son's cross, I know what to do when I sin—come to You for forgiveness and the power to change. Thank You for Your mercy, even when I rebel against You. Please change me from the inside out so I can be more like Jesus. In His name I pray. Amen.

He Keeps Forgiving

Because your heart was responsive and you humbled yourself before God . . . because you humbled yourself before me and tore your robes and wept in my presence, I have heard you, declares the LORD (2 Chronicles 34:27).

Scripture: 2 Chronicles 34:22-28
Song: "Redeemed, Restored, Forgiven"

I've never torn my robes over my sins, but the good Lord has seen plenty of weeping in His presence. I thought I was humble. I was certainly unhappy with myself, aware of my shortcomings, and imploring Him to change me.

A spiritual perfectionist, I kept trying to do better. I didn't understand that heaping condemnation upon myself didn't make me humble; instead, punishing myself spurned God's grace.

Thankfully, God heard my cries. Humbling came in the form of four children in six years. Here's what I mean: My deepest desire was to be a good mother, so I determined that I'd *always* be fun and cheerful and *never* lose my temper.

But I soon realized I couldn't be the perfect mom, and I found it impossible to let myself off the hook. As I groveled before the Lord, repenting once again, He whispered to my heart, *Do you really think I didn't know you would sin today? That it surprised me? My grace is for every sin you've committed . . . and every sin you will commit.*

As I accepted grace, He changed me. I became more humble before Him, not less, as I stopped living in condemnation.

Father, sometimes in my efforts to please You, I forget how much I need You. Teach me the kind of humility that relies on my need of Your grace. In Jesus' name, amen.

Still Full of Ourselves?

Come, let us build ourselves a city, with a tower that reaches to the heavens, so that we may make a name for ourselves (Genesis 11:4).

Scripture: Genesis 11:1-9
Song: "Clothe Yourself with Humility"

The 100th anniversary of the launching—and sinking—of the Titanic was April 2012. Perhaps the most famous quote about that mighty vessel is, "God himself cannot sink this ship." While this pronouncement was likely a product of Hollywood, not history, it is accurate to say that—before it sailed—the Titanic was indeed considered beyond any potential harm. When the New York office of White Star Lines heard that the ship was possibly in trouble, a vice president announced: "We place absolute confidence in the Titanic. We believe the boat is unsinkable."

It wasn't just the shipbuilders who bought into the idea. Before boarding the Titanic, one passenger wrote home, "We are changing ships and coming home in a new unsinkable boat."

Ouch. I guess we humans never learn. Thousands of years before the Titanic sailed, we were already bragging on our great accomplishments. The builders of the Tower of Babel lauded their newfound ability to make better bricks, saying their tower would reach the heavens, and they would be famous. We are still full of ourselves, even after 6,000 years.

Father, I have the audacity to think I'm incapable of the arrogance of the builders of the Titanic or the tower of Babel. Then I'm shocked when something I've built my hope upon fails. There is nothing worthy of my complete faith except You. Help me build on the Rock alone! In Jesus' name I pray. Amen.

Recalculating!

By faith Abraham . . . obeyed . . . went out, not knowing where he was going (Hebrews 11:8, *New American Standard Bible*).

Scripture: Hebrews 11:8-16
Song: "Lead On, O King Eternal"

On my first trip in my new 30-foot RV, I found myself in road construction on I-90, along the northern border of Indiana. Traffic was bumper-to-bumper but flowing at 75 mph. I was sandwiched between semis, so close I could see my reflection in the rearview mirror of the one in front of me. Suddenly my lane became an exit, and I was totally lost.

A few years later I bought a GPS, which keeps that from happening again. As long as it knows my destination, it talks me through all confusion, patiently suggesting, "Make a legal U-turn when possible" when I miss a turn, and offering, "Recalculating" when I've gone hopelessly astray.

I see my GPS as a symbol of the Holy Spirit. He too knows exactly where I'm supposed to be going and the best way for me to travel. He doesn't lose patience when I willfully go off in my own direction, but reminds me to turn around, go back, and regain my focus. I can almost hear Him whispering, "Recalculating!"

Loving Father, thank You for guiding me! Thank You for continuing to love me, even when I wander off after my own ideas and desires, even when I foolishly turn my back on You. Help me to trust You and follow You, through Christ my Lord. Amen.

September 30. **Elsi Dodge,** of Boulder, Colorado, sings, coleads Bible study, works with a youth group, and travels in an RV when she's not writing.

My Prayer Notes

_____

_____

_____

_____

_____

_____

_____

_____

_____

_____

_____

_____

_____

_____

_____

_____

_____

_____

_____

_____

_____

_____

_____

_____

_____

DEVOTIONS®

OCTOBER

> Your kingdom is an everlasting kingdom . . . The
> LORD is trustworthy in all he promises and faithful
> in all he does.
>
> —*Psalm 145:13*

Gary Wilde, Editor   **Margaret Williams,** Project Editor   Photo © iStockphoto | Thinkstock®

When the Checkbook Follows

Abram took Sarai his wife and Lot his nephew, and all their possessions which they had accumulated, and the persons which they had acquired in Haran, and they set out for the land of Canaan (Genesis 12:5, *New American Standard Bible*).

Scripture: Genesis 12:1-7
Song: "I Surrender All"

I've been on the road in my RV for eight weeks at a time, perfectly content with a week's worth of clothes. I carry my printer and computer with me, my bedding, dog and cat food—really, the only things I miss from my house are books. (However, e-book readers keep me from feeling too deprived in that area.)

I think about my house and all that it contains. I've accumulated so much stuff: what would Abram think? Yes, at home I need clothes for church and for winter, and I have hundreds of books that I treasure. But do I really need all this?

I walk through a superstore humming "I Surrender All," picking up a pretty shirt, an attractive knickknack, and a gift for a friend next Christmas, not considering whether these purchases are essential.

My financial advisor glares at me when I impulsively give money to a missionary, orphanage, or homeless shelter. But those are probably my best moments—when my heart and God's are aligned . . . and my checkbook follows.

O God, thank You for loving me so much, for being so bountiful and generous to me. Give me Your heart, and loosen my grip on my possessions. Through Christ, amen.

October 1–6. **Elsi Dodge,** of Boulder, Colorado, sings, coleads Bible study, works with a youth group, and travels in an RV when she's not writing.

Gift of Gratitude

Go, walk through the length and breadth of the land, for I am giving it to you (Genesis 13:17).

Scripture: Genesis 13:8-18
Song: "All Creatures of Our God and King"

My family was really good at giving and receiving gifts. No ripping open the wrapping paper, calling out "thanks!" and moving on—not for us. First, you admired the paper, read the card aloud, and tried to guess what was inside, while those in the know chuckled and hinted. Then you opened your present. You removed it from its packaging and held it up, looking at it closely, admiring and commenting on details.

"Oh, thank you! I love this author, and the title is fascinating. Look at the beautiful illustrations . . . and it has that wonderful new-book smell too. Thank you so much!" We could take five hours opening Christmas presents—and there were only three of us.

How dare I give the Lord less gratitude than I do my friends at Christmas? Abram walked every inch of the land God gave him, seeing the details, thanking the Lord for His gift.

But how do I pray? My tendency is to rush straight to requests: "Please heal John, and help Sue find another job, and give Annette a safe trip." When I do remember to slow down and start by thanking the Lord, I find my own soul is blessed—a precious gift!

O Father, thank You for this day! I loved seeing the sunrise reflecting off the mountain peaks this morning, the snow and clouds melting together in pink and gold. Thank You for all the blessings You pour into my life each day. In Jesus' name, amen.

Every Breath I Take

No longer shall your name be called Abram, but your name shall be Abraham; for I have made you the father of a multitude of nations (Genesis 17:5, *New American Standard Bible*).

Scripture: Genesis 17:1-8
Song: "Breathe on Me, Breath of Life"

The boy shifted uncomfortably in his chair at the conference table as his parents, the social worker, and I discussed the details of his transfer to my classroom.

"You know," I said to him, "your file here says you're David. Your teacher has been calling you Dave, and your mom calls you Davie. What do you want me to call you?"

He sat a moment, apparently thinking. "Maybe Christopher?" he suggested, then looked baffled when we laughed.

Maybe you were named for a grandparent, or you changed your name to erase a painful connection. (And did I mention there's no E on the end of my name, Elsi?) Names are important because they seem to define us, reflect who we are.

The Lord changed people's names throughout the Bible, often giving a new name to highlight a new responsibility or gift. But when He changed Abram ("exalted father") to Abraham ("father of many") and Sarai ("my princess") to Sarah ("princess"), He did more than that. He added an aspirant—the breathy H-sound—to each name. In a sense, He breathed into them a fresh breath of life (see Genesis 2:7 and John 20:22).

You've given me new life, **Lord,** and I'm so grateful. Everything changed when You came into my heart. Help me take in Your love and forgiveness with every breath and share those incomparable gifts each time I exhale. In Jesus' name, amen.

Promise? Really?

I took your father Abraham from the land beyond the Euphrates and led him throughout Canaan and gave him many descendants. I gave him Isaac (Joshua 24:3).

Scripture: Joshua 24:1-13
Song: "God Said It, I Believe It"

"Are we going to lunch, Grandma?" My friend smiled at her little granddaughter. "Yes, dear, as soon as I'm done here."

"OK!" The child ran off. Soon another grandchild appeared. "Are we really going to lunch, Grandma? Are you sure? Are we really?"

"Really," my friend said firmly.

"But Grandma, do you promise?"

"Honey, I told you we are. And I've never lied to you, have I? You can count on it!"

It was interesting to compare the two children. One believed her grandmother and was willing to play patiently until it was time to leave. The other couldn't stop worrying that what her grandmother had said wouldn't really happen. The grandmother hadn't ever lied to either child, but one was able to trust; the other was fearful.

Which am I? I wondered as we waited. Do I trust the Lord, or do I nag Him, asking if He really means what He said?

That's what the Lord was saying to the Israelites: "Hey, you can trust me! I've always done what I told you I'd do, haven't I? So you can believe me this time too."

Loving Father, You've given me no reason to doubt, but I still wonder sometimes. Help me believe Your Word. In Christ I pray. Amen.

Make Time for the Lord

Look to the LORD and his strength; seek his face always. Remember the wonders he has done (Psalm 105:4, 5).

Scripture: Psalm 105:1-11
Song: "What a Friend We Have in Jesus"

King Soopers, my Boulder, Colorado, grocery store, has recently installed a computerized system to keep track of the number of customers and available checkout lanes. This keeps the lines short and makes the customers happy.

There's one problem, though. When the manager says, "We're opening another lane and can take you right over here, ma'am," I refuse.

"Thanks, but I'm happy to wait for Dave King," I say. And the manager sighs and asks someone else. Often there are six or eight of us in Dave's line, while other checkers stand idle. I call us the "Dave King fan club."

Waiting patiently in line, I remember Dave's smiling face. He knows our names, makes eye contact with each of his customers, and makes us feel we're the most important person in the store. I'm more than willing to stand in line to have a few moments with him. It seems to make the whole day go better.

What are some of the wonders the Lord has done for me? Well, there's sunshine, the smell of spring, soft beagle ears, good books, friends, the Bible, salvation . . . I could go on and on. Today may I eagerly make time to seek His face, talk with Him, feel His love, and read His Word.

Lord, thanks for smiling at me, listening to me, and speaking to me through Your Word. When I wait for You, the whole day goes better! In Jesus' name, amen.

Star-Namer

"Now look toward the heavens, and count the stars, if you are able to count them." And He said to him, "So shall your descendants be" (Genesis 15:5, *New American Standard Bible*).

Scripture: Genesis 15:5-21
Song: "Trust in the Promise"

"It's one o'clock in the morning! You said we could go see the Perseid meteor shower."

The Boulder Church must have the only teens in the nation whose youth group is led by two women who are over 60 years old. At this August retreat, Vicki and I were in a mountain house with 11 girls, 5th grade through college age.

We sat on blankets, eyes fixed on the sky. Nothing happened. Finally, someone said, "Let's sing!" Lying on the deck, staring at the stars, we sang. And—I'm not making this up—as we got to the line, "You placed the stars in the sky and You call them by name," we saw a shooting star. Then another, and another.

Someone started "Amazing Grace," and the meteors came again. "I think they're coming because we're singing," a girl said in awed tones. We sang for an hour or so, until sleepiness and the chilly night air drove us back inside.

I was humming as I crawled back into my bed. He made the stars, uncountable, and spread them throughout the heavens. The stars sang at creation, and the Bible confidently says God knows each one by name. He knows your name too.

Abba Father, You know my name, and my heart, my fears and worries, my sins, my desire to be with You. I am loved by the Creator of the universe. Amazing! All praise and glory to You, in the name of Your Son, Jesus. Amen.

He's There, in Joy and Sadness

Haran died in the presence of his father Terah in the land of his birth, in Ur of the Chaldeans (Genesis 11:28, *New American Standard Bible*).

Scripture: Genesis 11:27-32
Song: "Now Thank We All Our God"

"My lilacs are finally blooming, and the bush is so full this year," I told my husband. I felt excited as I admired the lavender blooms. But my mood was marred by sorrow, as I glanced at the empty house just beyond my backyard fence, recalling Alice's recent death. *Who will I give my lilacs to this year?*

Alice loved lilacs and their scent but didn't have any bushes, so I shared mine with her for more than two decades. She'd wanted to die in the home she'd shared with her husband for 40 years, so my sadness grew deeper as I thought of how she died in a hospital among strangers. *I've got to shake this sorrowful attitude, or the rest of the day will be gloomy.*

But then I recalled a tree-lined highway from a recent road trip. What caught my attention were the intermittent dark green pines peeking out among the other varieties of bright green trees. The scene called to mind the occasional dark spots that creep in among the bright spots in my life. They are so subtly blended in—and God's presence and blessing are a part of the mix too—a tapestry of joy and sadness.

My dear Lord, You are with me always, in joy and sorrow. I thank You for Your goodness and loving care in every moment of my days. In Jesus' name, amen.

October 7–13. **Bernita Caesar** lives in Arvada, Colorado, with her husband. She enjoys quilting, scrapbooking, and spending time with her children and grandchildren.

Just Ask

Please say that you are my sister so that it may go well with me because of you, and that I may live on account of you (Genesis 12:13, *New American Standard Bible*).

Scripture: Genesis 12:10-20
Song: "Greater Is He That Is in Me"

As I spilled out the story to a trusted friend, I could see the faintly disguised shock on her face. I hadn't told anyone because I was ashamed of my selfishness.

As an eager new Christian, I wore a small gold angel pin on my collar. I asked the Lord to send my way those whom He wanted me to comfort or just listen to. Coworkers often approached me during my break time and began their conversations with comments about my pin. Eventually, I grew weary of these interruptions. Selfishly, I asked God to stop sending me people.

Guess what? He did. After weeks of peaceful, uninterrupted breaks, I noticed the change. *Whoa, I'd better be more careful, because God takes me at my word.*

I wondered what was happening to those who needed some encouragement or a listening ear. I even visualized the disappointment on God's face. It was a wretched time for me.

After I told my friend all of this, she said, "Just apologize and ask God to change things back." Could it be that easy?

Lord, just as Abraham did, I sometimes ask for the wrong things. I can't thank You enough, though, for allowing me to look at myself and giving me a second chance. Please help me not to become weary in Your service, but to keep trusting You for the strength to minister in Your name. Through Jesus Christ I pray. Amen.

Tracking with Sarai

Sarai said to Abram, "Now behold, the LORD has prevented me from bearing children. Please go in to my maid; perhaps I shall obtain children through her." And Abram listened to the voice of Sarai (Genesis 16:2, *New American Standard Bible*).

Scripture: Genesis 16:1-6
Song: "The Christ of Every Crisis"

The speaker placed a large purse on the podium. She removed the contents, one by one, as she continued to speak about the various ways we could pray. For the next 20 minutes, we heard suggestions for time of day and places to use for prayer. She encouraged us to be unique and creative with our choices and not to copy someone else.

Our lecturer also suggested that the format for our daily prayers could start with praise, followed by confession, continuing with intercession, and closing with our petitions.

"When you ask God for help," she continued, "how many of you really leave your answers up to Him?" Then she took the items from the podium and placed them, individually, back into the purse. "Many of us give God our prayers and worries in the morning," she said. "And then, throughout the day, we take them back, one at a time." My eyes were moist as I thought of how I did this too. It was as if I didn't trust God to do things His way without my help. *Sarai, sometimes we're on the same wavelength, aren't we?*

O Lord God, I am sorry for getting in the way of Your work and trying to engineer the circumstances of my life. Please help me to let go and focus more on trusting in Your omnipotent power. In the Holy name of Jesus, amen.

Repairing the Damage

As for Ishmael, I have heard you; behold, I will bless him, and will make him fruitful and will multiply him exceedingly. He shall become the father of twelve princes, and I will make him a great nation (Genesis 17:20, *New American Standard Bible*).

Scripture: Genesis 17:18-22
Song: "Jesus Is the Answer"

"Now what should I do?" I moaned. I'd discovered a large hole at the bottom edge of the beautiful new friendship shawl I was knitting. It was well over halfway completed, and somewhere along the way I had dropped stitches. The thought of ripping out many inches of work was daunting, so I decided to try and repair it.

The task reminded me of Ishmael's situation. Though he was Abraham's son, he wasn't eligible for the covenant. Abraham knew he and Sarah had made a mistake, and he was concerned for Ishmael's future. God told Abraham He had a plan and would take care of Ishmael, thus repairing the damage, promising to make Ishmael's descendants into a strong, great nation.

I needed a plan too. Before starting, I said a quick prayer because the work would be slow and tedious. Yet the result turned out to be worth my time and effort. Not only did I reinforce the base of the shawl, but the new work blended in perfectly with the whole pattern (just as God does with His plans for us).

O my God, I so often jump ahead of Your plans and make serious mistakes. Please help me to stop, listen, and rely on Your wisdom as You strengthen my life's foundation. I pray this in the name of Jesus. Amen.

Why Pray When You Can Worry?

The matter distressed Abraham greatly because of his son (Genesis 21:11, *New American Standard Bible*).

Scripture: Genesis 21:8-14
Song: "I'll Walk with God"

The sign on a neighborhood church said, "Why Pray When You Can Worry?" This seemed like a strange saying to me as a child, and I used to laugh at it.

Now I'm doing it! In fact I'm known as "the family worrier," and my children joke about it, but I'm not amused. The older I get the more frequently it happens. Even after I think I've left my dismal projections of the future with God, I spend the rest of the day wondering how He's going to help me. My tendency to worry makes me feel as if I'm letting God down.

I've noticed that Abraham usually brought his worries to God, or so it seems, and mostly he waited for God's timing. When he didn't, though, God responded with forgiveness and mercy.

I haven't found a solution to my worrying, but my current plan is to walk more closely with God by talking to Him about every care, large or small. I know this will make my concerns lighter on my shoulders.

There is a tiny wooden sign in my kitchen that says, "Trust in the Lord with all your heart" (Proverbs 3:5). I'll try to take notice of that little plaque more often while reminding myself of the New Testament version: "Cast all your anxiety on him because he cares for you" (1 Peter 5:7).

Faithful God, I know that when I worry, I lose strength for the day. Please give me the grace to keep looking up amidst all circumstances. In Jesus' precious name, amen.

Tie a Knot and Hang On

Sarah died in Kireath-arba (that is, Hebron) in the land of Canaan; and Abraham went in to mourn for Sarah and to weep for her (Genesis 23:2, *New American Standard Bible*).

Scripture: Genesis 23:1-6
Song: "Through It All"

Not again, Lord; it's too much too soon. I had just learned that a friend lost her husband unexpectedly. They were on vacation when he collapsed in a motel room, dying the next day at the hospital. She was the fourth friend of mine who'd lost her husband in the past six months. They'd become widows with no warning.

I'm not sure whether my anguish was from grief or fear that it could happen to me. *I know that You give us trials to make us strong, Lord, but this seems like too much.* I wondered how I would cope with such a heavy, seemingly impossible burden, the kind my friends were facing.

I'm not sure why, but the phrase "tie a knot and hang on" came to mind. It seemed to be God's answer to my earlier prayer. I remembered a large rope I'd seen hanging from a barn with thick knots up the length of it. I saw the rope as God's support, with each knot as either a snag or a handhold.

Abraham has been a good example for me. He mourned Sarah and buried her. Then he trusted the Lord for his next move, just as he'd done all along his journey.

Almighty and faithful Lord, help me to cling to You in times of need. Remind me to trust in Your support and hang on to Your promises. In the name of the Father, the Son, and the Holy Spirit, I pray. Amen.

A Laughing Matter

Is anything too difficult for the LORD? At the appointed time I will return to you, at this time next year, and Sarah will have a son (Genesis 18:14, *New American Standard Bible*).

Scripture: Genesis 17:15-17; 18:9-15; 21:1-7
Song: "God Will Take Care of You"

"This is a surprise! Where are you moving?" said yet another neighbor. She had just seen the unexpected "For Sale" sign in our yard. To each of the inquiries regarding location, schools, and my husband's job (which was ending soon), I had to answer: "We don't know yet."

This was the biggest step my husband and I had ever taken. We were fairly new at leaving decisions in God's hands, so it was a weird and funny situation, although scary. I wasn't sure how to explain it.

I thought of Sarah conceiving Isaac in her 90s. Isaac's name means "laughter," and both Sarah and Abraham did laugh when they heard God foretell the birth of the child. Their son became a permanent reminder, both for them and all generations, that God can be trusted, even when the situation seems laughable.

Well, we sold our home in three weeks, months sooner than expected. Then our out-of-state buyer allowed us to rent it back until the end of the school year. My husband had a job interview two hours after we closed on our new home, and he was hired. God worked out the details in His own way—and better than we could have imagined.

Dear Lord, thank You for Your wise guidance in my life. Please increase my faith and help me to trust in Your timing, no matter how unexplainable. In Jesus' name, amen.

Righteous Faith

Abram believed the LORD, and he credited it to him as righteousness (Genesis 15:6).

Scripture: Genesis 15:1-6
Song: "Faith Is the Victory"

"Ah, here is our very own Abraham," said our minister as he greeted my husband on the first Sunday in our new ministry. He hadn't come across too many men who would leave a lucrative, fulfilling career in the secular world to go into full-time Christian work for a third of the salary.

But it wasn't the first time I'd observed my husband's seemingly casual but committed faith in God. We'd been married only a few months when Roger informed me we'd be moving back to his hometown with seemingly no prospect of jobs. When I asked why, he just said, "I don't know, exactly. But I can't get away from the fact that God has told me we need to go."

So, feeling a little like Abram's wife, Sarai, I packed our few household goods and followed my husband from Texas to Illinois. There I saw firsthand how God confirmed Roger's decision over and over. Now, 17 years later, he unquestioningly followed God to Colorado.

Hudson Taylor once said, "We do not need a great faith, but faith in a great God." Like Abraham and many others before him, Roger believes that what God promises, He accomplishes.

Father, I confess that many times my faith is weak. In my humanness I forget how great You are. I believe—but help my unbelief. In Jesus' name, amen.

October 14–20. **Marjorie Vawter** lives in Colorado and is a freelance editor and writer for various Christian publishers. She has published numerous devotionals.

The God Who Sees

[Hagar] said, "I have now seen the One who sees me" (Genesis 16:13).

Scripture: Genesis 16:7-16
Song: "Open Mine Eyes"

Known as one of the most prolific hymn writers in history, Fanny Crosby penned many of the hymns we still sing today. As a result of an incompetent doctor, Fanny was permanently blinded when she was only 6-weeks-old.

Even though she was physically blind, Fanny wouldn't have it any other way. She said, "It seemed intended by the blessed providence of God that I should be blind all my life, and I thank him for the dispensation. If perfect earthly sight were offered me tomorrow, I would not accept it. I might not have sung hymns to the praise of God if I had been distracted by the beautiful and interesting things about me."

Fanny often spoke of her "spiritual sight" in her hymns. In "Blessed Assurance," for example, she wrote: "visions of rapture now burst on my sight."

As Hagar did, Fanny saw the "well of Thy full salvation that sparkles and flows for me." And she looked forward to the blessed day when she would "see Him face to face" and "know Him by the print of the nails in His hand." As Hagar saw the one who saw her in her need, so also did Fanny Crosby.

Almighty and everlasting God, open my eyes that I may see You, that I may see others as You see them, and that I may see Jesus my Savior and Redeemer. In the name of this same Jesus, who lives and reigns with You and the Holy Spirit, one God, now and forever, amen.

The Ultimate Promise-keeper

You must keep my covenant, you and your descendants after you for the generations to come (Genesis 17:9).

Scripture: Genesis 17:9-14
Song: "Standing on the Promises"

Several weeks ago, our son got married. As the bride and groom exchanged vows, I rejoiced at seeing them willingly enter into their marriage covenant. They chose the traditional vows from the *Book of Common Prayer*: "In the Name of God, I take you to be my wife/husband, to have and to hold from this day forward, for better for worse, for richer for poorer, in sickness and in health, to love and to cherish, until we are parted by death. This is my solemn vow."

Genesis tells us of the vows that were exchanged when God made a covenant with Abraham. Entering into a covenant in Abraham's time was serious business, not taken lightly. God made some pretty awesome promises to Abraham, promises that still stand today. All He asked in return was obedience.

As Randy and Nikki accepted each other's vows, they then exchanged rings as a token of those vows. So God requested a token from Abraham and his descendants when they accepted God's promises—their complete obedience symbolized by circumcision. Similarly, God enters into a covenant relationship with us when we believe and accept the gift of salvation through His Son, Jesus Christ. The symbol? Baptism.

Father, today I recommit my heart, my soul, my life to You. I can do no less when I consider the extent of Your love as You sacrificed Your Son to pay my sin debt. Thank You for Your saving covenant with all who trust in You. In Jesus' name, amen.

God Will Provide

Isaac said, "But where is the lamb for the burnt offering?" Abraham answered, "God himself will provide the lamb for the burnt offering, my son" (Genesis 22:7, 8).

Scripture: Genesis 22:1-8
Song: "Behold! Behold the Lamb of God"

When my husband called me in the middle of the day right after the first of the year, I had no idea how his words would change our lives: "I talked to my boss a little while ago . . . and they're letting me go."

Our country's leaders kept saying we had "turned the corner" and the economy was improving. But the company my husband had worked for during the last 11 years wasn't getting new projects. And they could not afford to keep him on staff.

My first thought was, "What are we going to do?" My income as a freelance editor and writer was sporadic but adequate—as a *supplemental* income. I was already doing as much as I could possibly handle alone. Yet the apostle Paul's words to the Philippians sprang into mind: "My God will meet all your needs according to the riches of his glory in Christ Jesus" (4:19). These words soon became my watchwords of faith.

The job search has lasted nine months now. While we are still waiting on God to provide the job He has for Roger, we have seen His provision, over and over again. Through a variety of people and ways, He has proved faithful.

Father God, You indeed are faithful. You not only provide for my daily needs, You have provided the way of salvation through Your Son, Jesus. I praise You for giving me what I don't deserve and supplying all my needs as well. In Jesus' name, amen.

Faith in Action

"Abraham! Abraham!" . . . **"I know that God is first in your life—you have not withheld even your beloved son from me"** (Genesis 22:11, 12, *The Living Bible*).

Scripture: Genesis 22:9-18
Song: "All for Jesus"

Jim Elliot once said, "He is no fool who gives what he cannot keep to gain what he cannot lose." In early 1956, Jim and four other missionaries to Equador were martyred for their faith by the Auca Indians.

In laying the groundwork for their mission, the five families established a mission compound before searching for Auca villages, using Nate Saint's plane. They found one village and made contact with the people, dropping gifts and messages into the village from the plane. The gifts were received, and several gifts expressing friendship were returned. Soon they received permission from the Aucas to land on Palm Beach, an island in the Curray River. There they met several Aucas and were encouraged by their response. On January 8, Jim radioed his wife, Elisabeth, saying they were going into the village and that they would report back three hours later.

When there was no message, Elisabeth and the other wives contacted the authorities. They found the five men brutally murdered at their campsite. These men had given the ultimate sacrifice of their lives in service to the Lord Jesus Christ.

Father, may I be willing to give my all in Your service as Jim Elliot and many other martyrs of the faith have done in the past. I desire to live out my faith before others, relinquishing all I have to You, so that others see Christ in me. In Jesus' name, amen.

Transparent Living

We can plainly see that the LORD is with you. . . . Look how the LORD has blessed you! (Genesis 26:28, 29, *New Living Translation*).

Scripture: Genesis 26:26-31
Song: "I Am the Vine"

When I "grow up," I want to be like my mother. Oh, not in her looks, necessarily. Nor even with all her health problems, though I have inherited a few of those. But in her heart's desire: that Christ would be seen in her.

Many times I've been with her when someone came and thanked her for reflecting Christ. I believe many will be in Heaven because of the way she lived her life. She sought Him every day, beginning her day early in His Word and prayer. (She was a nurse and often worked the 7–3 day shift). She truly believed that for her to live meant Christ alone. As a result, she overflowed with love for Him and His Word—a love that she passed down to her three children and many others.

The apostle Paul's prayer for the Colossians was the prayer of my mom's heart: ""We continually ask God to fill you with the knowledge of his will through all the wisdom and understanding that the Spirit gives, so that you may live a life worthy of the Lord and please him in every way: bearing fruit in every good work, growing in the knowledge of God" (1:9, 10). This is now my desire too.

Father in Heaven, my heart's desire is that others see Christ in me. It doesn't come easily, for in learning more of Christ, I must enter into His life of suffering. But drawing others to You—by His life lived in me—is worth it all. I pray this prayer in the name of Jesus, my merciful Savior and Lord. Amen.

Reward of Obedience

Do as I say. . . . If you do, I will be with you and bless you (Genesis 26:2, 3, *The Living Bible*).

Scripture: Genesis 21:12-14, 17-21; 26:2-5, 12, 13
Song: "There Shall Be Showers of Blessing"

"Obedience is the very best way to show that you believe," my young daughter warbled joyfully, as she went out to play. "Doing exactly what the Lord commands."

I stood inside the screen door watching her and shaking my head. Not at the truth she was singing but at how quickly and glibly it poured out. Especially as she had just been disciplined for disobedience. Obviously, our talk on what obedience looked like triggered the song she'd heard and sung many times before.

As she went on into the chorus, spelling out the word *obedience*, the thought crossed my mind that I was no better than she was when it came to my obedience to the Lord. Could others see through my actions to my reluctance at times to obey? Did they see the avoidance measures, the "exception clauses" I created in order to look good in my disobedience?

God reminded me that day that while He demands my obedience, He also blesses His children who do what He says. As I listened to one of His greatest blessings to me (my daughter) finish the song, I recommitted to obeying my heavenly Father . . . right away. With joy.

Father, I'm reminded that I need to learn obedience. Even Your perfect, spotless Son had to learn this lesson through His suffering. But You have also promised that when I have learned it, You will shower me with Your blessings. Thank You for Your faithfulness and goodness. In Your holy name I pray. Amen.

Insatiable Quest for Guidance

Everyone who drinks this water will be thirsty again, but whoever drinks the water I give them will never thirst (John 4:13, 14).

Scripture: John 4:1-15
Song: "We're Feeding on the Living Bread"

A young mother of three was debating with friends about the kind of discipline she should use with her 6-year-old daughter. The little girl hadn't treated her younger sister respectfully, and Mom was frustrated with her behavior. She told the young girl that she was not allowed to have a birthday party with all of her friends, only with her family.

In the social media outlet the mother uses frequently, she asked her friends to comment on whether she had done the right thing. After several comments, the mother added that the young girl had already told her friends at school that she was having a party—and the friends were excited about celebrating her special day with her. Therefore, this mother felt as though she had already lost the battle and had no choice but to give in to the little girl.

In all of the comments that people shared, no one directed Mom to what God has to say about disciplining children. She couldn't find peace with her decisions from her friends. But if we allow God the opportunity, He will fill us with wisdom and peace.

Lord, when I am listening to the ramblings of others, may I run to You for guidance, understanding, and wisdom. In Jesus' name, amen.

October 21–27. **Dawn Cherie Olson** is an international business virtual professor and stewardship ministry leader. She writes about finances and relationships from Nashville, Tennessee.

Noting Preferences

Now, my son, listen carefully and do what I tell you: Go out to the flock and bring me two choice young goats, so I can prepare some tasty food for your father, just the way he likes it (Genesis 27:8, 9).

Scripture: Genesis 27:1-10
Song: "Come and Dine"

"All things are ready, come to the feast." As a traditional southern family, we knew that food is the center of socializing in the home. There was never an event, holiday, celebration, or death that didn't involve massive amounts of food.

The most important of these meals for our family was Sunday dinner. As a young girl learning to prepare the meals, I was taught how my father preferred his food. I followed my mother's ways, and I watched the pleasure of a well-cooked meal shine in my father's eyes as he savored each and every bite.

As a child, though I wasn't skilled enough to prepare those fried chicken dinners, I'd rummage around in the refrigerator looking for the cold cuts for Dad's sandwich. I would serve him a sandwich with just the right amount of tomato, crisp lettuce, and bologna—on a plate with a napkin gently tucked underneath. He'd be listening to the Kentucky Wildcats game over the radio in his dusky office and always welcomed my tasty interruptions.

Bringing something pleasing to him made me feel loved and appreciated. Isn't it that way with the heavenly Father too?

Lord, may I prepare for You in a way that is pleasing to Your eyes and heart. Please guide me in my kingdom work. In Jesus' name, amen.

Under the Disguise

Then Rebekah took the best clothes of Esau her older son, which she had in the house, and put them on her younger son Jacob. She also covered his hands and the smooth part of his neck with the goatskins (Genesis 27:15, 16).

Scripture: Genesis 27:11-17
Song: "Remove My Covering, Lord"

As my daughter approached her first Halloween, we read books about finding costumes, trick-or-treating, and the disguises that people wear for fun. She seemed excited about the holiday, and I felt I had adequately prepared her for it.

We started with the fall festival at church where they were hosting a "trunk-or-treat." It was during the early evening, and she had so much fun walking up to the decorated cars filled with candy. We arrived home at dusk, and my husband joyfully prepared to take her trick-or-treating. She held his hand tightly as the many children raced from house to house, asking for their treats. After a few minutes, she was running too and having a great time.

The best part of Halloween, of course, is simply recalling that the word is short for "All Hallow's Eve" in the traditional church year. It's the day before what is often refered to All Saints' Day, when we remember loved ones and Christian martyrs who have gone on before us.

Lord, let us recognize Your graceful presence in all things, and give us clear vision to see past others' disguises. And may we be assured that nothing can cover us from Your view and Your love. In Jesus' name, amen.

A Unique Scent

So he went to him and kissed him. When Isaac caught the smell of his clothes, he blessed him and said, "Ah, the smell of my son is like the smell of a field that the LORD has blessed" (Genesis 27:27).

Scripture: Genesis 27:18-29
Song: "Christ, from Whom All Blessings Flow"

How exciting to prepare for the arrival of a child! One of the most rewarding times for me, as a mother, was sorting all of the baby clothes. After washing those new baby clothes, I opened the dryer, and the aroma of baby detergent filled the air.

I breathed deeply and took in all of the sweet smells of the clean, new clothes. Being highly sensitive to scents during pregnancy, this was a welcome change.

I folded each of the little outfits and placed them gently in the drawers. My mom had always said to put a bar of scented soap in your drawers to keep the clothes smelling fresh, and I had chosen some lightly fragrant ones for my daughter's dresser.

I was ready for her little sweetness to arrive. But once she came into our lives, her sweet smell often collided with the foul odor of used diapers and spit-up!

So, my laundry pile was large, but each time I opened the dryer, the aroma of the baby detergent would once again fill the air. Except now, the clothes also had her scent, unique and wonderful to me.

Lord, may we savor the gentle reminders of Your presence through the natural aromas of Your world. Help us to appreciate all things that You have created in their own uniqueness. Through Christ I pray. Amen.

Ongoing Battle—for "Stuff"?

Your name will no longer be Jacob, but Israel, because you have struggled with God and with humans and have overcome (Genesis 32:28).

Scripture: Genesis 32:22-30
Song: "Fight the Battle in the Body"

In my professional life, I've had many adventures that were generally driven by financial need. My first jobs were the typical teenager jobs: video store, pizza place, hamburger and ice cream shop, and franchise restaurants. During those times, I was beginning to earn my own money and discover what it was like to be "independently wealthy."

In the decade that followed, I began training and searching for jobs that would further my financial well-being. And during this whole time, I battled with God about what I was supposed to have and how I was supposed to get it. My problem was that I so often sacrificed family, friends, and coworkers to forward my own agenda. I was once in a lawsuit over a $12 late fee for video rentals.

Through all of these battles, I did not prepare. I had no armor, no vision of the goal, and no strategy. I was financially driven to obtain the things "society" seemed to tell me I needed. I had far more than most at an early age. And yet, I selfishly held on to my stuff. During the 10 years after that, I began to lose my stuff and recognize that what God provided was more than enough.

Lord, may I begin each day by cloaking myself in Your armor. Guide me through each trial with Your wisdom. Though I may not always know how I will get through, I ask that You strengthen me by prayer and the Word. In Christ, amen.

A Sacred Place

Jacob set up a stone pillar at the place where God had talked with him, and he poured out a drink offering on it; he also poured oil on it (Genesis 35:14).

Scripture: Genesis 35:9-15
Song: "Hush! Blessed Are the Dead"

Jean slowly walked through the cemetery, arm in arm with her two daughters. They were visiting the family grave site to place flowers around her husband's resting place. It was nearly two years ago, on this day, when she had heard the news from the doctor that it was time to "make him comfortable" at home. They had ordered the appropriate hospital bed and walkers, but she wasn't sure how much time she had with him.

When they brought him home, she turned on his favorite John Wayne movie and sat near him. He couldn't talk much, but he gently squeezed her hand when she reached out to him. Three months later, he passed away in his sleep.

Jean wandered around and looked at the places around their home that she wouldn't change. Although her health was failing too, she wanted to honor her husband and the life they had shared together. She gave away all of his clothes and shoes, but she left his hats hanging neatly on the hall stand, right where he left them. In the beautiful rolling hills of the Kentucky countryside, she knelt down. Laying the flowers gently next to the headstone, she ran her fingers over his engraved name and prayed.

God of all the saints, living and dead, may I honor You in this sacred place where You have spoken with me. May I be still and listen as You bless me with Your grace and mercy. In the holy name of Jesus, my Lord and Savior, I pray. Amen.

A New Land

The LORD will be my God and this stone that I have set up as a pillar will be God's house, and of all that you give me I will give you a tenth (Genesis 28:21, 22).

Scripture: Genesis 28:1, 10-22
Song: "God Has Set the Land Before Us"

Bryson had been packing for weeks to move to their new apartment. Though he'd been actively looking for jobs, he hadn't yet received an offer of employment. His mother called every day, trying to talk him out of moving to another state.

He was moving with his wife and their two small children. Cara had been a stay-at-home mom for several years now and was ready to return to work. As a result, she wanted to move close to her family for support. He could see the pain in her eyes and the longing for a fresh start.

Yet his mother and father couldn't understand this "leap of faith." Bryson believed God would provide for him and his family as long as he continued to be obedient. Yet how could he explain this faith to his family?

With significant anxiety, he called them and told about how many doors had been opened to him and his wife since they had decided to move. There was no denying that God had a guiding hand in their journey. As they sat on their new patio, he sighed with relief at the blessings that continued to come through for them.

O Lord, I praise You for all the blessings You've poured into my life down through the years. Today, help me recognize every good thing You provide— and lift up my heart in gratitude. In the name of the Father, the Son, and the Holy Spirit, I pray. Amen.

What Kind of Legacy?

Then a new king, to whom Joseph meant nothing, came to power in Egypt (Exodus 1:8).

Scripture: Exodus 1:7-14
Song: "Make Me a Blessing"

What child doesn't remember the story of Joseph, his colorful coat, and the dreams—oh yes, the dreams that came true. Joseph saw the sun, moon, and stars bowing down to him. And picture the lean cows eating up the fat ones in the Pharaoh's dreams. Through these dreams, Joseph was shown God's plan for his life.

God worked through Joseph to protect the lives of the Egyptians and the children of Israel. But even with Joseph's great accomplishments, there came a time when the kings of Egypt would remember him no more.

Do you ever wonder how you'll be remembered? Do you feel that someday your good deeds will be buried along with your body? As the years pass, I consider whether my life story will have any meaning for my children and grandchildren. Will the way I've lived my life influence them positively? I'm not sure, but today I'll take the time to look at my legacy and consider the effect of my deeds on God's work in the world. I want to be creating a "life story" that God will honor and remember, even if the world forgets.

Dear Father, today I examine my actions in the light of Your perfection. Help me to see where I'm pleasing You—and where I can improve. In Jesus' name, amen.

October 28–31. **Diane Gruchow** lives in the Colorado mountains with her husband of 50 years. She spends her time writing, mentoring single moms, and riding her horses.

Quiet Courage

The midwives, however, feared God and did not do what the king of Egypt had told them to do; they let the boys live (Exodus 1:17).

Scripture: Exodus 1:15-22
Song: "I Know Who Holds Tomorrow"

The young father ran back toward the house. His right sleeve was on fire, but he didn't even notice. "Help me, they're in there! Help me! My boys!" He shattered the door with his burning arm and threw himself inside. His two little guys were huddled together by the bedroom door. The man lifted them from the inferno and ran.

Bravery comes in many forms. This Texas dad, who saved the lives of his children from their burning mobile home, demonstrated courage amidst extreme physical danger. But there's another type of courage that sometimes goes unnoticed. It's the quiet strength that we gain by depending upon the Holy Spirit to guide our actions.

Recently I hurt a friend and needed to apologize for my actions. But I was afraid she might reject my attempt to make things right. Through prayer, God gave me the courage to call her, and our relationship was mended. It seems such a small thing now, but facing even one of those everyday fears becomes a big hurdle to jump if we try to do it without God's help.

Dear Lord, may I have the courage to give You every one of my fears, to place them in Your beautiful, strong hands. Sometimes I feel so afraid of what this life will bring, but I do truly believe that You are king over all. You control everything that I fear. Thank You, my Father, in Jesus' name. Amen.

Are You Watching?

When she could hide him no longer, she got a papyrus basket for him and coated it with tar and pitch. Then she placed the child in it and put it among the reeds along the bank of the Nile. His sister stood at a distance to see what would happen to him (Exodus 2:3, 4).

Scripture: Exodus 2:1-10
Song: "How Strong and Sweet My Father's Care"

The clock ticks its seconds, one by one. The sun begins to rise in the gray morning sky, and all the while I watch and wait. I watch to see what's happening in the forest around me. Are the tiny new rabbits safe? Is the young coyote still around? Will I see deer this morning?

Waiting and watching can bring us a sense of calm and peace. But sometimes the specters of fear or pain march along with those waiting ticks of the clock. So often, our watching is more important than my early morning musing. Sometimes it involves weightier matters.

Moses' sister was on guard duty. She was making sure that he would be safe. You can be certain that, if there was danger, she would rescue him. But for now, she was *watching* and *waiting*.

Sometimes it's all we can do, and it's hard. You may be waiting to see if that wayward child will see the light and come back to God. You may be watching over a seriously ill loved one. These are painful things, but remember, God is watching too.

Father God, I know You see everything in my life, and You love me so much that my waiting and watching touches Your heart. Help me to feel Your presence while I wait and to know that You have my whole world in Your hands. In Jesus' name, amen.

No Longer a Stranger

Zipporah gave birth to a son, and Moses named him Gershom, saying, "I have become a foreigner in a foreign land" (Exodus 2:22).

Scripture: Exodus 2:15-25
Song: "I'm But a Stranger Here"

My grandfather, Gustav, immigrated to the United States from Lithuania as a young man. Honest and upright, he worked hard to develop his land and became respected by his neighbors as a diligent man, true to his word. However, within a few years, things changed.

A world war caused uncertainty, anger, and uneasiness among the people. Those same neighbors, whose respect he had earned, turned against him. Since Gustav and his family spoke German in their home, they were suspect, and he was now viewed as an alien, even an enemy in his adopted land.

Neighbors conjured up lies about him. The FBI searched his barns for anything that would tie him to Germany. His wife and children suffered name-calling and other abuse. No longer accepted, he truly became a stranger in a foreign land.

When you feel like a stranger in your world, don't despair. If you claim Jesus as your Savior, you belong. You belong to the Creator of the universe. You are God's child, and that's a pretty impressive lineage. You're no longer a stranger, but a member of the family cherished and valued by God, your Father.

My loving Father, thank You for making me part of Your family. Sometimes I feel like a stranger in this world; I don't always fit. But God, please help me remember that I do belong to You. In Your Son's name I ask this. Amen.

DEVOTIONS®

NOVEMBER

Who among the gods is like you, LORD? Who is like you—majestic in holiness, awesome in glory, working wonders?

—Exodus 15:11.

Gary Wilde, Editor   **Margaret Williams,** Project Editor   Photo © Hemera | Thinkstock®

DEVOTIONS® is published quarterly by Standard Publishing, Cincinnati, Ohio, www.standardpub.com. © 2012 by Standard Publishing. All rights reserved. Topics based on the Home Daily Bible Readings, International Sunday School Lessons. © 2010 by the Committee on the Uniform Series. Printed in the U.S.A. All Scripture quotations, unless otherwise indicated, are taken from the HOLY BIBLE, *NEW INTERNATIONAL VERSION®. NIV®.* Copyright © 2011 by Biblica. Used by permission of Zondervan. All rights reserved. *The Living Bible (TLB)* © 1971 by Tyndale House Publishers, Wheaton, IL. Holy Bible, *New Living Translation (NLT),* © 1996, 2004. Used by permission Tyndale House Publishers. All rights reserved.

God Doesn't Cover His Eyes

When they heard that the LORD **was concerned about them and had seen their misery, they bowed down and worshiped** (Exodus 4:31).

Scripture: Exodus 4:27-31
Song: "Somebody Cares"

After the car accident that almost took the life of her husband, Shirley sat by his bedside watching his chest rise and fall. She watched as he groaned in pain and struggled for breath. Day after day, she watched and prayed and, at times, she just covered her eyes. She didn't want to see him this way.

Looking at someone in great pain hurts, doesn't it? And the hurt is compounded many times over when we love that person dearly. I wonder if God hurts when He sees the misery and pain in this world. I wonder if He wishes that He didn't have to see it, especially since He loves us so completely.

The Scripture says that He saw the misery of His people and was concerned about them. In 2 Corinthians 1:3, the Bible describes God as "the Father of compassion and the God of all comfort." What a warm feeling it gives me to know of God's compassion for all of His people.

So when we're in pain, whether physical or emotional, we can be assured that the "God of all comfort" is watching. He's not hiding His eyes. He looks on our pain and comforts us in love.

Father, there is so much hurt and pain around me, but I know how much You care for Your people. So I praise and worship You for Your love. In Jesus' name, amen.

November 1–3. **Diane Gruchow** lives in the Colorado Mountains with her husband of 50 years. She spends her time writing, mentoring single moms, and riding her horses.

Take Off Your Sandals

"Do not come any closer," God said. "Take off your sandals, for the place where you are standing is holy ground" (Exodus 3:5).

Scripture: Exodus 3:1-6
Song: "We Are Standing on Holy Ground"

The old Marine tried to stand at attention while the flag was passing by. It was difficult for him to raise his body out of his wheelchair, but he would allow himself no excuses. He would stand, and he would salute. This flag was the symbol of the country he loved, respected, and had fought for.

A woman sitting next to him tried to help but didn't have the strength. As a young man walked by, he saw the struggle. He saw the tears beginning to form in the old Marine's eyes, and he stopped, lifted the old man to a standing position, and removed his own baseball cap. The people around them noticed what was happening and, one by one, stood in silent respect for this soldier and the symbol of the country he loved.

God told Moses to show respect, to take off his sandals. This was holy ground. God was there, and respect for the awesome king of the universe was clearly demanded. It's worship, and worship is all about giving God the respect due Him in His presence. As I think of my Master, my God—as I try to do His will, and as I pray to Him—I'm standing on holy ground, always in His presence.

My Father, I praise Your name. Thank You for the example of Moses, his life and desire to serve You. May You smile at my small efforts to show the respect You deserve. Because Jesus opened the door to your throne room, I pray. Amen.

He Sees That Pink Pumpkin!

Moses said to God, "Who am I that I should go to Pharaoh and bring the Israelites out of Egypt?" And God said, "I will be with you" (Exodus 3:11, 12).

Scripture: Exodus 3:7-17
Song: "My God, Accept My Heart This Day"

God answered Moses with these words, "I will be with you." It's interesting to me that the Lord didn't try to talk Moses out of his lack of confidence. Maybe that tells us something.

When my child proudly hands me a drawing of a pink circle with three black dots, I'd better be a little careful what I say. If I pretend to understand his rough drawing and say, "It looks just like you," he may burst into tears, and I will have forfeited the trust he had in me. (Or at the very least, he will wonder at my poor eyesight!)

Couldn't I recognize that this was a pink pumpkin? I don't help him by pretending to understand his picture, and God doesn't pretend either. He knows our abilities and wants us to use them.

If there is something God asks us to do, we can trust Him to know what can be accomplished with our abilities and to bridge any difficulties. So, if God asks you to speak to Pharaoh—or to a group of teens or to your neighbor—you can be sure that He knows your limitations, and that He will recognize the "pink pumpkin" of your efforts. God didn't tell Moses, "You can do it." He told Moses, and He tells us, "I will be with you."

My Father, today I will do my best to paint a beautiful picture for You. Please help me see my abilities and inabilities with Your eyes. In Jesus' name, amen.

Early Morning

Jesus walked by. John looked at him intently and then declared, "See! There is the Lamb of God!" (John 1:36, *The Living Bible*).

Scripture: John 1:29-37
Song: "Behold the Glories of the Lamb"

The earth is hard under my feet. A frosty, chilly morning alerts me to summer's end. The sweet smell of sagebrush fills the air as I walk a mile trying to maintain a steady pace.

Along the mountain trail, I come to a standstill. A heavy mist blankets the valley below while distant mountain peaks seem to burst above the fog, moisture hanging like teardrops under the foliage.

Then a single ray of sun, shining through the droplets, creates a myriad of color—a tiny rainbow. *God is near.* I can feel His presence walking with me. When I arrive at the bridge, I know I'm at my halfway point. Gazing up the river, I look to the heavens and say, "Lord, wash over me, as the river washes over the rocks below. In this beautiful moment, please cleanse me!"

It's a habit now—this morning walk with Jesus. When I look at the sky, I realize without a shadow of a doubt that He is my redeemer, "The Lamb of God, who takes away the sin of the world" (John 1:29).

Lord, why am I in such a hurry? I wonder how many times You pass me by and I don't notice? Don't allow me to miss a moment with You. Help me be more aware of Your constant presence. In the name of Jesus, I pray. Amen.

November 4–10. **Shirley Reynolds** is a freelance writer living in a rural community in the mountains of Idaho. Besides writing, one of her passions is riding her 4-wheeler through the back country.

He Answers: But How and When?

Moses went back to the LORD. "LORD," he protested, **"How can you mistreat your own people like this? Why did you ever send me, if you were going to do this to them?"** (Exodus 5:22, *The Living Bible*).

Scripture: Exodus 5:19-23
Song: "Wherever He Leads I'll Go"

Listening intently to an account of the murders of Korean orphans, I asked God, "How can anyone harm innocent children? Why, Lord, do you allow these things to happen?"

When the conference speaker was finished, she asked: "Will you please pick up a wooden cross from the front table, as a reminder to pray for abused children around the world?"

I was tired from attending classes all day at the Colorado Christian Writer's conference, but I took a cross and held it in my hand. Heading out the door into the chilly night air, I walked to my room.

"Lord," I said, "I don't understand why children have to die!"

When I stepped into my room, I looked through my window at the snowcapped peaks of the Rockies, and I stood and prayed. "O God, I know that in all things, You work for the good, and that even amidst great evil, there is hope for redemption. But it's so hard for me to grasp."

I felt like Moses, who speaks in our Scripture today. I know God will answer me—but I still don't know how, I still don't know when.

God, I know that while we live in this world, bad things will happen. I put my hope in that day when You make all things right by Your omnipotent power. In Christ, amen.

His Power: to Thunder . . . to Care

I am Jehovah, the Almighty God who appeared to Abraham, Isaac, and Jacob—though I did not reveal my name, Jehovah, to them (Exodus 6:2, 3, *The Living Bible*).

Scripture: Exodus 6:2-9
Song: "How Majestic Is Your Name"

The words *Father, God, Jehovah,* and *Almighty* reveal a stronger, higher power than any of us. There are times, though, when I forget that awesome majesty in the busyness of my life.

My father used to say that every time it thundered, it meant that the angels were bowling. But one night, when my grandson was staying with us in our mountain cabin, we experienced a horrific storm. Trying not to show my fear, I watched the lightning flash across the sky. Yet when the thunder crashed, rattling the windows, I trembled.

My grandson and I watched, while I tried to comfort him. Ponderosa Pines swayed back and forth, and the wind blew branches and pine needles across our deck. I started to say, "That's quite a bowling game in Heaven," when 7-year-old Mikie looked at me and said, "Come on, Grandma, don't be afraid—it's just a storm."

I thought about his comment and God's awesome power displayed in this frightening thunderstorm. The Lord is so much bigger than I could ever understand. Then I felt a little hand on my shoulder. "Don't worry, Grandma; God will take care of us."

My awesome Heavenly Father, help me to see Your wonder in simple things and not question Your intent in my life. Help me to accept Your mighty power and majesty in all things—even in Your ability to take care of me. Through Christ I pray. Amen.

Wasn't It a Miracle?

The LORD had told Moses, "Pharaoh won't listen, and this will give me the opportunity of doing mighty miracles to demonstrate my power" (Exodus 11:9, *The Living Bible*).

Scripture: Exodus 11
Song: "Under His Wings"

As God told Moses that "Pharaoh won't listen, and this will give me the opportunity of doing mighty miracles," I've wondered, *Do we expect miracles today?*

A blood clot in my brain put me in a coma for three days. Even while asleep, I heard every word between the doctor and my family. Evidently, the doctors didn't believe I would survive.

Thankfully, God had another plan. In my comatose dreams, I walked down a narrow path with Jesus and begged Him to let me live and tell others about Him. I wanted to write.

Jesus walked with me, and then I awakened. It was Sunday morning, and it took awhile for me to open my eyes and realize that I had indeed survived. My first request was, "Please call my husband!"

In my humble opinion, God performed a miracle in my life. But I've wondered since, "Did the hospital staff see a miracle in my awakening?"

"There will be side effects," the doctors had said—but there were none. I've wondered about the nurse who took my blood each day. What did she think when I opened my eyes . . . and she screamed?

Lord, thanks for the miracle of salvation by grace. Help me live in such a way that I'll always expect miracles to happen, large and small. In Jesus' name, amen.

All Through the Years

Your children ask, "What does all this mean? What is this ceremony about?" (Exodus 12:26, *The Living Bible*).

Scripture: Exodus 12:21-28
Song: "God's Word Is Our Great Heritage"

"Daddy, why do you tell me stories about the church, the Bible, and God?" I asked.

"Because God wants us to pass these stories on to our families and friends," he said. "Then you can tell them to your own children some day."

I've thought about my heritage. I was raised in the church from birth. I've thought about special people in my life, who have passed on tidbits of truth to me, and in turn, I've passed those stories on to my children and my grandson.

My family used to spend part of each summer at our local church camp meeting, parking our trailer on a site we'd purchased. Evening services were held beneath a canvas tent with a carpet of straw, and there a certain tall Texas preacher made a lasting impact on my life — Dr. B. V. Seals. He had a booming voice, and I was captivated with his stories.

My father repeated many camp meeting stories to me as I sat on his lap before bedtime. When I asked my father, "Why do people go to the altar?" His answer was, "God meets you there. He forgives your sins and He loves you." The words spoken by great evangelists — and the words spoken by my own father — have stayed with me all through the years.

Father, may I never forget the times when I've felt You were so near me. Remind me to share those experiences with other people too. In Jesus' name, amen.

A Church Choir Miracle

The people of Israel followed all of Jehovah's instructions to Moses and Aaron (Exodus 12:50, *The Living Bible*).

Scripture: Exodus 12:43-51
Song: "The Blood Will Never Lose Its Power"

One morning I felt as if God were instructing me to "Assemble the church choir and go to Memory's bedside and perform the Easter musical!"

"You want us to perform the musical at a hospital?" Had this indeed been the Holy Spirit's nudging? My friend, Memory, was dying of brain cancer. And I know that her one great wish was to hear the Easter musical before she died.

I made a few calls, and eight choir members arrived at the hospital. With God's help, we performed the entire cantata for a dying friend.

We sang with gusto. Memory smiled, with tears flowing down her cheeks. When we finished, she hugged each one of us and said, "Thank you for making my wish come true!" Her family was seated in the hallway, and her son walked into the room weeping. He hugged me, and said, "There is nothing more you could have done to give her happiness—except what you did today. Thank you!"

As we walked from her room, we saw doctors and nurses quietly clapping. They lined the hallway. It was then I knew God had orchestrated more than just the music. Later that afternoon, Memory went to be with the Lord.

Dear Father, help me listen closely, each day, for Your still, small voice. Let me never miss an opportunity to follow Your instructions! In Jesus' name, amen.

Ready for the Lord's Visit?

This is how you are to eat it: with your cloak tucked into your belt, your sandals on your feet and your staff in your hand. Eat it in haste; it is the LORD'S Passover (Exodus 12:11).

Scripture: Exodus 12:1-14
Song: "Since Jesus Passed By"

Dad lived his life as if each day were his last. In his later years, he often said he was "ready to go home." When he suffered a severe stroke, his care became my responsibility.

He was hardly able to speak, but we walked the aisles of the care center, and I talked to him about my life. He loved to sit in the courtyard, but in his small room, he sat in his own rocking chair. In the midst of my conversations with him, he would walk over to the window, gaze up at the sky, and lose himself in his own thoughts. Every now and then he'd cry.

I held his hands and thought about all the things Dad had taught me through the years. "Always be ready to go," he'd say. "Never lay your head on your pillow, unless you are ready."

I've thought about those words since and try to make each day count for God. Some days I may not accomplish a whole lot—but I know all my days are blessed with God's presence. When Dad passed away, he left this earth but he also left me a heritage beyond value. When I feel distressed over some problem, I often remember his words: "Be ever ready!"

O Eternal Lord God, show me how to be ready at all times for Your direction. Help me to have my traveling clothes on—to be prepared—and ready to go with my walking stick. I don't want to miss Your visit. In the holy name of Jesus, my Lord and Savior, I pray. Amen.

Intentional Living

Let the Holy Spirit guide your lives. Then you won't be do-ing what your sinful nature craves (Galatians 5:16, *New Living Translation*).

Scripture: Galatians 5:13-21
Song: "Draw Me Close"

While we were shopping, my 3-year-old daughter found a pocket sewing kit. Oblivious to the hazardous needles, she fo-cused on the bright thread and sparkly buttons. Excitedly she asked if she could have it. I explained to her what it was, told her no, and moved on.

We had made our purchases and had buckled ourselves in the car when I noticed she was being oddly quiet. "What are you holding?" I asked. Very slowly she pulled the little sewing kit out from her coat. "I really wanted it, Mama."

I could see that my daughter was in great turmoil. Some-thing inside her knew it was wrong, yet she wanted it so badly. My first thought: *I can't believe my child is a shoplifter!* My second thought: *We are all born sinners—and this is a teachable moment.* The lesson unfolded as we returned to the store.

Because sin is natural to us, our struggles will never get easier until we surrender control to the Holy Spirit. Yet, as we lay down our own desires, we realize that all we really need is Him.

Father, my deepest desire is to live by the power of the Holy Spirit, but I am a work in progress, and I know You don't expect perfection in my Christian growth. Thankfully, the perfection came in the work of Jesus on the cross. Through Him I pray. Amen.

November 11–17. **Tami Lambertson** was born and raised in the Midwest. She is a freelance writer and licensed minister.

The Little Things

In the future, your children will ask you, "What does all this mean?" Then you will tell them, "With the power of his mighty hand, the LORD brought us out of Egypt, the place of our slavery" (Exodus 13:14, *New Living Translation*).

Scripture: Exodus 13:11-16
Song: "He Saved Us to Show His Glory"

As a stay-at-home mother of three, I often babysit for a bit of extra cash. So it's common to have six or seven little ones gathered around the table for lunch. On one such occasion, I reminded one of our guests not to eat until we had prayed. With an incredulous look he blurted, "You pray in the daytime? We wait until we go to bed at our house!"

When the laughter subsided, my son seized the opportunity to explain how we choose to thank God for providing our food before we eat it. The rest of our dinner conversation revolved around the Lord, His Word, and His promises to us. That simple act of praying became a witness to God's goodness.

My approach to everyday situations should be a testimony of His faithfulness. Telling others about what Jesus has done isn't a presentation; it's simply part of an ongoing conversation. It's the little things — things I might not give a second thought to — that provide such immense opportunities to speak of the Lord to tell about all He has done for us.

O God, the King of glory, thank You that I am no longer a slave to sin. As I quietly live for You, let my actions shout the difference in my life, because of Your goodness and grace toward me. When curious souls begin to question, may I be quick to give You the glory. In Jesus' name I pray. Amen.

You Are My Light

The LORD went ahead of them. He guided them during the day with a pillar of cloud, and he provided light at night with a pillar of fire (Exodus 13:21, *New Living Translation*).

Scripture: Exodus 13:17-22
Song: "Lead Me, Lord"

The hour was late. I was lost. Without much choice, I decided to keep following the confident voice of my car's GPS. My stomach was in knots as I made turn after turn, driving deeper into some rough-looking neighborhoods of a huge city. I knew I would reach my last stop, but the current route seemed to have no outlet. And . . . this definitely wasn't a place to get out and ask for directions, so I just kept looking into the distance for signs.

Finally, I turned onto a main avenue and, within half a block, arrived at my desired destination. Before venturing anywhere else, I changed the settings on the navigation system from "shortest route" to "fastest time" to avoid the back roads in this unfamiliar territory.

I'm so grateful the Lord promises to be my guide, just as He guided His people through the desert so long ago. I can depend on Him to lead the way, even in the darkest hour, through the scariest situations. If I make a wrong turn or get off course, I can get back on track by allowing His Word to light my path and by listening for the confident whispers to my heart.

Father, I know You might not take me through on the "fastest time," but You guarantee I'll reach my destination. You truly know what's best for me, so thank You for being my light and guiding me. Help me to trust the directions You give. Lead me, Lord, in Jesus' name. Amen.

Hot Pursuit

The Egyptians chased after them with all the forces in Pharaoh's army—all his horses and chariots, his charioteers, and his troops (Exodus 14:9, *New Living Translation*).

Scripture: Exodus 14:5-9
Song: "Power of Your Love"

Several years ago, Charlotte was diagnosed with a chronic illness. With no known cause and no known cure, she was depending on God to heal her body. Eventually, Charlotte had no choice but to check into the hospital until her flare-up was under control.

The initial news was devastating: she had no medical coverage for her preexisting condition. All her summer plans came to a screeching halt. *Why did this have to happen now?* Between the pain and an uncertain future, Charlotte felt the *enemy* known as discouragement closing in.

Nevertheless, Charlotte put her faith in high gear. She decided that if she was going to be confined to a bed, it wasn't going to be wasted time. What the enemy meant for harm, God would use for good. Instead of looking at the problem, she looked at those around her. Charlotte made the most of every opportunity and shared God's love with all who entered her room.

The way Charlotte walked through her trial proved the old adage, "The greater the test, the greater the testimony." In moments of life when you feel chased by every adversary, look to Jesus. He has a bigger plan in mind.

Dear Heavenly Father, thank You for Your constant protection. I know that whatever I face, it is covered by the power of Your love. In Jesus' name, amen.

Remain Calm

The LORD himself will fight for you. Just stay calm (Exodus 14:14, *New Living Translation*).

Scripture: Exodus 14:10-14
Song: "I Don't Need Anything but You"

The bills piled up, and Adam and Julia were in a real mess. Since their daughter's surgery, they just couldn't seem to catch up. Yet the couple was determined to make ends meet on one income; that would keep Julia home with their young brood.

However, she was growing tired of the lifestyle of sacrifice. God had given her two hands and a solid work ethic—wasn't it time to put them to use?

As she browsed the classifieds for opportunities, her son approached. "Mommy, when I go to Heaven, can I give Jesus a hug?" Julia pulled the child near for a conversation about the person of Jesus, His love, and His closeness to them. In her attempt to teach her boy, she received encouragement of her own. Julia threw away the newspaper with a renewed sense of hope that God's faithfulness never ends.

When facing our enemies, it's hard to see the face of the Lord. We strategize about how to take care of a problem, thinking we can fix things quicker and easier. Being still has the appearance of doing nothing. But often the act of being still or remaining calm requires more wisdom and discipline than immediately attempting to repair things on our own.

Heavenly Father, help me to look to You in the midst of the battles of Christian growth. As I remain calm, You will fight the fight. Let me not grow weary or impatient, knowing that Your plan is always the best. In Christ's name I pray. Amen.

Just Wishin' and Whinin'?

Then the LORD said to Moses, "Why are you crying out to me? Tell the people to get moving!" (Exodus 14:15, *New Living Translation*).

Scripture: Exodus 14:15-20
Song: "The Great Adventure"

Last summer Tiffany learned to ride her bike without training wheels. She could zip around the block, ride over to a friend's house, and leave everyone in the dust as she sped by. Her new-found freedom was obvious to all and envied by her little brother, Darin. "She never waits for me! She always goes too fast! I can't do it!" It wasn't that he wanted her to wait for him, but he wanted to feel the rush of wind as she did, to pedal faster and go farther than he ever had before. He sat on the curb just a-wishin' and a-whinin'.

"If you want to keep up, then learn to ride your bike," his mother suggested. The next day, Darin was on a mission. He didn't give up; he believed he could do it. After a couple hours of sweat, frustration, and skinned knees, he raced his sister down the block. With unmatched elation he put his face into the wind.

Serving the Lord isn't always comfortable. Hard work, frustration, and the risk of getting hurt are part of the package. But we can't put our faith into action until we get up and move. Once we stop wishin' and whinin', we can start believin' and receivin'.

Dear Heavenly Father, help me get up and move by faith. As I step out, I believe You will prepare the way. Thank You for giving me the strength and courage to move forward to receive all You have planned for me. In Jesus' name, amen.

Just One

The waters returned and covered all the chariots and charioteers—the entire army of Pharaoh. Of all the Egyptians who had chased the Israelites into the sea, not a single one survived (Exodus 14:28, *New Living Translation*).

Scripture: Exodus 14:21-30
Song: "Faith Is the Victory"

I will never forget the day my mother was diagnosed with breast cancer. With one phone call her life flipped upside down. After radical surgery, her doctor told us that everything looked great, and he was sure they'd removed all abnormal cells.

The celebration, however, was short-lived. Upon further examination of the tissue, he discovered a micro-tumor that would need further testing. The positive result meant extra chemotherapy and more surgery. Lymph nodes that are next to malignant tumors are often removed because, if even one cancerous cell gets into those channels, the disease will likely return. It is the most common way cancer spreads. Due to the doctor's meticulous procedures and my mother's unwavering faith, today she is cancer free.

Just as it only takes a single cancer cell to destroy a human body, it only takes a single sin to destroy your soul. The good news is: the Lord has already fought that battle and won. We can live in victory instead of sickening with sin. God wiped out Egypt's entire army with the waters of the Red Sea, and Jesus wiped out sin and death with the atonement of the cross.

Father, my soul was dying with the disease of sin, and the prescription was the blood of Your Son. I am in awe of Your mercy and grace. In Christ's name, amen.

Given, Not Taken

Everyone who is willing is to bring to the LORD an offering (Exodus 35:5).

Scripture: Exodus 35:4-9
Song: "Take My Life and Let It Be"

My 2-year-old daughter, Zephani, is learning how to share. Whenever there is an extra toy, cookie, or chair, we show her how important it is to let others use our things. Most of the time, she understands and shares happily. However, my older children have found a sure way to rile her up. Instead of asking her to share, they snatch her things away. This violation of her personal space and dominion always results in a howl of protest.

It isn't that she is unwilling to share. It isn't that she needs or even wants all the toys to herself. It's just that there's a big difference between sharing and having things taken away.

Sharing requires a willing heart. When materials were needed to construct the tabernacle, Moses could have required items from each household. Demanding jewelry, thread, skins, and spices could have met the need. Certainly, a worship center for God's redeemed people was worth mandatory common sacrifice. Instead, God was pleased to build and furnish His tabernacle with offerings given willingly by enthusiastic worshippers. Offerings are given, not taken, and it still pleases God when worshippers willingly share their resources to honor Him.

Redeeming God, I marvel at Your generosity toward me. You gave lavishly and willingly to offer me forgiveness and eternal life. Thank You, in Jesus' name. Amen.

November 18–24. **Matthew Boardwell** is an avid nonfiction reader and enthusiastic musician. More importantly, he is husband to Pam, father of nine children, and a minister in Erie, Colorado.

Given with Skill

All who are skilled among you are to come and make everything the LORD has commanded (Exodus 35:10).

Scripture: Exodus 35:10-19
Song: "Give of Your Best to the Master"

In our church entrance hangs a beautiful painting encouraging everyone to delight in the corporate worship of God. The artwork is all the more inspiring once the artist's story is known.

"I turned to drawing and painting as an escape," Greg says. "It was a way for me to express my anger and sadness. Although I had an architecture degree, I really wanted to be an artist. I thought I could work in an architecture office during the day to support myself and at night experiment and improve my artwork. I really wanted to make a living at it." But when his dream career eluded him, in bitterness Greg turned to alcohol —and his artwork turned to blasphemy. The dark, brooding subjects he pursued mocked God and those whom God loves.

Then a coworker approached Greg with the gospel, highlighting Christ's forgiveness. Soon Greg placed his faith in Jesus, and his life changed forever. Now the beauty of his art brings glory to God. The same skill is focused in a new direction.

Moses invited anyone with a skill to employ it for God's glory. Seamstresses, goldsmiths, woodworkers, and tanners volunteered their talents to produce a corporate work of art, the tabernacle. However they used their skills before, now they were used for the Lord.

Father, I have used my gifts for many things, both good and bad. Help me to remember that the gifts You give can be given back to You in love. In Christ my Lord, Amen.

Giving Together

Everyone who was willing and whose heart moved them came and brought an offering to the LORD for the work on the tent of meeting (Exodus 35:21).

Scripture: Exodus 35:20-29
Song: "We Are God's People"

Once a month, our members show up at church with food in hand. A remarkable variety of foods—pasta salads, casseroles, roasts, cakes, and cobblers—line the counters in the kitchen adjacent to our worship space. The delicious aromas seep in throughout the service, making the mouth water even during the driest of sermons. The anticipation ends when we gather around the kitchen, offer thanks, and dig into our meal.

None of the dishes on that table makes a balanced meal by itself. And no single talented cook provided the variety we enjoy. Instead, *together* we indulge in the benefits of one another's talented cooking.

When the Israelites came together to build the tabernacle, they contributed diverse talents, abilities, and materials. Some brought their jewelry. Others donated fine wood. Still others gave spices. Each contribution was only a part. No single craftsman could lay claim to the whole accomplishment.

Churches still live this way today when members generously offer their own passions, skills, and resources together with others. This is how we build one another up for greater service.

Gracious Lord, by Your wisdom You created me with abilities and resources that can benefit others. Forgive me when I withhold them, and prompt me to give generously when my offering can help. All I have is Yours. In Christ's name I pray. Amen.

Spiritually Gifted to Give

The LORD has chosen Bezalel son of Uri, . . . and he has filled him with the Spirit of God, with wisdom, with understanding with knowledge and with all kinds of skills. And he has given [him] . . . the ability to teach others (Exodus 35:30, 31, 34).

Scripture: Exodus 35:30-35
Song: "We Give Thee but Thine Own"

When I worked construction the summer before my junior year of college, I was expected to show up with some tools of my own: hammer, tape measure, pencil, and utility knife in my own tool belt, the sort of standard tools that every construction worker needs to carry. But my boss assigned us a lot of tasks that those simple tools could not accomplish. For those assignments, we would rummage through his construction trailer. If the job required special tools, he provided them for us.

Bezalel is the first person in Scripture said to be filled with the Spirit. This filling was not merely for Bezalel's own benefit, but to equip him to accomplish the God-sized task of building the tabernacle. This assignment required special tools, so God provided them. Bezalel needed the inspiration of the Lord to do the artistic work of the Lord.

Christians have been assigned many tasks that are impossible without the spiritual gifts God provides. We show up for duty with our natural abilities and physical strength, but when special tools are needed, God provides them.

Spirit of God, I thank You for giving us all we need to do all You require. Help me recognize the spiritual gifts You have given me. Show me how and when to use them to do Your kingdom work. In Christ, amen.

Extraordinary Generosity

The people were restrained from bringing more, because what they already had was more than enough to do all the work (Exodus 36:6, 7).

Scripture: Exodus 36:2-7
Song: "Because I Have Been Given Much"

Normally, the Red Cross has a blood supply sufficient for only one to three days of ordinary hospital use. However, after the World Trade Center attacks of September 2001, Americans donated more blood than could be used up. But even though they had more than enough, Red Cross leaders couldn't bring themselves to announce it. They didn't want to discourage anyone from giving.

Can you imagine any charity organization calling a moratorium on fund drives? Can you imagine envelopes overflowing the sides of the offering plates and fluttering to the floor? Can you picture the offeratory music grinding to a halt halfway through as the minister urges people to stop giving? As hard as it is to imagine today, that is what happened when Moses asked Israel to contribute to the building of the tabernacle. The people were so enthusiastic about giving to that effort that the artisans were overwhelmed with materials.

How extraordinary it is when ministries have more than enough. That kind of giving takes extraordinary generosity, sacrifice, and faith.

O Lord my Shepherd, my cup overflows. You give me much more than I need. How delightful it would be if Your church and its ministries were supplied with more than enough! Grant me extraordinary faith to help make it happen. Through Jesus, amen.

Blessed for Giving

Moses inspected the work and saw that they had done it just as the LORD had commanded. So Moses blessed them (Exodus 39:43).

Scripture: Exodus 39:32-43
Song: "Something for Thee"

When a contractor purchases a building permit for a home, he agrees to a series of inspections. The foundation, framing, mechanical, and drywall all have to be examined carefully before the project progresses to the next stage. Each time an official signs the permit, it's a tribute to the diligence and expertise of the workers.

After all the officials have signed off and occupancy is approved, then comes the most important inspection of all. It's the final walk-through with the homeowners. Their response will indicate whether the contractor kept his promises. Theirs is the last word, the final assessment of a job well done . . . or not.

The artisans must have been watching Moses breathlessly as he scrutinized their work. Was the tabernacle worthy of the one who had commissioned it? For their generosity and diligence, they received the approval of Moses and the blessing of God.

Whenever we give or volunteer, let us keep in mind the "final inspection." At the final walk-through, our "work will be shown for what it is" (1 Corinthians 3:13). Will our life's work receive God's approval and blessing?

Blessed Father, I know my salvation comes through the work of Jesus alone. But You will reward the works I do, out of gratitude, in the power of Your Spirit. Teach me that my efforts for others are ultimately offerings to You. Through Christ, amen.

Glory Through Giving

Then the cloud covered the tent of meeting, and the glory of the LORD filled the tabernacle (Exodus 40:34).

Scripture: Exodus 40:16-30, 34, 38
Song: "Trust, Try, and Prove Me"

For a year our church prepared for a soccer skills camp outreach in the community. Some did the paperwork, approving the use of the fields. Others prepared Bible lessons for the kids who attended. Some arranged for food at the closing barbecue. Others bought the prizes to give away that night.

To staff the camp, a team of soccer players and their coach traveled from Missouri to Colorado. To host them, church families volunteered their spare bedrooms. Scores of kids showed up that week, learning soccer skills and Bible truths while having a lot of fun and making new friends.

During the closing barbecue, while I gave the talk, the supernatural hush of God's Spirit fell over the crowd. The simple gospel presentation brought tears to some eyes and repentance to one soul. Years later, that single decision to follow Jesus is still bearing fruit.

We applied all our resources, our skills, and our spiritual gifts, and God filled our completed work with His own glory. How gratifying it must have been for the whole community of Israel when God's glory filled the tabernacle!

Lord God Almighty, it is such a privilege to be part of Your church. Draw us together as we serve You. Help us recognize Your presence among us and fill us with Your glory. Guide us by Your Holy Spirit in all our work for You. I pray this prayer in the name of Jesus, my merciful Savior and Lord. Amen.

Made to Sing!

I will sing of the LORD's great love forever; with my mouth I will make your faithfulness known through all generations (Psalm 89:1).

Scripture: Psalm 89:1-7
Song: "All Praise to Thee, Eternal Lord"

You know the feeling, that moment when your heart sings! When I stand at the edge of the ocean at sunset or sit on a rock overlooking the mountains, or even when I walk the dog and look up at a full moon, my heart fills with song. *Yes, Lord, Your creation speaks!* Like the psalmist, I can say with all sincerity, "I will sing of the Lord's great love . . ." as I take in the overwhelming beauty here on earth. And I want to praise Him forever.

It doesn't matter whether I'm singing in tune or not, just as long as my heart, mind, and body take a moment to resonate with those holy ones who sing around the throne of God, day and night (see Revelation 5:6). And it doesn't matter whether I'm singing an ancient hymn or a recent praise song. Because of what Jesus Christ did for us on the cross, I can sing of God's love—forever. Not just now in my mortal body will I sing or even after other memories escape me in old age; I will sing in my new body in His presence forever.

Dear Lord, as a child, I thought that praising You in Heaven might be a boring way to spend eternity. But I'm beginning to understand. Like the psalmist, I was made to sing of Your love for eternity—while You give me work to do in Your kingdom come! All praise to You, in Jesus' name. Amen.

November 25–30. **Carol McLean** is digital products manager for ValPak in Naples, Florida. She lives with her husband on the gulf coast and enjoys the sunsets at beautiful Bonita Beach.

Who's the Leader?

I have found David my servant; with my sacred oil I have anointed him. My hand will sustain him; surely my arm will strengthen him (Psalm 89:20, 21).

Scripture: Psalm 89:19-24
Song: "Servant of God, Well Done!"

God chose a *servant* to be His king over His people. Today in the modern halls of business and power, we usually look for the strongest candidate, the best one on his or her feet at the interview. Who has the most support, the best connections—politically and financially? Who has the most experience, the best public record? Who shares our values or fights for our favorite cause?

That's how people choose leaders, but God selects His leaders differently. He sees the heart and looks for humility, for a servant attitude.

That's pretty much all God requires of His leaders: a humble heart, like the one in young David, the shepherd. The Lord promoted David from the dirty, lowly, isolated life of a shepherd to the most powerful seat in His kingdom.

I can only conclude: Those counting on their superhero strengths need not apply. God's own hand takes care of any opposition. And that's the kind of support I need in this daily battle of living the Christian life. Most of all, it's the kind of humility I need while I serve where I am now, to the glory of the Lord.

Father, You know my tendency to assert my strengths and try to engineer my circumstances. Please give me a sense of balance in these things—an appropriate strength under the control of Your Holy Spirit; that is: humility. In Jesus' name, amen.

He Remains True

I will not violate my covenant or alter what my lips have uttered (Psalm 89:34).

Scripture: Psalm 89:26-34
Song: "There's a Wideness in God's Mercy"

Ever make a deal with your family or friends that you just couldn't keep? In an attempt to lose weight recently, I agreed to either lose a certain number of pounds by a certain date or pay big bucks to my husband and two sons. They also set personal goals and dates.

We all shook hands on the deal and agreed to hold each other accountable—no matter what! Well, as the end date came closer, each of us feared we would not reach our goals. We tried to renegotiate, either for more time or to avoid paying at all. Finally, after much stress on our relationships, we all agreed to call off the deal (and vowed never to do *that* again).

We all had good intentions, but in the end, we just couldn't reach our goals . . . and we also couldn't afford to pay up. Thankfully, when God makes a covenant with us, He not only keeps His Word, but He also forgives us when we fail to keep up our part. That forgiveness was won for us at the cross.

Of course, there are temporal consequences to David's descendants who "do not follow [God's] statues" (v. 30). Punishment came to Israel, but the Lord never took away His love and mercy. He faithfully kept His covenant completely through the work of His Son, Jesus.

I praise You, **Father,** for Your unfailing faithfulness—and for the price of my forgiveness paid by Jesus. I rely on Your grace today in all things. Through Christ, amen.

Thanks, in the Tough Times

How great you are, Sovereign LORD! There is no one like you, and there is no God but you, as we have heard with our own ears. . . . and with your blessing the house of your servant will be blessed forever (2 Samuel 7:22, 29).

Scripture: 2 Samuel 7:18-29
Song: "God Is So Good"

David, the man who composed many great songs of thanksgiving as psalms, leaves us another example here in 2 Samuel. His passionate prayer of thanks and praise to God for His goodness in the present, past, and future would make a glorious hymn today.

You might think that he prayed these words in a moment of joy, feeling full with happiness. No, David speaks this prayer after experiencing great disappointment: God would not allow him to build the temple. Instead, that coveted honor would go to David's son, Solomon.

When I experience the deep hurt of true disappointment, I naturally respond in anger as I express my feelings to God and those around me. But David showed just how humble he was, even as king. He thanked God and pleaded the case for God's faithfulness in keeping His Word.

In other words, he blessed God instead of turning his back in angry defeat. What an example for me, as I experience impatience with God's plans or even disappointment in His apparent lack of care.

Lord God in Heaven, I know You care about every detail and problem in my life. Help me to know and feel Your love today! I pray in the name of Jesus. Amen.

Seeking Sincerely?

Again the LORD spoke to Ahaz, "Ask the LORD your God for a sign, whether in the deepest depths or in the highest heights." But Ahaz said, "I will not ask; I will not put the LORD to the test" (Isaiah 7:10-12).

Scripture: Isaiah 7:10-15
Song: "Prayer Is the Soul's Sincere Desire"

Recently, while praying for God's guidance about a potential new job and move, I asked that God be very clear to me in His answer. No, I didn't ask for a "sign," but I knew I wouldn't mind receiving direction from His Word.

Sure enough, I began to notice certain Bible verses that said things like: "keep doing what you have been doing" and "be content where you are." Well, that was not the answer I wanted, so I held out hope until I got the final word in a phone call, "No. You're not going anywhere right now."

King Ahaz had other plans too. That's why he wasn't open to asking God for a sign—he wouldn't follow God's plan anyway. But he didn't want to admit it to Isaiah, so he piously said, "I will not put the Lord to the test."

He really didn't want to know God's plan for him or for the future of Israel. That's when Isaiah made things very clear, and God gave him a sign for all to see and recognize: the virgin birth of Immanuel, God with us.

Almighty and merciful God, sometimes my heart isn't really in it when I pray for Your guidance. I know what I want, and so I try to get You to endorse my plans. Forgive me, Lord! Help me seek Your will in all sincerity. In the name of Jesus, who lives and reigns with You and the Holy Spirit, amen.

Encouragement from a Friend

When Elizabeth heard Mary's greeting, the baby leaped in her womb, and Elizabeth was filled with the Holy Spirit. In a loud voice she exclaimed: "Blessed are you among women, and blessed is the child you will bear!" (Luke 1:41, 42).

Scripture: Luke 1:41-45
Song: "Blest Be the Tie That Binds"

Today we can check news online—"on the go"—with our wireless mobile devices. We can even get directions for avoiding accidents and traffic jams spoken right from our car's dashboard. We can chat back and forth on Instant Messenger.

But back in Mary and Elizabeth's day, news traveled slowly, person to person. Distances between family members kept them apart—except when God sent the message through His Holy Spirit messenger.

I was at a prayer retreat years ago and jotted notes in my journal when the speaker said things that touched my heart. Here is one entry (a poor paraphrase) that still blesses me today: "The Lord raises up among us some marvelous friends to help us along the way. They aren't perfect people, but they have received a large amount of grace that shines as the reflected glory of God. They can love us in a way that our own souls are lighted by God's light." I apply those words to the strong bond between Elizabeth and Mary. They both knew the love and grace of God and, in reflecting that love, they strengthened one another.

Father, I thank You for deep and lasting friendships within the body of Christ. Use me in these relationships to reflect Your love for those I love. And when I need it, may I draw from the love of my friends. In Jesus' name, amen.

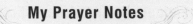

My Prayer Notes

_____

_____

_____

_____

_____

_____

_____

_____

_____

_____

_____

_____

_____

_____

_____

_____

_____

_____

_____

_____

_____

_____

_____

DEVOTIONS®

December

Who in the skies above can compare with the
Lord?

— *Psalm 89:6*

Gary Wilde, Editor   **Margaret Williams,** Project Editor   Photo iStockphoto | Thinkstock®

DEVOTIONS® is published quarterly by Standard Publishing, Cincinnati, Ohio, www.standardpub.com.
© 2012 by Standard Publishing. All rights reserved. Topics based on the Home Daily Bible Readings,
International Sunday School Lessons. © 2010 by the Committee on the Uniform Series. Printed in
the U.S.A. All Scripture quotations, unless otherwise indicated, are taken from the *HOLY BIBLE,
NEW INTERNATIONAL VERSION®. NIV®.* Copyright © 1973, 1978, 1984, 2011 by Biblica, Inc.™.
Used by permission of Zondervan. All rights reserved. *King James Version (KJV),* public domain.

Obedience Doesn't Make Sense

"I am the Lord's servant," Mary answered. **"May your word to me be fulfilled." Then the angel left her** (Luke 1:38).

Scripture: Luke 1:26-40
Song: "Breath of Heaven"

My husband and I are in the midst of some financial struggles. For the first time in our lives, we don't always know how we're going to pay all our bills, and we're living paycheck to paycheck. Nevertheless, we feel convinced that God wants us to bless others with what little we have. So we've decided to tithe anyway, even though the numbers don't add up. Through it all, we're learning to trust that God will provide, and so far He hasn't failed us.

When the angel told Mary she would give birth to Jesus, she replied, "How will this be . . . since I am a virgin?"(v. 34). The angel's announcement that Mary would carry God's Son into the world didn't make sense to her, but she still agreed to follow God's plans.

Is God asking you to do something that doesn't make sense to you? Consider the story of Mary. God asked her to help bring His Son into the world. She obeyed, and the whole world was blessed.

Thank You, **Lord,** for Mary's example of faith and obedience. Thank You for sending Your Son to our world. Today I will face problems that seem to have no solutions, and I will need Your guidance in order to move forward in faith. Please help me to be obedient to You, even when it doesn't make sense. Through Christ I pray. Amen.

December 1–7. **Andrea Osmun** is a freelance writer from Cleveland, Ohio, who finds her inspiration to write flowing from her loving Savior and from her precious family.

He's the Source

The LORD sends poverty and wealth; he humbles and he exalts (1 Samuel 2:7).

Scripture: 1 Samuel 2:1-10
Song: "Blessed Be the Name"

When I was a kid, I always thought that if I worked hard enough, I would have everything I needed in life: money, a good job, a house, cars. Basically, I thought I could live comfortably. Life doesn't come together that easily, though.

I survived two layoffs and left a company just before it went bankrupt. I kept wondering why God would allow that to happen to me, since I had always worked so hard. However, as I've been learning lately, possessions and financial security are only temporary. The security that comes from God is eternal.

In the Bible, Hannah had a wonderful dream, a deep desire, but it was withheld from her for awhile: She couldn't bear children. And to make matters worse, her husband's other wife was taunting her because of it. She cried out to God in the temple, and He listened. He gave her a baby boy, Samuel, and she dedicated him to God. In her dedication prayer, instead of focusing on the amazing gift she had received, Hannah acknowledged the gift-giver.

Isn't that what God wants from us, as well? To acknowledge Him as the source of everything we have and everything we need? Whether He gives us a little or a lot, every good thing comes from His hand.

Dear God, thank You for meeting all of my needs—and for every good thing You give me. I acknowledge You as the source of everything I have. In Jesus' name, amen.

Just Try It!

Taste and see that the LORD is good; blessed is the one who takes refuge in him (Psalm 34:8)

Scripture: Psalm 34:1-8
Song: "Taste and See"

My husband, Keith, is the pickiest eater I know. He could eat peanut butter and jelly sandwiches for lunch every day of the week and be happy. The only vegetables he'll eat are green beans and corn; he hates berries of all kinds, and he doesn't like creams or sauces.

Being from a Croatian family, I'm used to trying all kinds of new foods. Sometimes I'll come across a food that tastes so delicious, I just have to convince Keith to try it. Often he's reluctant, but I've been able to persuade him.

In today's Scripture, David seems to be saying about God what I've been saying to my husband all this time about food: "Just try it. I know you'll like it."

David, the psalm writer, was in a tough situation, harassed and pursued by a murderous king. Yet David encouraged God's people to rejoice in the Lord and trust in Him, because God answers prayer and delivers His beloved ones from trouble. From personal experience, David could say: "God is good" (Psalm 73:1).

When you're not sure of God's goodness in your troubles, just "taste and see" (v. 8) what it means to enjoy fellowship with Him throughout each day. You won't be disappointed.

Dear Lord, thank You for David's example in tough times. When I doubt Your goodness in my life, please help me to turn to You, trusting that You will come through for me, in Your way and in Your time. In Jesus' name, amen.

Joy Through Thanksgiving

Enter his gates with thanksgiving and his courts with praise; give thanks to him and praise his name (Psalm 100:4).

Scripture: Psalm 100
Song: "Give to Our God Immortal Praise"

In the past two weeks, my husband has lost his job, we lost our family health insurance, our car broke down, and a family member was diagnosed with cancer. Yet somehow, we are finding joy in being grateful for the blessings God has poured into our lives down through the years.

Of course, it's so easy to focus on the negatives! But when we do, we end up feeling depressed and arguing with each other. So, Keith and I have determined to focus on the goodness of God, knowing He's in complete control of our circumstances.

One of my favorite Bible passages is Philippians 4:6, 7, which says, "Do not be anxious about anything, but in every situation, by prayer and petition, with thanksgiving, present your requests to God. And the peace of God, which transcends all understanding, will guard your hearts and your minds in Christ Jesus."

When we come before God with thanksgiving and praise, focusing on His goodness instead of our troubles, we walk away with a supernatural peace. We're not sure what the future holds, but we do know that God is good. Therefore, we have reason to thank and praise Him each new day.

Dear Father, thank You for all the good things You give me and my family. Even when we struggle through difficult times, we know that You are in control. I thank You and praise You today, through Christ my Lord. Amen.

God the Loving Father

As a father has compassion on his children, so the LORD has compassion on those who fear him (Psalm 103:13).

Scripture: Psalm 103:13-22
Song: "Children of God"

Television these days doesn't offer many examples of good fathering, does it? Just turn on the TV, and you'll soon come across a dad who's fairly irresponsible in his approach to his family—and life in general. He's often portrayed as drinking, chasing after women, and spending his evenings on the couch immersed in sports.

Some of us can relate to these portrayals, because our own fathers are (or were), in fact, like this. Others of us grew up with good fathers who paid loving attention to us and conveyed a godly example to follow. This is important, because our "God image" is significantly shaped by our experience of earthly fatherhood. Even though we know what the Scriptures say about our heavenly Father's character, we can't deny the impact of our biological dad, for good or ill.

In any case, let us familiarize ourselves with what God says about His character in Scripture. Thus we can bring into focus the beautiful portrait of Him as the loving Father He is. He's certainly not the lackadaisical dad of television notoriety. He is never abusive and harsh toward us. He doesn't crush us with His power. Instead, He treats us with compassion and love, despite our frail, broken condition.

Dear Heavenly Father, thank You for Your compassionate fatherhood. Today I praise You for Your loving care in my life. In the name of Jesus, amen.

Legacy of Love: A Way of Life

The fear of the LORD is the beginning of wisdom; all who follow his precepts have good understanding. To him belongs eternal praise (Psalm 111:10).

Scripture: Psalm 111
Song: "Children of the World"

Every night, as part of my daughter's bedtime routine, I sing "Jesus, Jesus, Lord to Me" in remembrance of my grandmother, who sang it to me when I was little. My grandma lived with my family from when I was 11 years old until I was about 16. Every day, she woke up at sunrise and read her Bible. At night, she'd tuck my brother and me into our beds and sing us that lovely song.

In Psalm 111, David praised the Lord in front of other believers, recounting the many ways God had been faithful to them. He encouraged his people to fear God and obey His Word, because God was worthy of their reverence, obedience, and praise. David passed down to his son Solomon this "fear of the Lord," he repeated it throughout the book of Proverbs.

My grandmother didn't just pass a song down to me, a tune and some lyrics. No, she handed me *a way of life*, a life filled with praise for all the Lord is to us. I want to pass my grandmother's legacy of love to my own daughter. I want her to remember all the great works of our heavenly Father and pass the good news of His love to future generations.

Dear God, You are worthy of our praise because You have been faithful to us for generations. May I hand Your legacy of love on to my children and their children. In Jesus' name I pray. Amen.

Change We Can Believe In

Do not put your trust in princes, in human beings, who cannot save (Psalm 146:3).

Scripture: Psalm 146
Song: "Trust in Jesus"

Every year we have elections, whether for local, state, or federal government positions. And every year we watch as candidates make promises they can't keep. We do our best to vote with the knowledge available to us, hoping that our candidate of choice will take office and then make the changes we desire.

But we should always ask ourselves: *How much are we trusting others to fix our problems?*

The psalmist reminds us that, ultimately, only God can deliver us. He champions our cause, knows all of our struggles, sets us free from the chains of sin, and provides for our needs. What politician can do that?

We Christians should vote, of course, because it is our right as American citizens, and we can thereby help influence society for the good. Nevertheless, we do well to remember that the promises of politicians are many . . . and fleeting. As one anonymous quipster put it: "To succeed in politics, it is often necessary to rise above your principles." Haven't we often seen it?

Promises from God aren't empty, though. They're eternal and flow from His holy character. So let us put our hope and trust in the only one who can make a lasting difference.

Dear God, thank You for championing our cause, for seeing our struggles, and providing for our needs. I claim You as my deliverer today, putting all my trust in You. In the name of the Father and of the Son and of the Holy Spirit, amen.

Let Us Glorify Him!

My soul doth magnify the Lord, and my spirit hath rejoiced in God my Saviour (Luke 1:46, *King James Version*).

Scripture: Luke 1:46-56
Song: "Mary's Boy Child"

Our Scripture today is known to Christians around the world as the Magnificat. The word comes from the first line in the Latin text: *Magnificat anima mea Dominum* ("My soul doth magnify the Lord"). *Magnificat,* then, is translated "magnify" or "glorify."

So what does it mean to *glorify* the Lord? In the original biblical languages, it conveys the idea of weightiness. For instance, we might say of someone that he's a "heavyweight" of a personality, or a "substantial" personage. We're not talking about weight in pounds; we're referring to a significance of character.

Thus to glorify God is to recognize, proclaim, and honor His weighty personhood, His heavy majesty, His substantial holiness. Jehovah is no small deity who created the cosmos, no "lightweight" who flung the stars into the universe.

Mary knew all this and proclaimed it. Even more, she acknowledged a heavenly mercy: the king of the universe bending down to her in order to use her mightily in the plan of salvation. Mary would bear the Messiah; she knew she was blessed.

Can we too think of good reasons to lift up a magnificat today? Has God blessed us, been merciful, shown us His mighty deeds, and filled us with good things? Let us glorify His name.

Father, I glorify You today for all the goodness and mercy You have poured into my life. Thank You, in Jesus' name. Amen.

December 8. **Gary Wilde** is a minister and freelance writer who lives in Bonita Springs, Florida.

Obedient Servant

Everyone who heard this wondered about it, asking, "What then is this child going to be? For the Lord's hand was with him" (Luke 1:66).

Scripture: Luke 1:59-66
Song: "O How Happy Are They Who the Savior Obey"

My father-in-law has trusted the Lord all of his life. He grew up poor, worked hard, earned five academic degrees, and had a distinguished career. The Lord blessed him with love, generosity, and a desire to help others.

For as long as I can remember, he has visited and encouraged people in hospitals and nursing homes. He has been an elder of his church for over 40 years and shared his professional expertise with family and friends. They all say the same thing: "I wish I could be like him." His passionate prayers have touched the hearts of listeners for years. So many lives have been transformed because he bowed to the Lord's will.

When we obey Him, the Lord's hand is with us. If Elizabeth and Zechariah hadn't obeyed God all of their lives, John the Baptist might never have been born to this once barren couple. And without John, who would have spread the word about the coming Messiah? It seems that obedience plays a large role in releasing God's activity in the world.

Father, thank You for the people in my life who serve as marvelous examples of Your love. Help me follow Your commands as I emulate those who went before me in faith and obedience. In all things, may I bring glory to Your name, through Christ. Amen.

December 9–15. **Nancy Dutton** is a freelance writer who lives in the Rocky Mountains of Colorado. She helps the elderly, loves her family and friends, and greatly enjoys the outdoors.

Baptized Together

He went into all the country around the Jordan, preaching a baptism of repentance for the forgiveness of sins (Luke 3:3).

Scripture: Luke 3:1-6
Song: "Shall We Gather at the River?"

At Christmas time, as lights glowed on the pine trees in the church sanctuary, my husband and I walked to the front and then stepped down into warm water to be baptized. The minister dipped me into the water first. I gladly surrendered myself in faith to the Lord. I already knew my previous lifestyle no longer worked for me: The stress of devoting all of my time to career and money had brought me illness and low energy.

When the minister submerged my husband, joy filled my soul, knowing we would share this new life in Christ together in the coming years. I never wanted that smile on my face to disappear. What a relief it was to let go of the past, accept God's forgiveness, and look forward to our exciting future as a team guided by Jesus, now and through eternity.

Yes, our baptism was a refreshing act of repentance—and dedication to the Lord. Now, incorporated into the body of Christ, we would seek to do His will each day.

Have you taken the plunge in His living water of spiritual life? Without Jesus, we would be drowning, with no hope. No wonder the preaching of John was so powerful!

O Merciful Father, the opportunity to repent and to be forgiven changed my life. I rejoice and thank You, God, for washing away my sins. Help me, each day, to seek Your will and follow Your ways. In the precious name of Jesus, amen.

What Could I Share?

John answered, "Anyone who has two shirts should share with the one who has none, and anyone who has food should do the same" (Luke 3:11).

Scripture: Luke 3:7-14
Song: "Lord, Thou Lov'st the Cheerful Giver"

God calls us to produce fruit by giving what we have. My friend Shirley is retired, living on a fixed income, but always eager to give to others. She lifts people's spirits wherever she goes. She sings for them, says an encouraging word, and compliments them. God has taught me much about giving through observing Shirley's way of life.

Once a month Shirley cleans and organizes her closet. She washes clothes she no longer wears and gives me her new-looking outfits. I give the ones that don't fit to the less fortunate and pass on the joy. Thus Shirley's sharing multiplies the blessings.

At her house, Shirley offers me chocolate cake and iced tea. When a church member grieves for a loved one, she takes them food for dinner. A smile, a kind word doesn't cost anything to give. When Shirley and I go shopping, she tells the saleslady about Jesus. Our next destination is usually a restaurant. When a waitress told us about a physical problem, Shirley put her hands on the woman and prayed. Tears streamed down the woman's face, and her eyes lit up with hope.

This Christmas season, could we help someone with Christ-like kindness? I'm thinking right now: What could I share?

Dear Father, You gave Your only Son to die for me. Please grant me a giving heart to share what I have. In Jesus' precious name I pray. Amen.

Cleansing Agent

John answered them all, "I baptize you with water. But one who is more powerful than I will come, the straps of whose sandals I am not worthy to untie. He will baptize you with the Holy Spirit and fire" (Luke 3:16).

Scripture: Luke 3:15-20
Song: "Holy Spirit, Truth Divine"

As my husband rode his bicycle around the lake near our house, he came to a small bridge over a gully. Up ahead he saw the grass below a cottonwood tree burst into flames. It happened so fast, it was as if someone threw a torch on that grass.

Firemen responded quickly, dousing out the blaze, but that parcel of grass—and half of the tree—were black. A few months later, though, the grass grew back greener than ever. A red-twig dogwood bush sprang up where one had never grown before. The fire cleansed the land and prepared it for new growth.

John was God's appointed messenger who prepared the way for Jesus. John baptized with water, a symbol of cleansing away sin. Jesus baptized with the Holy Spirit and fire. When we're baptized, God puts His Spirit into us. Through the Holy Spirit, we know the power of God, which is demonstrated in the resurrection of Jesus. The "fire" is the presence of the Holy Spirit, who acts as a cleansing agent, burning up what is not good in us—as we allow Him to do so. He purifies and prepares us for our life with the holy trinity in Heaven.

Almighty and gracious Father, I am grateful for being born anew, so I may live with You in Your kingdom forever. May I this day be "on fire" with the Holy Spirit. O Lord, cleanse and prepare me for new growth! In Jesus' name, amen.

I'm His Child Too

A voice from heaven said, "This is my Son, whom I love; with him I am well pleased" (Matthew 3:17).

Scripture: Matthew 3:13-17
Song: "The Family of God"

We enjoy a family reunion every Fourth of July in the woods near a lake and a river. The women arrange all of the homemade food, keep everyone fed, brew the coffee, and oversee the children (who have ongoing watermelon fights). The men barbecue meat while telling stories and flying remote-controlled aircraft. Another relative shows the old home movies. We treasure this time together as we catch up on our lives, connecting to our heritage and enjoying the companionship of our loved ones.

"When you believed," says Ephesians 1:13, 14, "you were marked in him with a seal, the promised Holy Spirit, who is a deposit guaranteeing our inheritance until the redemption of those who are God's possession."

In other words, when we receive the Holy Spirit in baptism, we become adopted children of God, full members of His family. After Jesus was baptized, the voice from Heaven identified Him as the Son of God, and—in Him—we too are now God's children, brothers and sisters in Christ, coheirs to His heavenly throne through eternity.

Today, I will remember that voice from Heaven, for it still speaks. I will listen for it when I have a chance to stop and recollect who I really am: a beloved daughter of the king.

O Loving Father, I am humbly honored to be a part of Your family. Thank You for sending the Holy Spirit to direct me in Your ways. In Jesus' name I pray. Amen.

Jesus, Our Healer

At that very time Jesus cured many who had diseases, sicknesses and evil spirits, and gave sight to many who were blind (Luke 7:21).

Scripture: Luke 7:18-27
Song: "Jesus Heals"

Gravely ill, I was afraid of dying as I suffered from severe and painful digestive issues that left me barely able to eat and swallow food. All I could do was lie in bed and sit up briefly. I prayed and then read Luke 7:21. Jesus healed many people plagued with diseases and illnesses. Why wouldn't He heal me too? Even if I didn't get completely well, any improvement would be an encouragement.

Every morning and evening I listened to a CD of Scriptures about healing. My faith that Jesus would renew my health increased. I read the Bible daily and started a prayer list. Praying for other people helped them, and it brought me closer to God. My hope grew.

And God started reviving my body. When I could sit up longer, I wrote poetry and short stories. A nutritionist guided me as to what foods to eat. Soon I could drive and shop at the grocery store half a mile away. I attended a weekly Bible study where others prayed over me, and the Word of God energized me. My digestive problems diminished. Jesus brought me from the brink of death to restored health.

Great Physician, I praise You for soothing my physical ailments. Most of all, thank You for granting me new life. I joyously look forward to the time we will be together in the new earth, where death and sickness no longer exist. Through Christ, amen.

Praise the Lord

Zechariah was filled with the Holy Spirit and prophesied: Praise be to the Lord, the God of Israel, because he has come to his people and redeemed them (Luke 1:67, 68).

Scripture: Luke 1:57, 58, 67-79
Song: "O for a Thousand Tongues to Sing"

The word *praise* appears in more than 300 verses of the Bible. The dictionary says *praise* means to worship, glorify, value, merit, commend, express a favorable judgment of. In Zechariah's song, the priest and prophet overflowed with thanks for the birth of his son, John the Baptist. He also gave thanks for the rescuing of his people.

Praising the Lord can transform your ho-hum or difficult day into a joyful experience. When the Holy Spirit came to live inside me, my eyes opened to how the Lord wanted me to live. Actions and omissions of a lifetime played through my head. A myriad of emotions raced in my heart. I felt deep sorrow for people I had hurt, forgiveness for those who'd hurt me, and happiness for the promise of eternal life. I exalted the Lord for delivering me from such an unsatisfying life.

Now whenever I feel grumpy, fearful, or overwhelmed, I glorify Him with grateful praises. Are you experiencing difficulties? Sing aloud praises to Him, feel His love for you, and rejoice in the hope that flows from His mercy.

Dear Father in Heaven, I praise You for waking me up to Your love and saving my soul, so I am free to enjoy each day in peace with Your love. Give me a spirit of gratitude amidst all the joys and sorrows of this life, until I enter the next life! In the name of Jesus, my Lord and Savior, amen.

Make Good Your Word

So now I give him to the Lord. For his whole life he will be given over to the Lord (1 Samuel 1:28).

Scripture: 1 Samuel 1:21-28
Song: "We Are an Offering"

"God, if you'll just let me make this putt, then I'll . . ." "God, if you'll just let us buy this house . . ." "God, if you'll just deliver me from this . . ." Have you ever bargained with God like that? Maybe it wasn't on the golf course or at the realtor's office. Maybe it was something far more serious, like the health of your child or the pending death of someone close. I think we've all at least *thought* about it, even if we haven't actually spoken the words. But when the deal has been struck, how many of us have kept our end of the bargain?

I'm intrigued by Elkanah's response in today's Scripture. He said in verse 23, "[Only may] the Lord make good his word." I'm not sure what he meant by this, but I chuckle to think that Elkanah was in some way questioning God's integrity. After all, when was the last time God failed to keep a promise?

I think the more pressing question is whether or not we'll make good *our* word. Hannah was true. She kept up her end of the deal and dedicated Samuel to the Lord. That's got to be our goal. May we always be faithful like Hannah. May we always be true to our word.

Lord, I pray that You'll be honored with my life. Strengthen me to keep every promise I've ever made to You, or before You. In Jesus' name I pray. Amen.

December 16–22. **Von Mitchell** is a high school teacher and basketball coach in Delta, Colorado. Married for 19 years to Marcia, the love of his life, he is also a big In-N-Out Burger fan.

The Power of a Smile

The LORD make his face shine upon you and be gracious to you (Numbers 6:25).

Scripture: Numbers 6:22-27
Song: "Revive Us Again"

It really is a universal statement. Smiles translate into every possible language and dialect under the sun. Smiles are a good thing, and we all know it. Smiles brighten up the world. I love smiles.

As a public high school teacher, I know that sometimes the students in my classroom are having a bad day. If I can get them to smile, everyone's day gets a little better. Many of my students' parents speak little or no English. But they understand it when I smile at them during parent/teacher conferences, and I understand it when they smile back at me. Smiles help create understanding. Smiles convey goodwill. Smiles help us bridge the communication gap.

Who wouldn't want a smile from God? If we thought that His face was shining upon us, wouldn't that be similar to a smile?

I don't know about you, but I'd travel many miles just to get a smile from the Creator. In my own life, I'm working out "with fear and trembling" (see Philippians 2:12, 13) just how much of that smile I will enjoy some day. But make no mistake, I long for God's face to shine upon me. How about you?

O God, Creator of Heaven and earth, I pray that Your face would shine upon me. And may my life be the best smile I can produce for Your glory. I pray this prayer in the name of Jesus, my merciful Savior and Lord. Amen.

The Great Light

The people walking in darkness have seen a great light; on those living in the land of deep darkness a light has dawned (Isaiah 9:2).

Scripture: Isaiah 9:1-5
Song: "Something Changed"

I once had to drive from Eureka Springs, Arkansas, to Cedaredge, Colorado, in one day, by myself. It's about an 18-hour trip. As you can imagine, I left quite early in the morning while it was still dark.

I was so sleepy! I couldn't wait for the sun to come out and wake up the day. Somewhere on the highway in the great state of Oklahoma, between turtles and tollbooths, a light dawned and dispelled my drowsy darkness. I felt much better (until "turnpike trance" settled in somewhere around Kansas). After that, I was on a beeline to get home.

How many times has your life felt like an isolated 18-hour road trip in the darkness—without a map? Even if you've walked with Christ for some time, you undoubtedly have still experienced difficult days. We all do. But the good news trumpeted in the book of Isaiah is for all of us. The Light has come!

Like merry sunshine on our souls is the dawning of Christ as Lord in our hearts. Even in the darkest hours of our lives, Jesus will light the way and ignite us with passion and purpose—until, eventually, we all make it home.

O Eternal Lord God, thank You for lighting my way and igniting my heart with a fire to serve you. May you be glorified in my life through the things I do and say, and think. This is my prayer, in the name of Jesus. Amen.

Pointing to Him

But you, Bethlehem Ephrathah, though you are small among the clans of Judah, out of you will come for me one who will be ruler over Israel. . . . And he will be our peace (Micah 5:2, 5).

Scripture: Micah 5:1-5
Song: "Peace, Peace, Wonderful Peace"

I have a friend who sees God's story in almost everything. If a runner falls down at a track meet—my friend the Father who picks us up when we fall. A falsely accused man spends 20 years of his life in prison—my friend sees the chance to forgive as Jesus did. A kid on the brink of suicide until a sports icon takes him to dinner—my friend sees *hope*. My friend's capacity to see all of life's events pointing to the Lord amazes me. But so does the Bible—for the written Word constantly points us to the *living word*.

I am amazed to know that the five verses in today's Scripture point to Jesus. This passage was written nearly 700 years before Jesus came to earth.

It seems the entire Bible is a tapestry with a constant thread: *Jesus*. It's a screenplay with a consistent theme: *for God so loved the world* (John 3:16). It's an essay with a life-changing thesis: *We exist to glorify Him*.

Will you be ready to see God's story in your circumstances today? No matter what you have scheduled, take a moment to see the hand of God in your life.

Dear God, I pray that all of my life would point to you—not to me, O Lord, or to anything else. Give me the peace that comes in knowing that all things are in Your sovereign hands. Through Christ, amen.

～ Victory! ～

You exalted me above my foes; from a violent man you rescued me. Therefore I will praise you, LORD, among the nations; I will sing the praises of your name (Psalm 18:48, 49).

Scripture: Psalm 18:46-50
Song: "Victory in Jesus"

Old-school Denver Broncos fans aren't likely to ever forget Super Bowl XXXII. That was the day the Broncos won their first Super Bowl over the heavily favored Green Bay Packers. It was a special day made even sweeter because Denver had suffered lopsided defeats on the big stage so many times before — first to the Cowboys back in 1978 (I cried my 8-year-old self to sleep that night), then to the Giants, Redskins, and 49ers in later years. But only tears of joy were flowing after Super Bowl XXXII. The reason? V-I-C-T-O-R-Y!

We all lose sometimes. No one goes undefeated through this life. And sometimes we even lose to the same opponent, over and over again.

But victory is in store for the upright (see Proverbs 2:7). As believers, we have a common foe who seeks to steal, kill, and destroy us (John 10:10). Yet think of how many victories God has marshaled despite the opposition — and those in a conflict much more important than football.

So, like my beloved Broncos, let's keep striving. Let's be strong in God's mighty power (Ephesians 6:10) and give Him praise for all the victories in our lives!

Lord, thank You for victory over an enemy who seeks to destroy me in any way possible. I praise You that You have exalted me above my foes. In Jesus' name, amen.

Really? Wow!

So you are no longer a slave, but God's child; and since you are his child, God has made you also an heir (Galatians 4:7).

Scripture: Galatians 4:1-7
Song: "Martyrs and Thieves"

Not too long ago, my wife and I watched the movie *Little Giants* starring actor Rick Moranis. There's a scene in the film where they hand the football to a little, timid kid whose dad is coming for the first time to see his son play.

Dad stands at the far goalpost, so the little boy weaves in and out of defenders as he runs. Those tacklers are trying to annihilate him en route to the end zone—and his father's arms. It's a telling scene about the love between a father and son. Both of us got a little misty.

Fast forward now to the father-child dynamic in your relationship with God. I don't know about you, but I struggle to grasp this concept: I am God's beloved child.

With my finite mind I try, but I fall short. *Are you serious, Lord? Really? Me, a son? You'd be waiting for me in the end zone?* It boggles my mind every time I think of it. But this biblical pronouncement has led me to one of the best conclusions I've made as an adult: God is not limited by my understanding. In fact, He's not limited by anything about me. Only I am.

So that settles it. God said it. I believe it. I'm not just a son. I'm an heir. Wow!

O gracious God, thank You for Your Word. Thank You for truth. I pray for insight and I cry out for understanding—to grasp what You have said about my adopted sonship. May I remember this great fact every day of my life. In Jesus' name, amen.

It Happened!

Today in the town of David a Savior has been born to you; he is the Messiah, the Lord (Luke 2:11).

Scripture: Luke 2:1-17
Song: "Joy to the World!"

My mother was born on Christmas Day in 1940. Before my grandma passed away, she used to tell me about that day. "Have you ever just wanted something so bad?" she'd ask. "Well, that's how it was when your mother was born. I wanted her with all I was worth. And then it happened. I got her. I got the best present in the whole world!"

I was always quick to agree. My mother is a present. She's the one who holds us all together. She's worth celebrating, every day of the year.

Close to 2,000 years before my mom entered the world, the person that all prophecy had been pointing to was born. It finally happened. And what a gift He was! To think that He split history into BC and AD—and that we still celebrate His birthday today. Talk about the best present.

Gram told me the story more than once of Mom being born and I never got tired of it. I've read or heard the Christmas story hundreds of times, but I never tire of it. That's the thing about great stories—they never get old. Jesus came down and made His home among us. He took on flesh and lived a sinless life on our behalf. Praise God. It happened!

O God, the king of glory, I praise You today for all you have done. Thank You for unwrapping the best present in our hearts and showing us how to live out the life He has put within us. Through this same Christ, my Lord and Savior, I pray. Amen.

This Baby Belongs to God!

Joseph and Mary took him to Jerusalem to present him to the Lord (as it is written in the Law of the Lord, "Every firstborn male is to be consecrated to the Lord") (Luke 2:22, 23).

Scripture: Luke 2:21-24
Song: "Silent Night"

Alone in my hospital bed, I held my first baby in my arms. No one else was in the room. A serene sense of holiness and peace seemed to surround my newborn son and me in the stillness of the night. It happened to be close to Christmas, which gave me a fresh new bond with Mary, thinking how the mother of my Lord must have felt holding baby Jesus.

What a miracle to hold my new baby and to consider this fact: though he was born from me, I did not make him or own him. Nor could I protect him from all the harsh things that come with simply being a human in this world.

Yet he had come through me and was put in my care for a season of time. It would be my job to nurture and raise him to know and love God who sent him. I knew I couldn't give my son all he needed on my own. I asked God to help me raise this child (who was really His.) Holding my newborn son before the Lord, I asked that my precious baby's life be blessed and set apart so that others might know he belonged to the Lord.

Father, it is impossible to know what You felt as You sent Jesus to be born as one of us in the form of a helpless baby. But thank You for giving Him! In His name, amen.

December 23–29. **Eva Juliuson,** who writes from Oklahoma City, Oklahoma, loves to see others grow deeper in the Lord through prayer.

The Only True Cleaner

How much more, then, will the blood of Christ, who through the eternal Spirit offered himself unblemished to God, cleanse our consciences from acts that lead to death, so that we may serve the living God! (Hebrews 9:14).

Scripture: Leviticus 12:1-5
Song: "Blood of His Covenant"

Cleaning the church I grew up in was an act of love for me. This particular night seemed even more special, since the next day would be a Christmas service. I vacuumed between the pews and prayed for those who regularly sat there. I recalled my baptism, my marriage, my children's baptisms, my husband's and my dad's funerals, and my kids' marriages; they were all held in that little church. I worked extra hard so the church would look sparkling clean for the service and for my whole church family.

The ladies' bathroom was the last place to clean. Everything had a fresh look . . . except for one stubborn brown stain in the sink. I had used some strong cleanser on it, but it just wouldn't come out. (I did know of a cleaner that would wipe out that stain, but I didn't have any.) Surely no one would notice; the rest of the church was so immaculate.)

You guessed it! The next day a lady pointed out that brown spot on the sink. Because it was Christmas, I was reminded that no matter how hard we try to look good, there is only one who can truly cleanse the stains of our sin.

Father, thank You for Jesus, who was born in a manger and willingly sacrificed himself for me. Thank You for His precious blood, the only solution to eternally cleanse our dark stain of sin. Through His holy name I pray. Amen.

Gift of Life!

Just as the Son of Man did not come to be served, but to serve, and to give His life as a ransom for many (Matthew 20:28).

Scripture: Leviticus 12:6-8
Song: "When I Survey the Wondrous Cross"

My neighbor had been on the heart transplant list for many years. Charles had far outlived the few years the doctors had predicted when he was still in his twenties. Though his life had been lived in and out of the hospital, he still had been able to raise his daughters and enjoy being a grandpa. But then a phone call came about a heart that was finally available.

After all those years of struggling for breath and energy and fighting huge battles for his very life, he received the heart of a 19-year-old young man who'd died in a motorcycle accident. Not only did Charles get a new lease on life, but so did four other people who received the young man's liver, kidney, eyes, and lungs.

My neighbor told me about the emotional meeting when the young man's parents met each of those who received new life through their son's organs. These parents never dreamed, when they held their newborn son, that someday he would lose his life and others would live.

Yet our heavenly Father knew all along His Son would take our death so we could have eternal life. We should be offering gifts to our king; instead, He made himself a sacrifice for us.

Heavenly Father, what an amazing gift! You gave Your own Son to be sacrificed so I could live. There is no greater gift, and I thank You! Through Christ, amen.

Tender Judgment

Speak tenderly to Jerusalem, and proclaim to her that her hard service has been completed, that her sin has been paid for, that she has received from the LORD'S hand double for all her sins (Isaiah 40:2).

Scripture: Isaiah 40:1-5
Song: "Amazing Grace"

My husband and I waited with dread outside the courtroom. We were guilty, and we knew it. We had borrowed money against land homesteaded by family to start a business. It seemed like a good idea at the time. In order to keep the business going, we ran up bills and had to borrow more money.

We worked long hours, desperate for the business to work. Our funding plans kept getting more complicated until we realized there was no way out of our mess. We needed to admit our guilt and declare our inability to pay our debts before a judge.

When we appeared before the judge, we held our heads in shame as creditors listed the debts we owed. As the judge looked at our list of assets (or lack of them) and the remorse we felt, he told our creditors to be quiet. He raised the gavel and declared us free of all the financial burdens that had held us prisoner for so long. With a kind look, he told us to go and make a new life.

This was such a marvelous picture of God's tender mercy in my life. All my unbearable sins were gone, and in their place was a fresh new start.

Holy Father! Thank You for open eyes to see my sin and guilt. Thank You for Jesus who has taken my shame and given me new life. In His name, I pray. Amen.

God's Wristwatch

This is what the LORD says: "In the time of my favor I will answer you, and in the day of salvation I will help you" (Isaiah 49:8).

Scripture: Isaiah 49:8-13
Song: "They That Wait Upon the Lord"

"I'm going to give God a wristwatch," my friend joked, "so He'll realize when it's time to help me!" She was known for complaining that God ran late a little too often. Don't we all feel like that at times—because we want God to synchronize His watch with ours? We think we know the right moment for things to happen. Yet God calls us to trust Him and His promises, even when we don't see much happening.

The Jewish people had been waiting for a promised Messiah forever. And they had their ideas about exactly *how* this Savior would save them. Most of them apparently believed He would release them from Roman rule. Yet all along, God had His perfect plan, one that far surpassed human comprehension. He sent Jesus at just the right time to offer eternal salvation.

When we willingly enter the waters of baptism, we can also accept God's timing for the rest of our lives. Then, whatever the circumstances are, we can take joy in knowing that God has deep compassion for us and travels the road with us. Our Lord wants the very best for us and is at work in our lives. When we trust Him, we can willingly synchronize our timing with His.

Eternal God, You look far beyond the concept of time as we know it. Thank You for guiding my life with infinite wisdom and unfailing compassion. I pray this prayer in the name of Jesus, my Savior and Lord. Amen.

Servant . . . Son . . . King!

Here is my servant, whom I uphold, my chosen one in whom I delight; I will put my Spirit on him, and he will bring justice to the nations (Isaiah 42:1).

Scripture: Isaiah 42:1-7
Song: "Above All"

It takes a lot of courage to run for president in our country. Another candidate's full-time staff is working to dig up dirt on you! They will surely find something on a presidential hopeful, for there is no such thing as a perfect candidate.

In fact, the Bible says that everyone has sinned and fallen short of the glory of God. All except for one! Jesus, pure and unblemished, lived the perfect life for us, fulfilling the commandments to the letter. As our high priest, He also offered the perfect sacrifice—both priest and victim—to completely atone for our sin.

Jesus, the second person of the Trinity, God Almighty, doesn't need our vote. He was already sovereign before He ever accepted the Father's request to humble himself as a servant to be born as one of us. Our king was sent to live life amidst the same human challenges we face daily. Only He never failed to do the right thing.

No one but Jesus was worthy to save us. No one but Jesus served so unselfishly. No one but Jesus reigns forevermore at the right hand of God. No one but Jesus deserves to be our king.

Father, how can we ever thank You for the gift of Your Son, Jesus? He reigns above all, yet lowered himself to be our servant. Thanks to You, in Jesus' name. Amen.

The Answer: Bundled in Blankets

Now there was a man in Jerusalem called Simeon, who was righteous and devout. He was waiting for the consolation of Israel, and the Holy Spirit was on him (Luke 2:25).

Scripture: Luke 2:25-38
Song: "Open the Eyes of My Heart, Lord"

Once a month, I invite all my grandchildren over for "Grandkids Night." We always hold hands around the table and pray before eating. More than once, when we are finished praying, one of them will say, "Mamaw! They had their eyes open!" I laugh and remind them that they wouldn't know unless their own eyes were open. Then I try to explain that there are times it's OK to pray with your eyes open (like when you're driving or walking outside).

Simeon and Anna had both been praying for many years with their eyes wide open. Scripture doesn't tell us if they kept their physical eyes open, but they had been waiting and watching for many years. They had dedicated their lives to watching to see when God would send His promised Messiah.

I don't know if they ever grew discouraged or thought about giving up. One thing I do know is this: They immediately recognized Jesus when Joseph and Mary brought Him to the temple. They saw the answer to all their prayers bundled in blankets. Maybe we should practice keeping our eyes open every time we pray—to see how God will lead us *this* time.

Gracious Father, as I bring my requests to You in prayer, help me watch for all the creative ways You will answer and lead. Remind me to watch and pray at all times! Thank You, in Jesus' name. Amen.

Mercy Incarnate

Wilt thou be made whole? (John 5:6, *King James Version*).

Scripture: John 5:2-17
Song: "Beside the Gospel Pool"

On cots and crutches, the blind, halt, and lame crowded the porches surrounding the healing pool. Each person hoped he'd be the first into the pool, when the water was stirred (v. 7) so that healing might follow.

For some, this was the first try; for others, perhaps the hundredth. For one, on his bed, unable to walk, it had been 38 years. When Jesus stopped to ask him "Wilt thou be made whole?" (v. 6), he replied with the reason he was still waiting: he had no one to put him in that pool called Bethesda ("the house of mercy").

Another passerby might have chided the man for laziness. (*What's the matter with you? Why haven't you made it down to the water yet?*)

Another might have accused him of languishing there on purpose, for pity or for money. (*Quit feeling sorry for yourself! Get a job!*) Still another might have cited some sin. (*Surely this is the result of . . .*)

Jesus—mercy incarnate, asked only if the man wanted to be healed. The man yielded, took up his bed, and walked. Jesus asks the sick—and the sick at heart—the same question today.

Merciful Father, I yield to Your saving, healing, and transforming power today. In the holy name of Jesus, my Lord and Savior, I pray. Amen.

December 30, 31. **Phyllis Beveridge Nissila** is a writer and instructor at Lane Community College in Eugene, Oregon. She is married and the mother of two daughters.

Still Reverberating

It is a good thing to give thanks unto the LORD, and to sing praises unto thy name, O most High (Psalm 92:1, *King James Version*).

Scripture: Psalm 92:1-8
Song: "He Has Made Me Glad"

I grew up thinking religion was only about sitting up straight, minding the rules, and not asking questions. In church, I pictured God frowning on me with my smudged shoes, dirty fingernails, and sermon yawns.

My Sunday song was hardly the joyful Sabbath day psalm of David. It was more like a funeral dirge. The only thing I was happy about: soon the service would end. Then I could exchange my starchy Sunday clothes for jeans and a T-shirt and go back outdoors to play.

As I grew in the knowledge of God's Word, I came to realize it isn't about sitting up straight in a pew. No, it's about "[sitting] together in heavenly places in Christ Jesus" (Ephesians 2:6). It isn't about perfecting lists of rigid rules; rather, it's about the delight found in doing God's will and observing His law implanted in my heart (Psalm 40:6). It isn't about blind obedience, but about the freedom to ask, seek, and knock (Matthew 7:7, 8).

Because of the faithful tutelage of the Holy Spirit—not just one day a week, but every day—my sad song became a glad song. It reverberates still.

Thank You, **Lord,** for a new song in my heart—the song of new life, of forgiveness and adoption into Your family, of redemption and of the indwelling Spirit. Help me to sing joyfully of Your goodness, this day and every day! In Jesus' name, amen.